I0810385

IMAGES
of America

EAGLE'S NEST

THE WILLIAM K. VANDERBILT II ESTATE

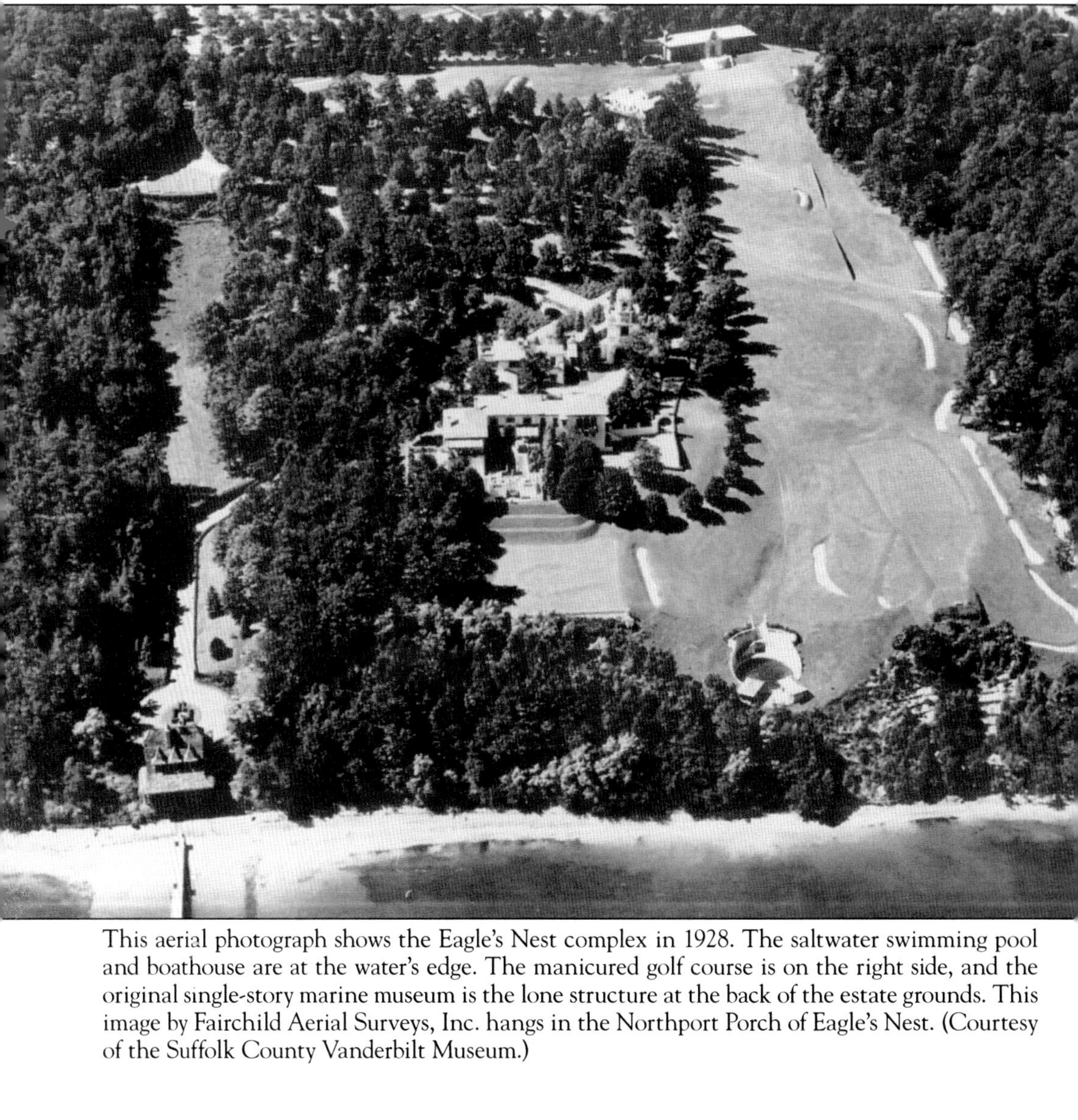

This aerial photograph shows the Eagle's Nest complex in 1928. The saltwater swimming pool and boathouse are at the water's edge. The manicured golf course is on the right side, and the original single-story marine museum is the lone structure at the back of the estate grounds. This image by Fairchild Aerial Surveys, Inc. hangs in the Northport Porch of Eagle's Nest. (Courtesy of the Suffolk County Vanderbilt Museum.)

On the Cover: This is Eagle's Nest as viewed from the north end of the golf course in an image from the late 1920s. The decorative arch marks the future site of the final wing added to the house in the mid-1930s. The photograph was taken for William K. Vanderbilt II by Drix Duryea. (Courtesy of the Suffolk County Vanderbilt Museum.)

IMAGES
of America

EAGLE'S NEST
THE WILLIAM K. VANDERBILT II ESTATE

Stephanie Gress

ARCADIA
PUBLISHING

ISBN 978-1-4671-2332-7

Published by Arcadia Publishing
Charleston, South Carolina

Printed in the United States of America

Library of Congress Control Number: 2014952478

For all general information, please contact Arcadia Publishing:
Telephone 843-853-2070
Fax 843-853-0044
E-mail sales@arcadiapublishing.com
For customer service and orders:
Toll-Free 1-888-313-2665

Visit us on the Internet at www.arcadiapublishing.com

Contents

ACKNOWLEDGMENTS

There are many who have contributed to the story of Eagle's Nest, most notably William K. Vanderbilt II, who had the foresight to document his life and times through publications, photographic images, and personal correspondence. The original architects, artists, craftsmen, designers, and scientists, all of whom were selected by him, are also recognized.

Those who participate in the stewardship of Eagle's Nest are integral to the story as well: the staff, volunteers, and board of the Suffolk County Vanderbilt Museum (past, present, and future). All of whom give so generously of themselves are acknowledged for their tireless dedication and true affection for Eagle's Nest: the Suffolk County legislature, parks department, department of public works, and the Society for the Preservation of Long Island Antiquities.

Thank you to Abby Walker of Arcadia Publishing for guidance and Maryann Zakshevsky, Brandon Williams, and Kirsten Amundsen of the Suffolk County Vanderbilt Museum curatorial staff for their help with this publication.

I am particularly grateful to the original employees of Eagle's Nest and their families for sharing their photographs, documents, and oral histories.

Unless otherwise noted, all images appear courtesy of the Suffolk County Vanderbilt Museum. The historical photographs of Eagle's Nest were taken by New York photographers (in chronological order by building phase): Pach Brothers, Drix Duryea, Fairchild Aviation Photographers, and Samuel Gottscho.

Introduction

The design of the Eagle's Nest estate provides a portal into the world of its owner and creator, William Kissam Vanderbilt II (1878–1944). "Willie K.," as he came to be known, was the great-grandson of Cornelius Vanderbilt, "The Commodore," who launched the family fortune via shipping and railroads. His grandfather William Henry, who inherited most of the Commodore's wealth, doubled the family fortune through the transportation empire. William Henry's three sons built the grandest private residences in the nation. Willie K. had the daunting task of following in these family footsteps and determined that he required a legacy of his own making. Eagle's Nest is part of that legacy.

Like his father, William K. Vanderbilt I, Willie K. ran the New York Central Railroad offices in New York City, but soon his interests led him elsewhere, and he embarked upon a series of adventures. While Vanderbilt's abiding passion was the sea, in the late 1890s he became enamored with the automobile—the invention that would change the world. A few short years later, Willie K. made history when he broke the land speed record in Ormond Beach, Florida, in 1904. Riding the wave of this exciting accomplishment, he returned to New York to establish and finance the Vanderbilt Cup Races on Long Island, the first organized automobile races in the United States. He also formed the Long Island Motor Parkway Corporation to build the road on which the races would be held. The parkway ran from Queens to Lake Ronkonkoma, with a portion of the road paved by 1908. Due to safety issues and competing venues, the final Long Island Vanderbilt Cup Race ran in 1910, the same year Willie K. purchased the first parcel of property on which Eagle's Nest would be built.

The history of Eagle's Nest, Willie K.'s summer home, is as interesting as the life of the man who built it, and in many ways the structure reveals much about him. Having the distinction of being the easternmost of the mansions on the Long Island Gold Coast, Eagle's Nest began as a refuge for him—then newly separated from his first wife, Virginia Graham Fair Vanderbilt. The selection of this remote waterfront location was purposeful in that Willie K. sought both a retreat far from the city and a deep harbor for his yachts, as he was an avid sailor, fisherman, and world explorer.

Influenced by his travels, with the guidance of renowned architects Warren and Wetmore and later their protégé Ronald Hoyt Pearce, Vanderbilt built one of the most unique estates imaginable. An eclectic version of Spanish Revival architecture, Eagle's Nest can best be described as a fairy tale made of stucco, iron, and tile. Remotely located on a north shore Long Island peninsula, the property is guarded by an undulating whitewashed stucco wall and black iron gates. The property cascades down to the water with views of the Long Island Sound to the shores of Connecticut. Winding cobblestone paths lead to a sturdy concrete bridge and down to a bell tower with a Medieval-style portcullis and heavy wooden gates. Lanterns and custom-made wrought-iron elements adorn each window and door. White stucco facades are capped by tile roofs, and the central courtyard is paved with cobblestone. Vanderbilt and his family would spend many happy summers here swimming, entertaining close friends, and setting off on their journeys.

The early structure of his estate had a modest beginning as a seven-room cottage of an English Arts and Crafts design, then in three separate building phases grew to be a sprawling Spanish Revival mansion. The transformation of Eagle's Nest over 25 years was guided by the changes in Vanderbilt's life and family. His marriage to Rosamund Lancaster Warburton in 1927 (the second for both) is an event discernible in design of the estate. Rosamund was a stylish woman with two young children and highly refined tastes. The French-paneled upstairs bedrooms are one obvious result of her influence on both the owner and the architects. Vanderbilt added a wing for her children and their nanny (and his new mother-in-law) at a comfortable distance from the adult accommodations.

Willie K. spent his time traveling the oceans of the world in his yachts and collecting natural history specimens, art, and artifacts from every locale. His vision was to have a museum at Eagle's Nest in order that he could share his world treasures with all who were interested in seeing them. To that end, he eventually constructed a separate building to house his collections. Completed in 1922, he called it the Hall of Fishes. Said to have been inspired by a church he visited in Guatemala, it was a single-story stucco structure with twisted columns and Spanish tile roof. By the late 1920s, his collections had already outgrown the space, necessitating the addition of a second story.

The untimely death of William K. Vanderbilt III in 1933 was the other major life event prompting the final construction phase of Eagle's Nest. In 1936, the Memorial Wing was added in homage to Vanderbilt's only son, who died in an automobile accident. The placement of this wing closed in the last open side of the courtyard as though the event was foretold in the architecture. A religious triptych placed in the front facade of the new wing is a powerful and permanent expression of the tragic loss. Imparting a somber greeting for visitors crossing through the portcullis into the courtyard, it does not allow for his son to be forgotten. Inside, the wing houses three museum galleries: two for Willie K.'s collections and one dedicated to his son, filled with trophies from his 1931 safari in the Anglo-Egyptian Sudan.

One

Young William K. Vanderbilt II

On October 26, 1878, Willie K. was born to William K. Vanderbilt I and Alva Erskine Smith Vanderbilt. He had one sister a year older, Consuelo (named for Alva's dear friend Consuelo Yznaga), and a brother six years his junior, Harold Stirling, whom they called Mike. His grandfather William Henry died in 1885, leaving millions of dollars to each of his children, one of whom was William K. Vanderbilt I. The Vanderbilts lived on Fifth Avenue in New York, and Willie K. summered at Marble House in Newport, Rhode Island, with his family. After his parents divorced in 1895, the children visited their father's Idle Hour estate in Oakdale, Long Island, during the summer. Given the history of Cornelius and his shipping empire, sailing was in the Vanderbilt blood. The family cruised to Europe in 1887 on their steam yacht, *Alva*, commissioned the year before. Shortly thereafter, Willie K. bought his first vessel, a half-rater named *Osprey*, marking the beginning of his most enduring love affair—the one he had with the sea.

Willie K. entered Harvard University in the fall of 1897, attempted to enlist in the US Army during the Spanish American War (he was rejected for health reasons), and would never return to school. By April 1899, he was married to Virginia Graham Fair (nicknamed "Birdie" for her tiny waistline), the daughter of Nevada senator and Comstock Lode millionaire James Fair. In 1902, Willie K. began constructing his Long Island estate, Deepdale, in Lake Success. In addition to working for his father at the New York Central Railroad offices in New York, Willie K. raised prize chickens, purchased interest in a vacuum cleaner company, and formed the Long Island Motor Parkway Corporation. Willie K. spent the better part of his 20s pursuing his latest passion, the automobile. In 1904, he broke a land speed record at Ormond Beach, Florida, and organized and financed the Vanderbilt Cup Races on Long Island. In September 1909, he and Birdie, with whom he had three children, formally announced their separation.

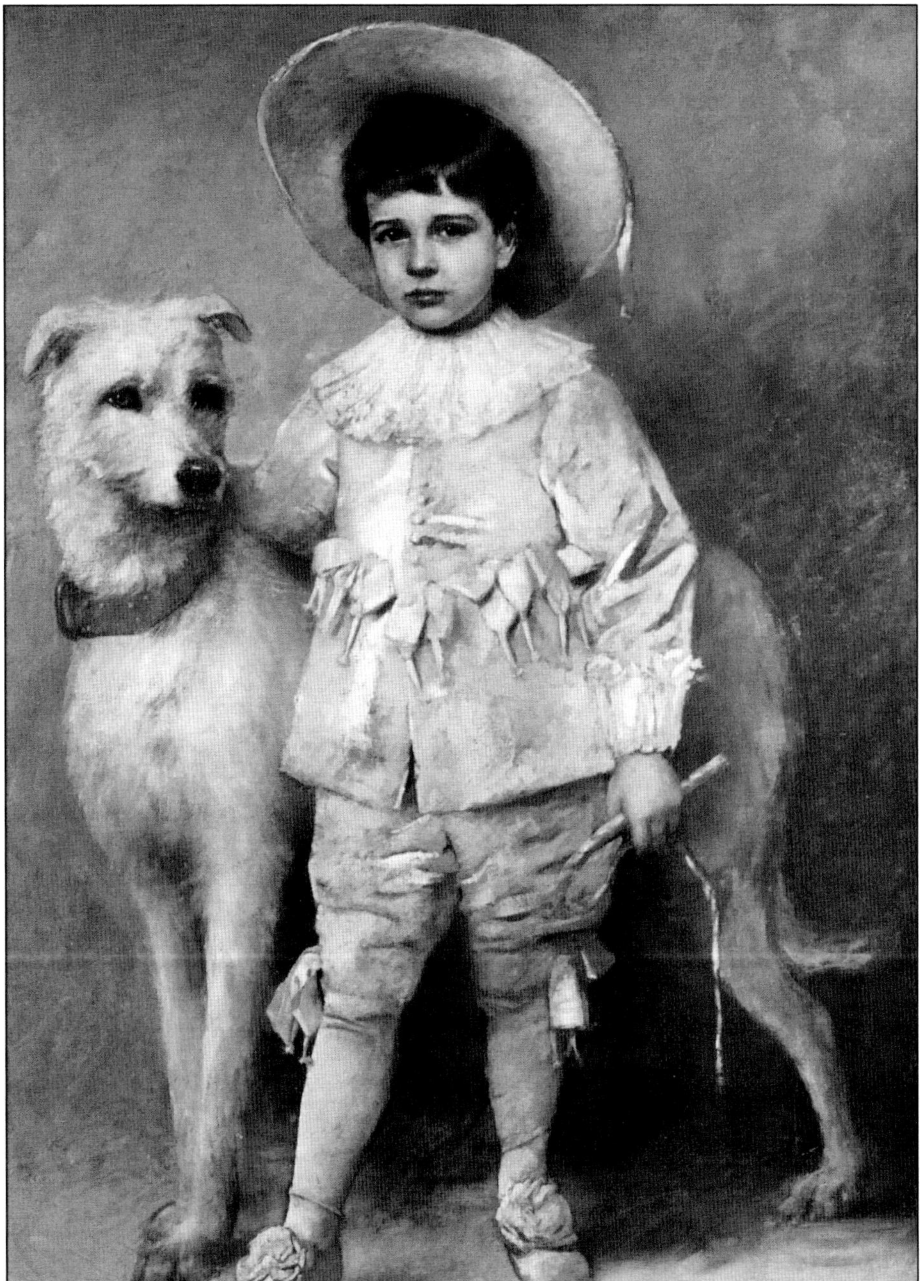

Willie K. is the subject of this painting at the age of six. This type of portrayal was most likely influenced by his mother, Alva, a Francophile, whose family retreated back to Paris, France, from Alabama at the end of the Civil War. The son of Alva and William K. Vanderbilt I, he was described as a sickly child. The artist's inclusion of a white rose to symbolize youth, purity, and innocence conflicts with a weighted facial expression suggesting he was already burdened by his illustrious family history. This portrait, painted by Benjamin Curtis Porter in 1884, hangs over the door to the main entrance of Eagle's Nest estate. The portraits that surround it on the other walls are of his parents and traditional Dutch portraits of unknown identity.

Cornelius Vanderbilt, the Commodore (1794–1877), great-grandfather of Willie K., founded the family fortune by building a transportation empire in shipping and railroads. He left over $100 million to one of his 11 surviving children (there were 13), allowing for that fortune to be doubled in a decade. Painted in 1935 by an artist signing only "K.F.," the style is after Jared B. Flagg. This painting hangs in the upper entrance hall to the Memorial Wing at Eagle's Nest.

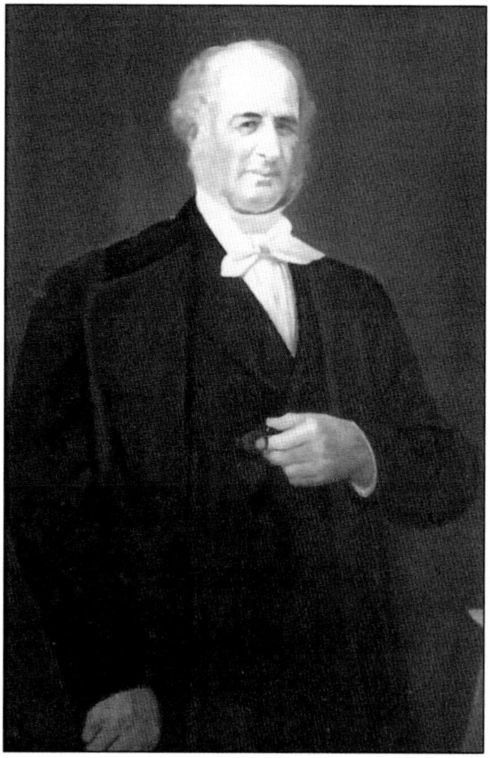

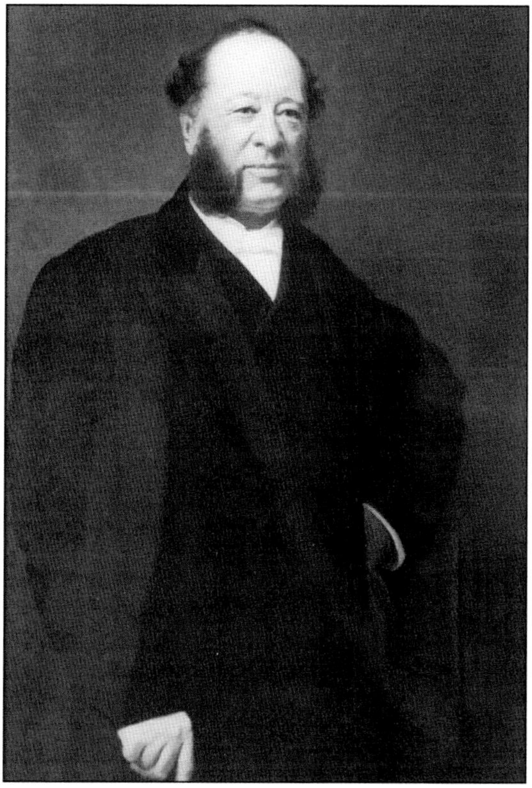

The portrait hanging immediately to the right of Cornelius is that of Willie K.'s grandfather William Henry (1821–1885), to whom Cornelius left the bulk of his fortune. Unlike Cornelius, he was a generous philanthropist and a discriminating art collector who helped to establish the Metropolitan Museum of Art in New York City. This portrait was painted in 1887 by Jared B. Flagg.

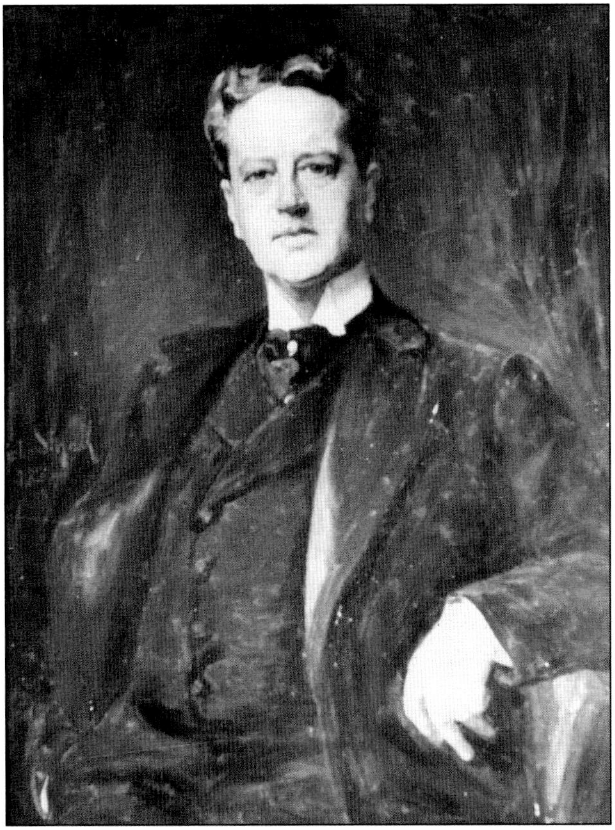

Willie K.'s father, William K. Vanderbilt I (1849–1920), was a breeder of horses and is famed for building Marble House in Newport, Rhode Island, for his wife, Alva. She divorced him, citing infidelity. He married Anne Harriman in 1903 after the divorce decree stipulating that he not marry during Alva's lifetime was overturned. This 1911 portrait by Richard V. Hall hangs to the right of William Henry's.

Willie K.'s strict upbringing is credited to his mother, Alva, a formidable woman by all accounts. Alva took up the cause of suffrage after the death of her second husband, Oliver H. P. Belmont. Alva is pictured here with her children Harold (left), Willie K. (center), and Consuelo. In Consuelo's autobiography, *The Glitter and the Gold*, she reveals that Willie K. very much disliked having to wear that sailor suit.

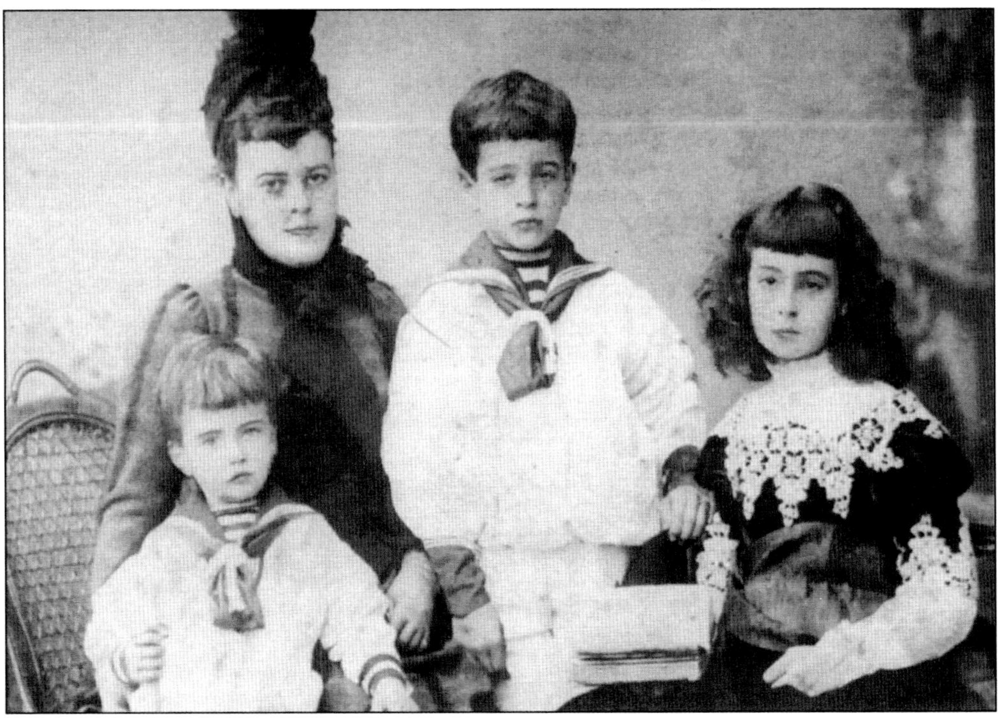

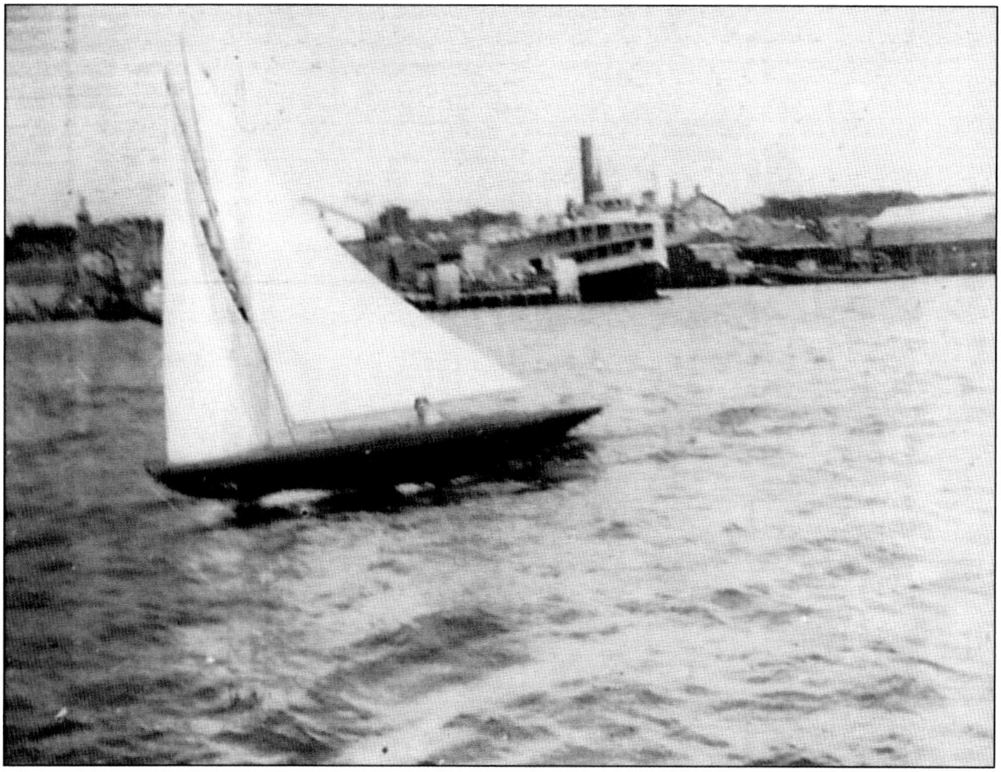

The half-rater *Osprey* purchased in 1895 was Willie K.'s first sailing vessel, built at Herreshoff Shipyard in Newport, Rhode Island. On August 3, 1895, the *Newport Mercury* reported that his new vessel was the last to be launched from their yard before they closed for summer vacation. Throughout his writings, Willie K. mentions his early ships affectionately and often, crediting them with training him for his job as captain.

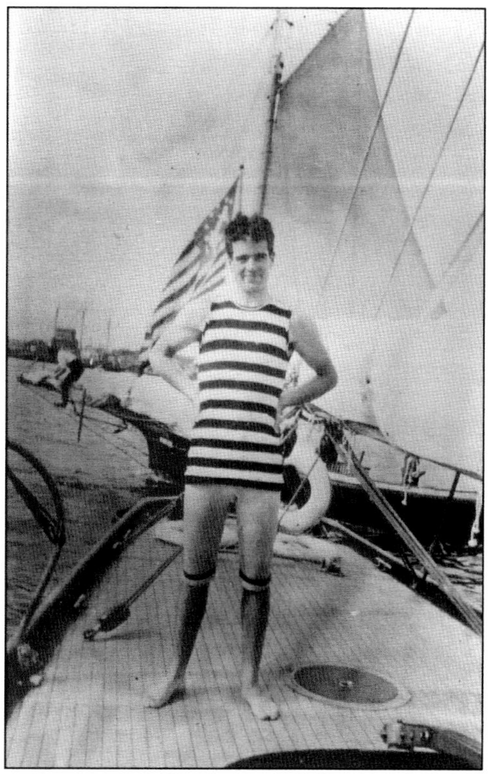

Willie K. is pictured aboard his sloop *Carmita*, which his family purchased for him in 1898 when he was a freshman at Harvard. He sold *Carmita* in 1900 and purchased the 70-foot-long sloop *Virginia*, named for his new wife. It was one of four crafts built by a racing syndicate off of Newport, Rhode Island.

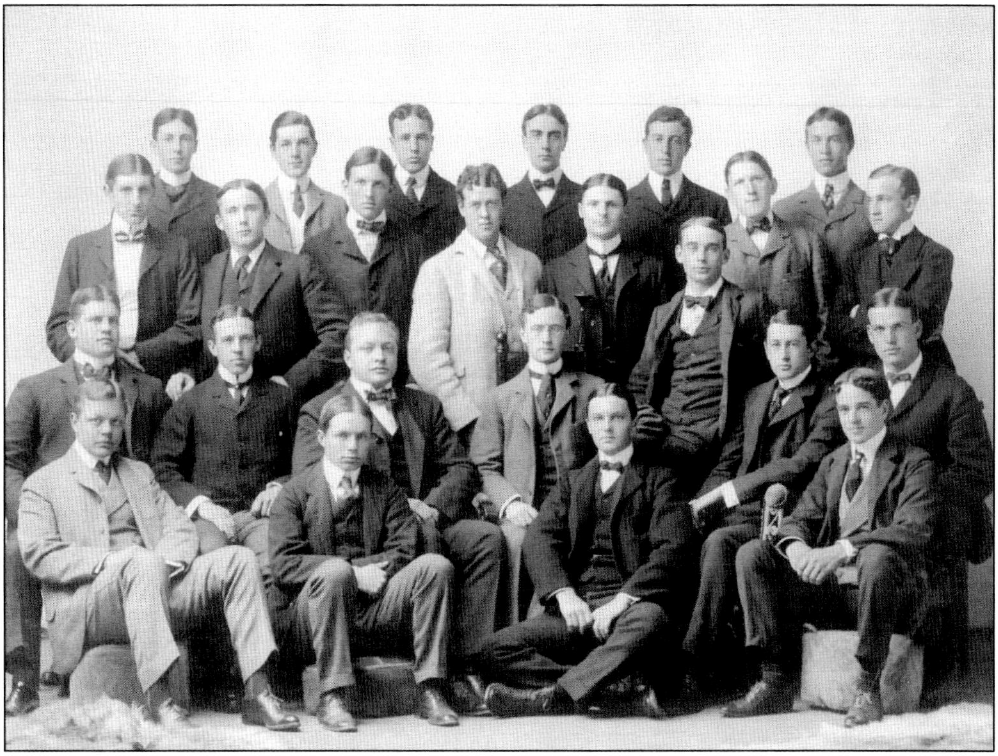

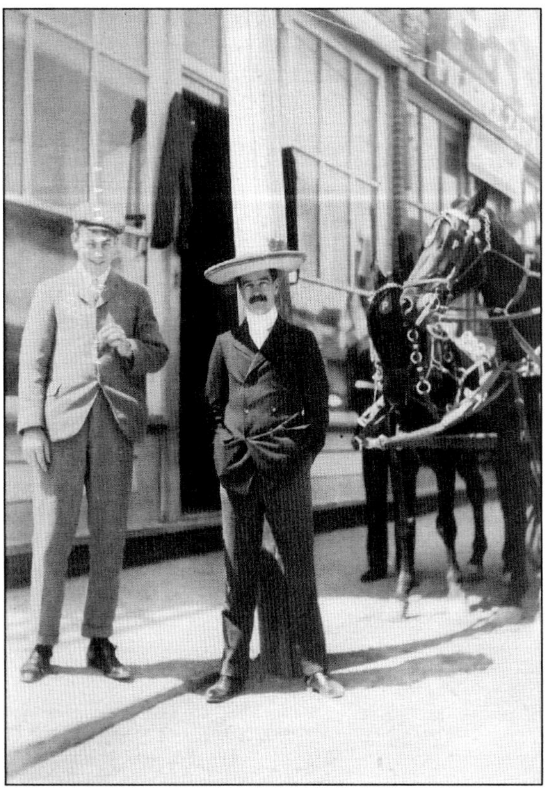

Willie K., seated at bottom right, is pictured with his Alpha Delta Phi fraternity at Harvard University in 1898. Having entered college in 1897, he left during his second year and never returned to school. After a failed attempt to enlist in the Army during the Spanish-American war, he married Birdie in 1900.

Willie K., posing in a sombrero in Ciudad Juárez, Mexico (just over the border of El Paso, Texas), is pictured here with his traveling companion identified as R.C. Watson Jr. The photograph was taken during a 1904 tour around the country at the behest of his father to report back on the operations and condition of various railroads.

Willie K. is pictured here in his automobile racing gear in 1905. Although he founded and financed the Vanderbilt Cup Races on Long Island in 1904, he never participated as a driver, but rather officiated. When the newspapers announced Willie K.'s appointment as an officer of the New York Central Railroad, the articles were accompanied by this photograph or a similar one with Willie K. wearing racing goggles atop his head.

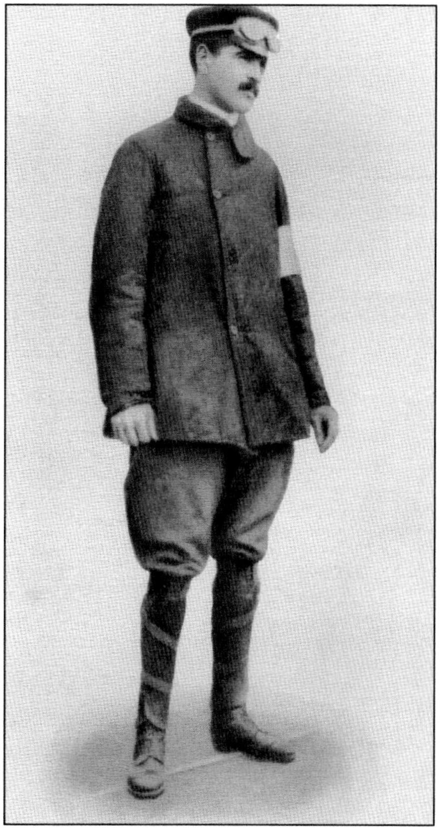

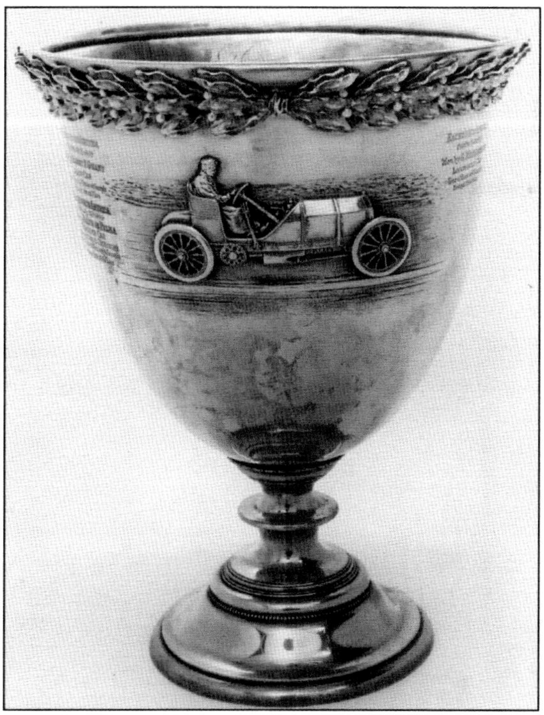

Willie K. commissioned Tiffany and Co. to design the Vanderbilt Cup Trophy for the winners of the Vanderbilt Cup Races, held on the Long Island Motor Parkway from 1904 to 1910. The 30-pound cup is made of sterling silver with Willie K.'s race car on one side and the names of each of the winners on the other. Once on display in the museum at Eagle's Nest, it was donated to the Smithsonian Museum in Washington, DC, in 1934.

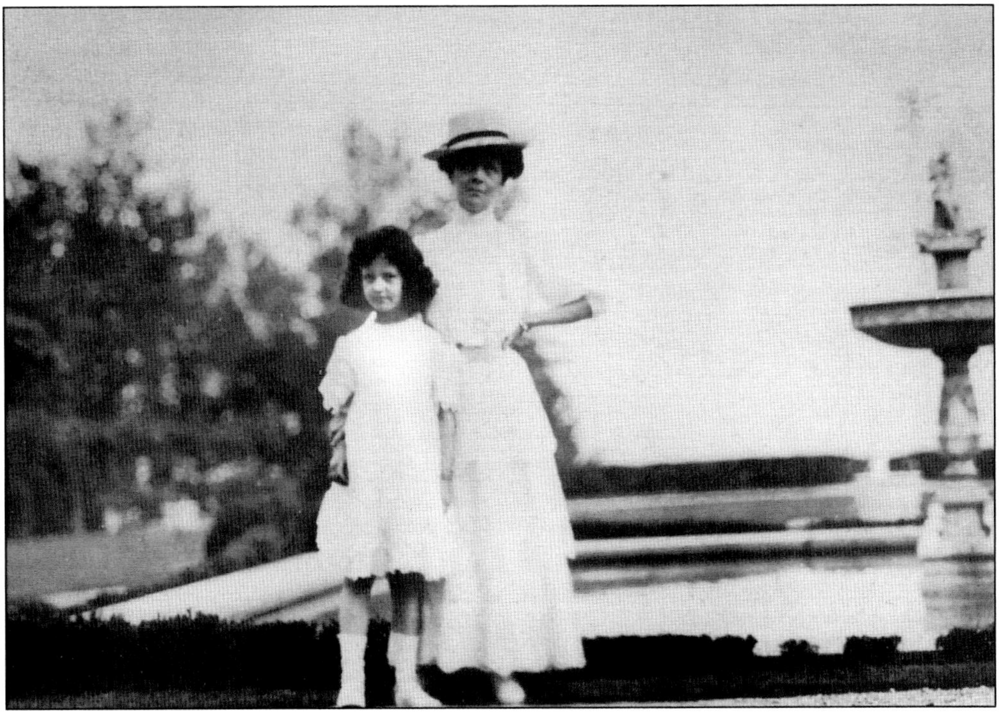

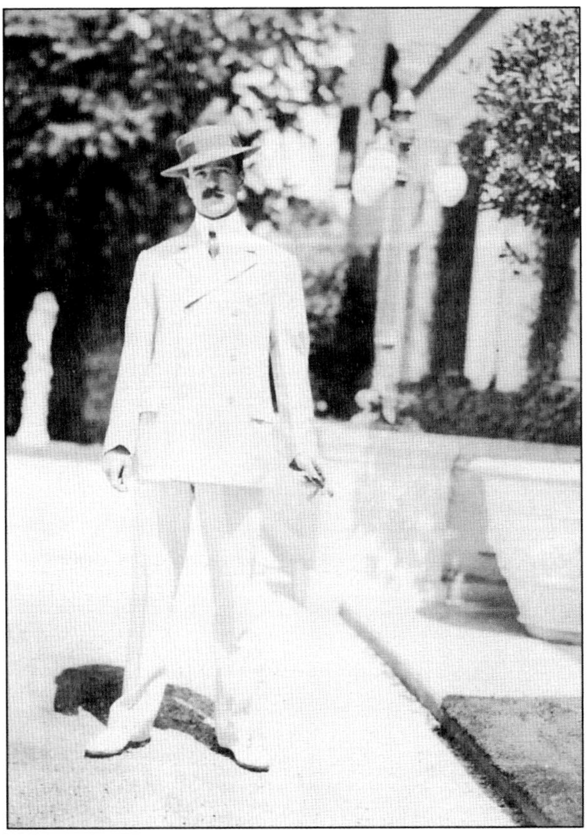

Virginia Vanderbilt is pictured here in 1908 with her eldest daughter, Muriel, at the family estate known as Deepdale. Birdie and Willie K. are not photographed together at this time, perhaps alluding to their impending separation. They made their home here with their three children: Muriel, Consuelo, and infant son, William K. III, born in 1907.

Willie K. is pictured here at his Deepdale estate in Lake Success, Long Island, in June 1908 in a double-breasted summer suit and Panama hat. These hats became wildly popular after Theodore Roosevelt was photographed wearing one in 1904 at the namesake canal site. Willie K. had plans to acquire a great deal more land here, including the lake. He did not succeed in doing so.

Two

The Early Years of Eagle's Nest

Shortly after separating from Birdie, and with the Vanderbilt Cup Races nearing their end on Long Island, Willie K. needed a place of retreat close to the water and far from the press. In 1910, he purchased land on a north shore peninsula of Long Island in the village of Northport. A single access road winding through the Little Neck peninsula divides the estate property with 40 acres on the east side of Little Neck Road and three on the west. Vanderbilt would acquire a total of 43 acres in all for his compound in three separate real estate transactions between 1910 and 1921.

He contracted Warren and Wetmore, a renowned New York City architectural firm, to help him plan and execute the estate. Between 1910 and 1912, they began excavating the site and planning for the first of the structures: the original seven-room, Craftsman-style cottage, a necessary bridge on the rolling hills of the acreage, the cast-iron eagles taken from New York's Grand Central Terminal at the estate entrance, the foundation for the boathouse, a terrace with six Corinthian-order columns from Carthage to frame the water view, and the golf course.

In 1914, the boathouse was completed, and in 1917 a house was built on the western side of the road where the superintendent for the estate lived with his family year-round. The superintendent's cottage, sometimes called Normandy Manor for its Tudor-style appearance, had gardens to provide fresh flowers and produce for the estate during the summer months.

During this time of his life, Willie K. worked for his father at the New York Central Railroad offices in New York City, motored, sailed, and fished. He documented each journey whether it was by sea or land, taking photographs and making meticulous logs of his travels. He self-published each of these journeys in bound volumes. While on his fishing adventures, he had his future museum in mind with every catch.

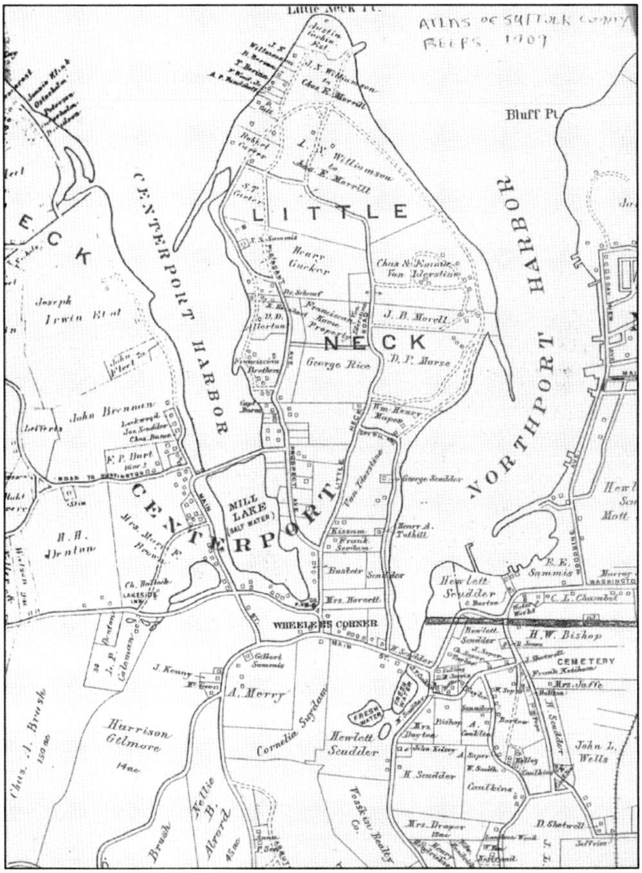

This map of Little Neck, dated 1909, is from the *Atlas of Suffolk County* and reflects the ownership of property parcels by name. This peninsula provided what Willie K. was looking for: a deep-water harbor for his boats, privacy from the press, and a prime Gold Coast location on Long Island's prestigious north shore.

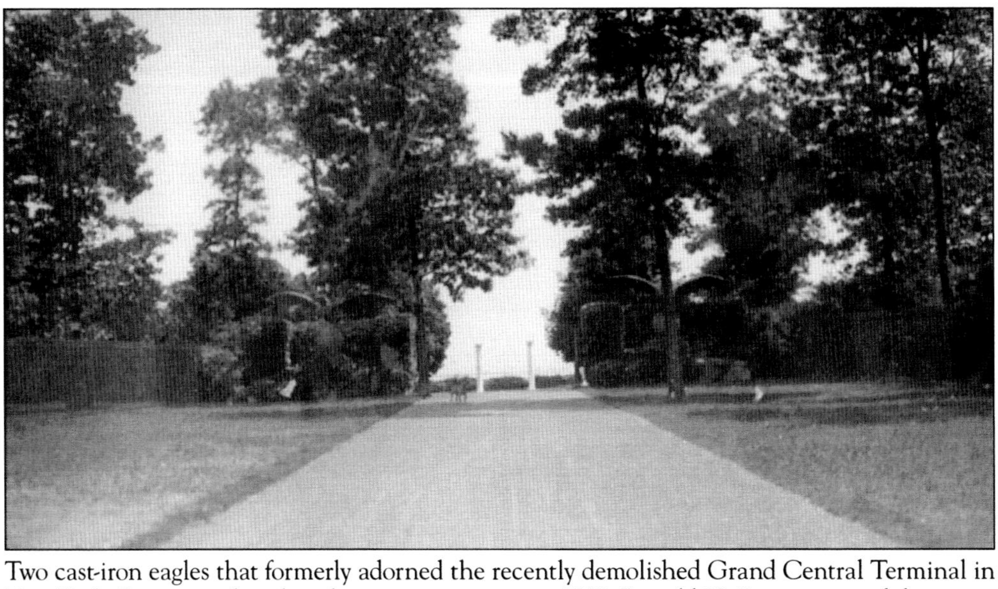

Two cast-iron eagles that formerly adorned the recently demolished Grand Central Terminal in New York City were placed at the estate entrance in 1910. Ronald H. Pearce, one of the estate architects, said the name Eagle's Nest does not derive from these statues, but rather from a sighting of an eagle flying from the trees at the water's edge during one of Willie K.'s early visits.

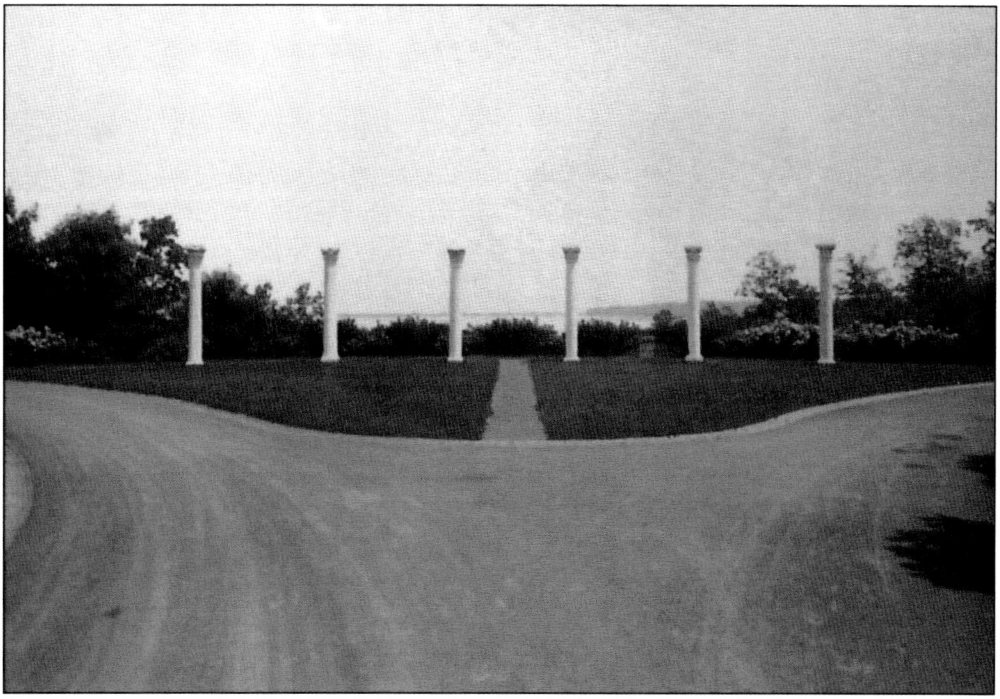

Six marble Corinthian-order columns frame the water view from an overlook just inside the entrance to the property. Over 1,000 years old, they are from Carthage in northern Africa. The road to the right leads to the estate's tennis courts, and the one to the left follows down toward the original residence cottage.

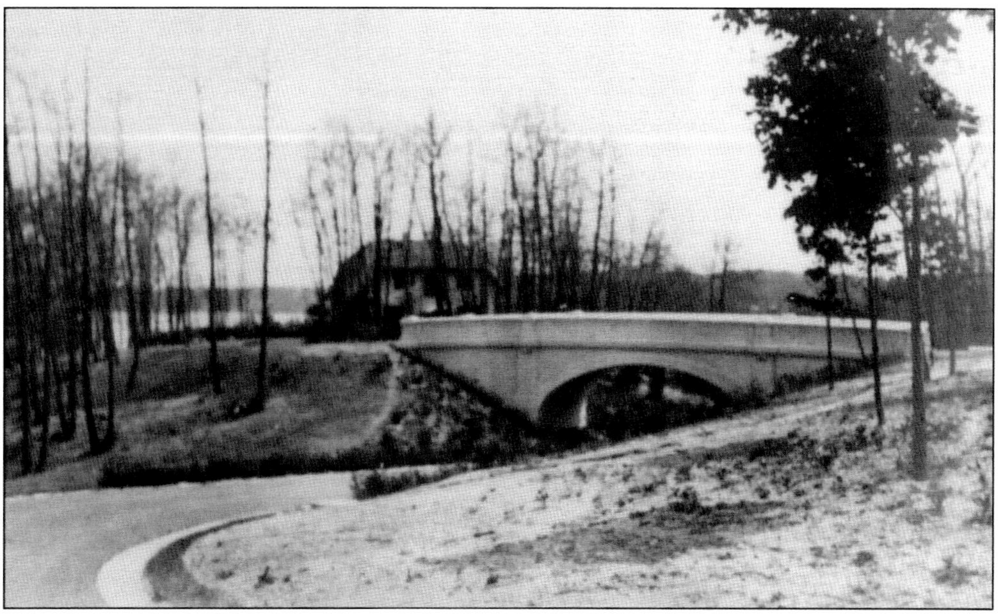

The extreme slope of the waterfront property necessitated that a bridge be among the first of the structures built to facilitate the passage of vehicles to the dwelling. In the earliest building stages at Eagle's Nest, between 1910 and 1912, the original seven-room cottage and the foundation for the boathouse were also constructed.

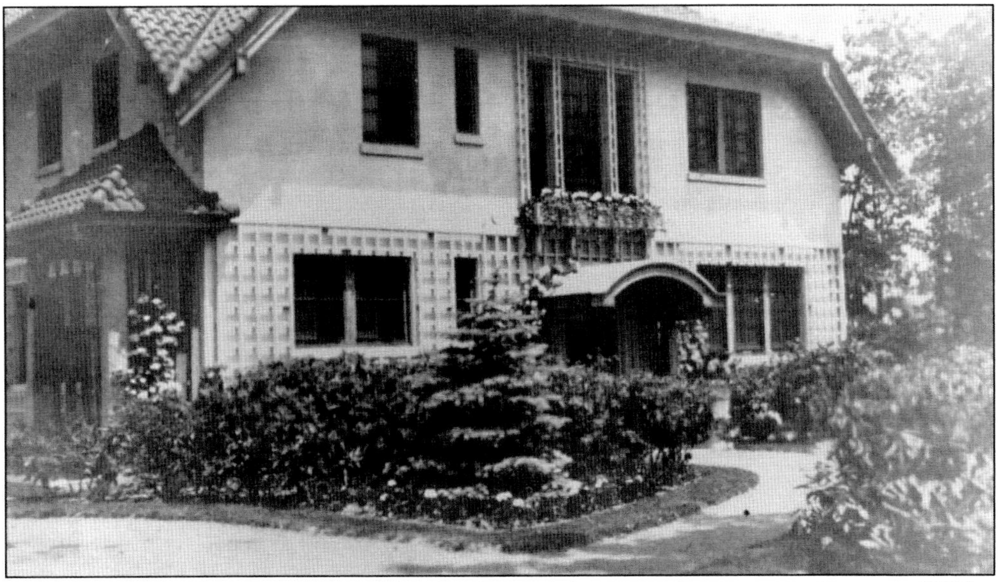

For most people, the dwelling would be the focus of the estate; however, in the case of Willie K., initially he was most concerned with the construction of his boathouse and museum. The seven-room cottage remained in its original state for a decade or so until the second construction phase, in which it was completely transformed, inspired no doubt, by the magnificent museum structure and Willie K.'s travels.

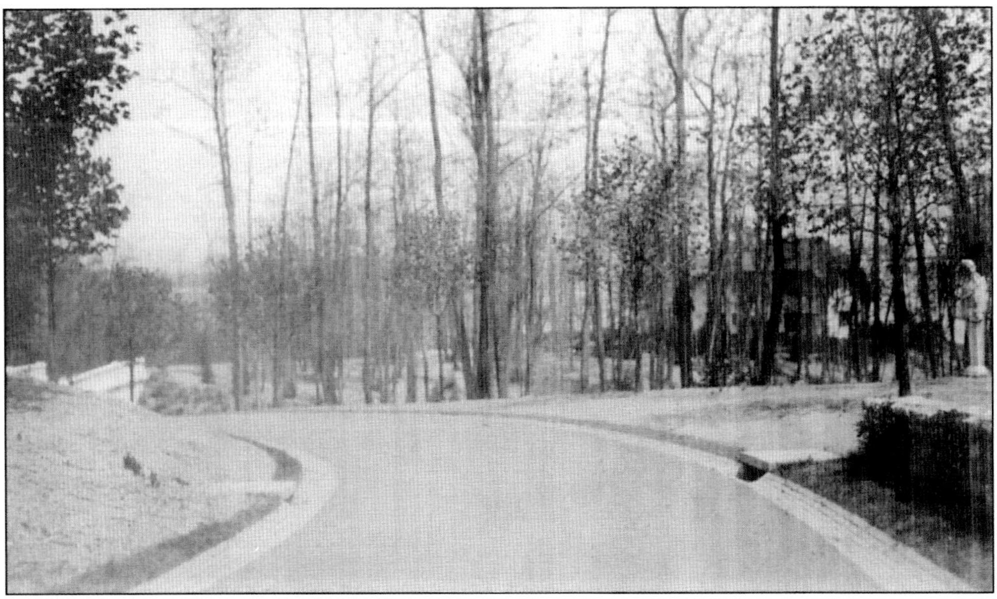

The road leads over the bridge and toward the cottage. Due to the hilly nature of the property, it was necessary to install an efficient drainage system to divert rainwater. The brick swales along the road's edge run throughout the estate access roads. The stone statuary on the right is appropriately an impish Pan-type character, the mythological hunter and god of the wild.

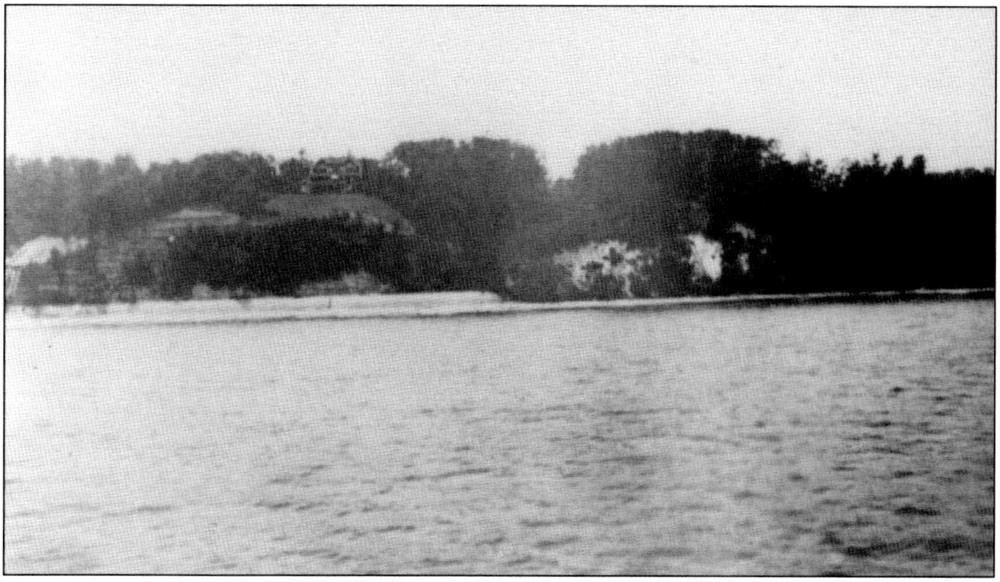

The original cottage, described as an English bungalow, is perched up on the Eagle's Nest property as seen in the 1913 photograph above taken from Northport Harbor. The boathouse had not yet been constructed, but the wharf is clearly visible. Willie K. could easily reach his estate by land or water from New York City. Below, an early photograph of a small boat docked there shows that the wharf had not yet been outfitted with lighting, making nighttime visits by water prohibitive. The construction of a boathouse and improved docking facilities were the next phase in the early development of the estate.

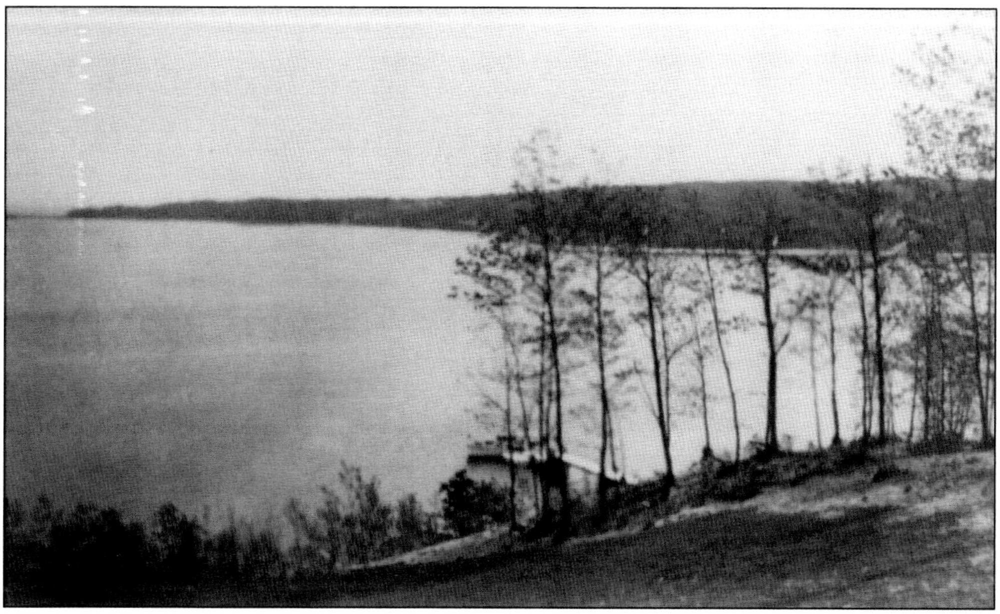

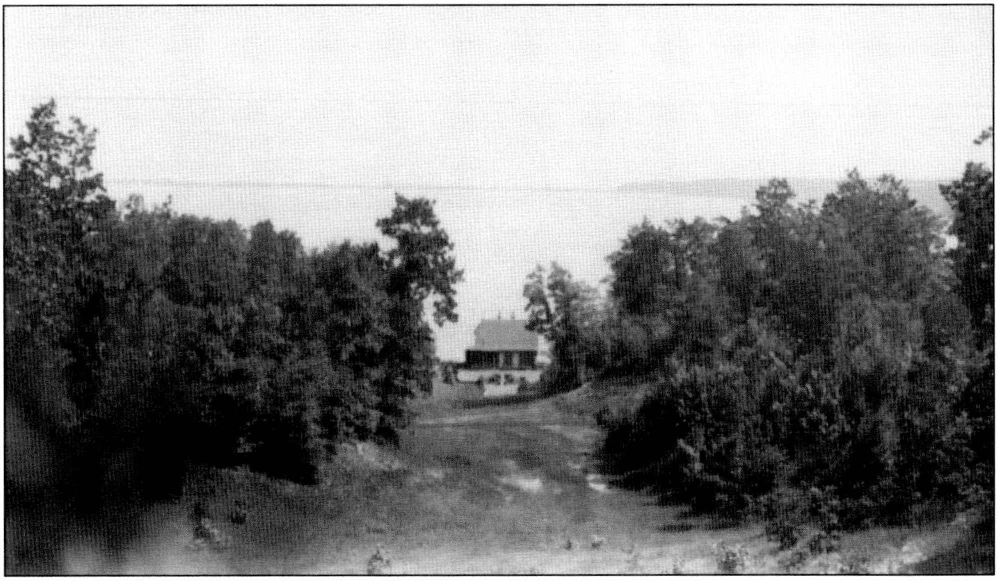

Designed and constructed by Warren and Wetmore, the Eagle's Nest boathouse is pictured above in a view from the overlook where the marble columns are located. The road that leads down to the boathouse from the upper part of the estate winds to the right, behind the cluster of small trees, and is barely discernible. A close-up view below of the Eagle's Nest boathouse wharf reveals that the decorative lighting standards had not yet been installed.

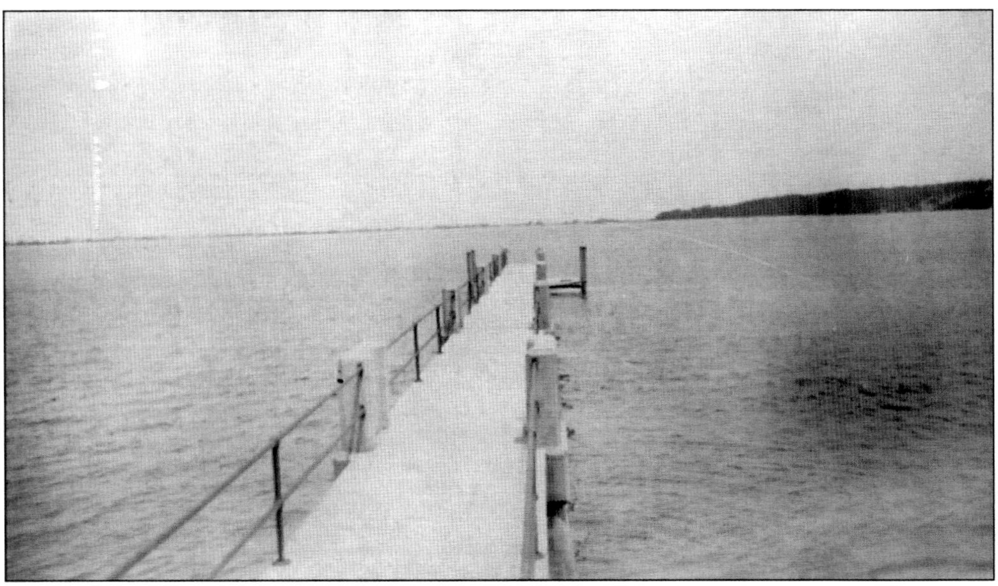

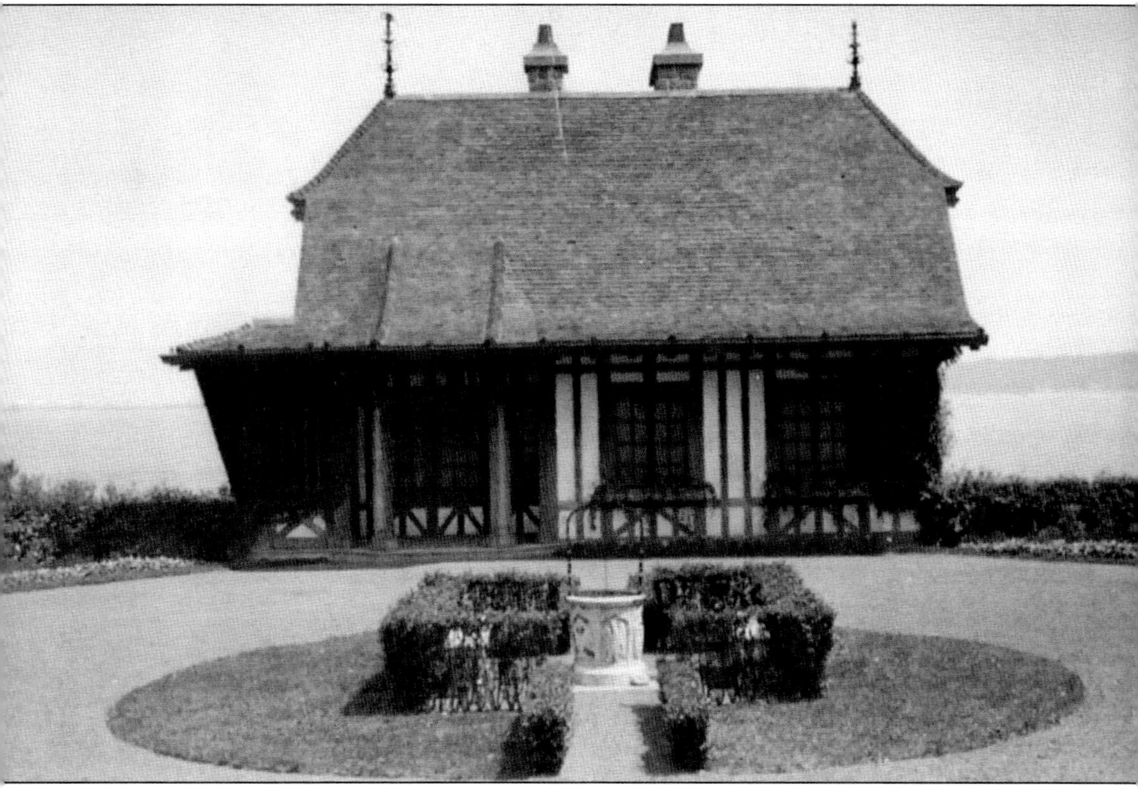

In this image of the boathouse from the access road, it appears to be a two-story structure with a slate roof and half-timbers to evoke the Tudor style. From this vantage point, it is uncertain what lies immediately beyond the house, other than a steep drop to the water's edge. This 1917 photograph shows the addition of a small well and two stone benches surrounded by a boxwood hedgerow. The superintendent's cottage, which was the next major structure built at Eagle's Nest by Warren and Wetmore on the parcel across Little Neck Road, matches the architectural style of the boathouse.

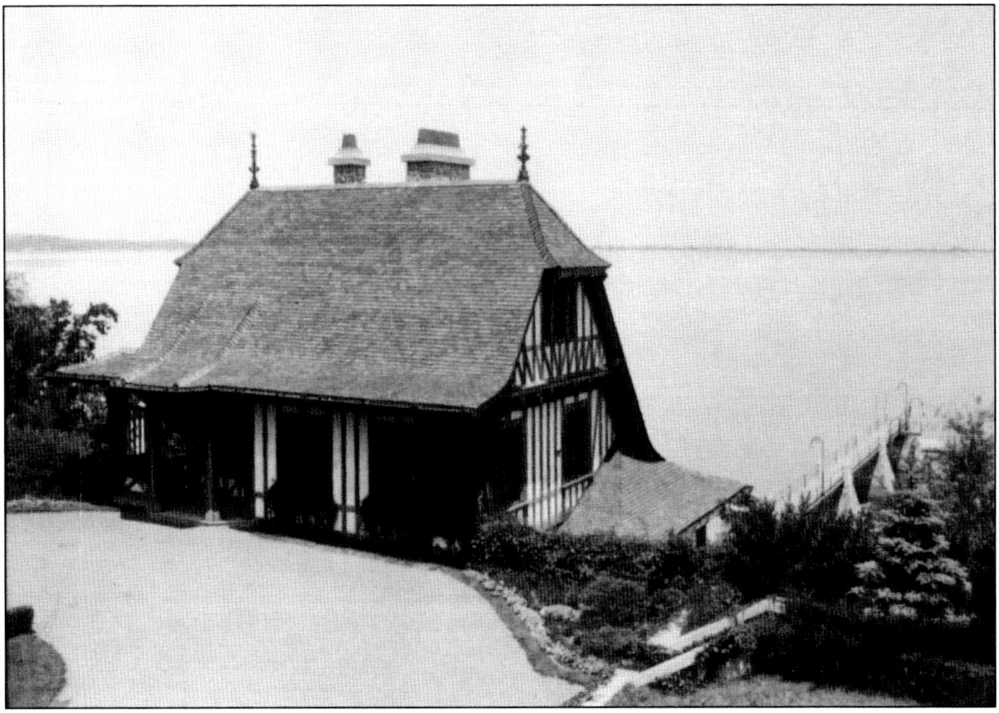

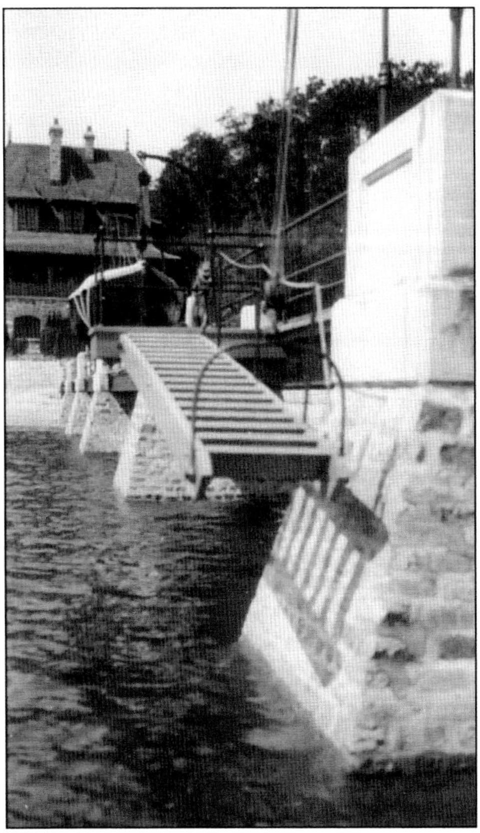

A photograph taken from the east side of the boathouse reveals what lies beyond. The two lower levels are visible, revealing that the structure has four stories. Decorative lighting standards have been added to the dock, and it becomes evident that the only way to access the waterfront is through the house.

A detail of the wharf shows the wooden gangway and pyramid-shaped stone pilings that support it. The view of the structure from the waterside shows a medieval-style facade in large slabs of hewn stone, unlike the Tudor treatments seen in the view from the property. There is also a large covered porch off the back of the house.

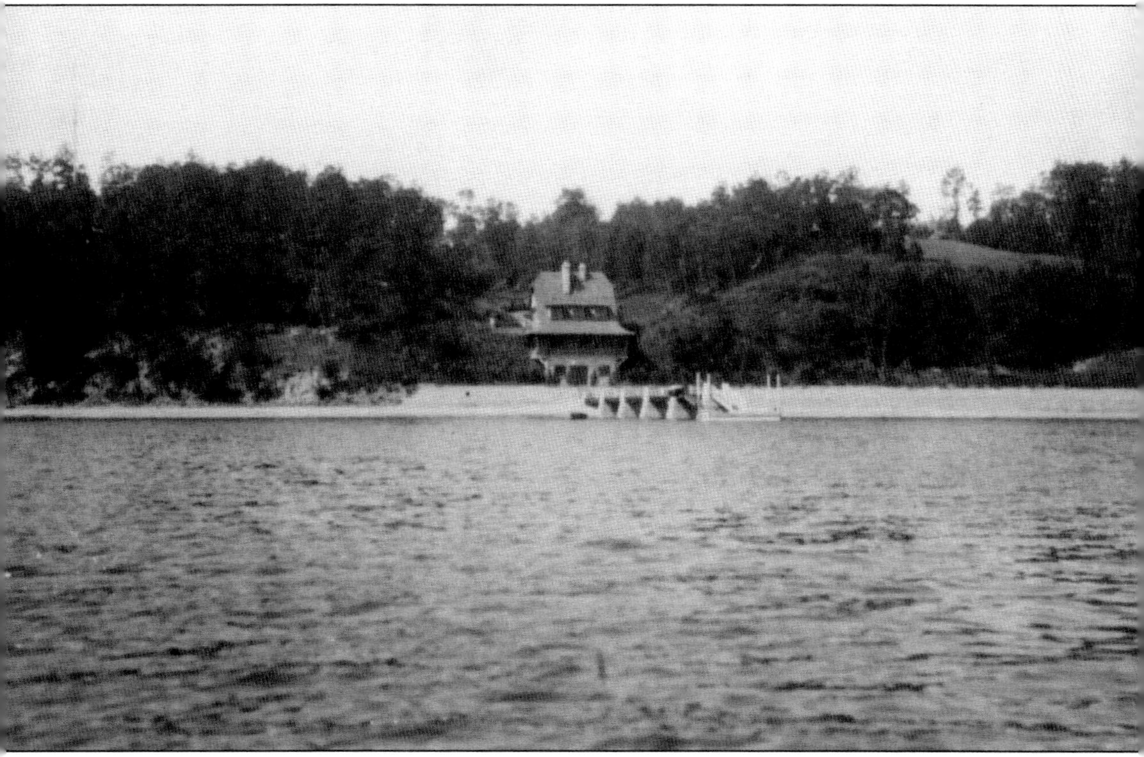

The entirety of the 621-square-foot boathouse structure can be seen in a photograph taken from Northport Harbor. The golf course had been added to the property by this time, and the road winding up to the estate can be seen to the left just behind the house. Making good use of his new facilities, Willie K. acquired a 213-foot-long ship, the *Ara*, from a Captain Heriot in Southampton, England, in 1922. With a crew of 35, Willie K. began making serious collecting voyages for his museum. He reports dropping anchor at Northport on August 1, 1924, in *Across the Atlantic with Ara—Summer 1924*.

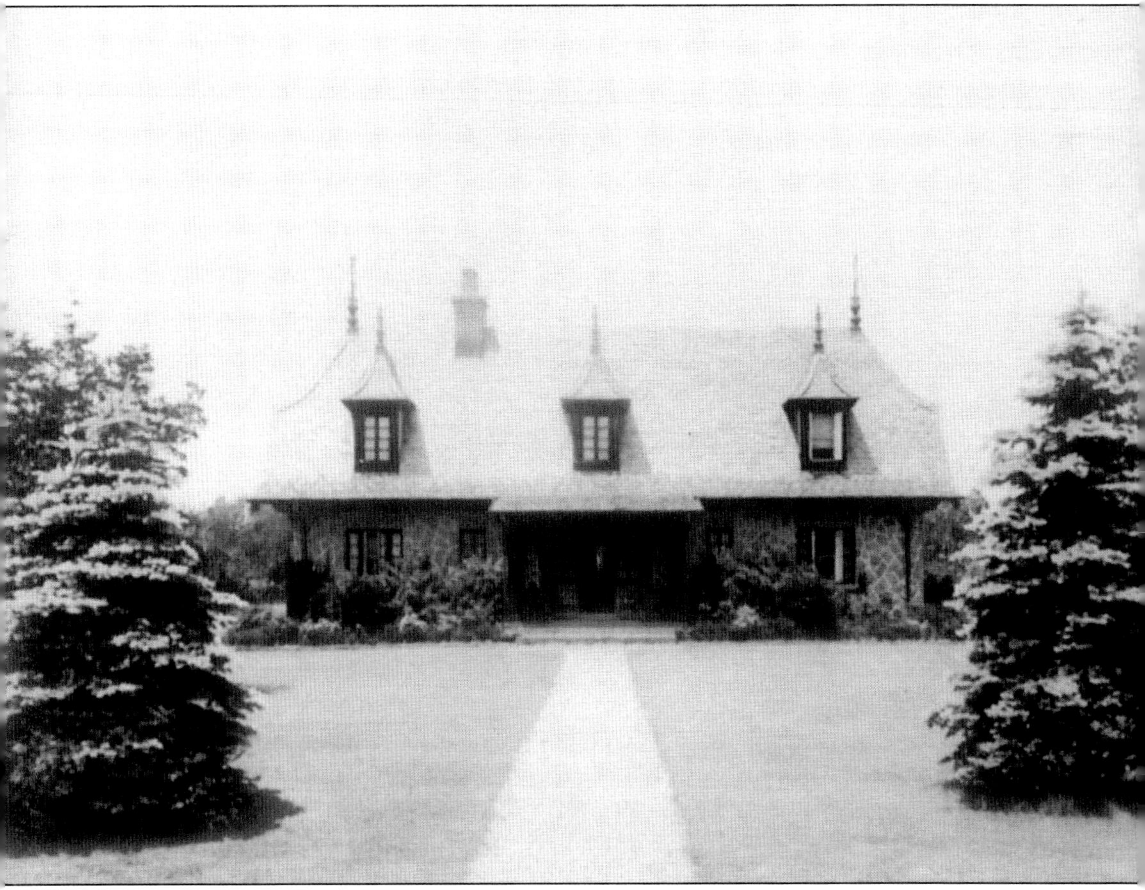

The superintendent's cottage of hewn stone was constructed by Warren and Wetmore in 1917 on the parcel on the west side of the road that divides the peninsula. The three acres surrounding it would be transformed into vegetable and flower gardens to supply Eagle's Nest during the summer months. A superintendent lived there year-round with his family to act as caretaker for the estate. The house is actually *L*-shaped, although it cannot be seen from this view. There are three upstairs bedrooms, and on the main floor there is a kitchen with a keeping room off of the back, a dining room, a main parlor, and another small bedroom.

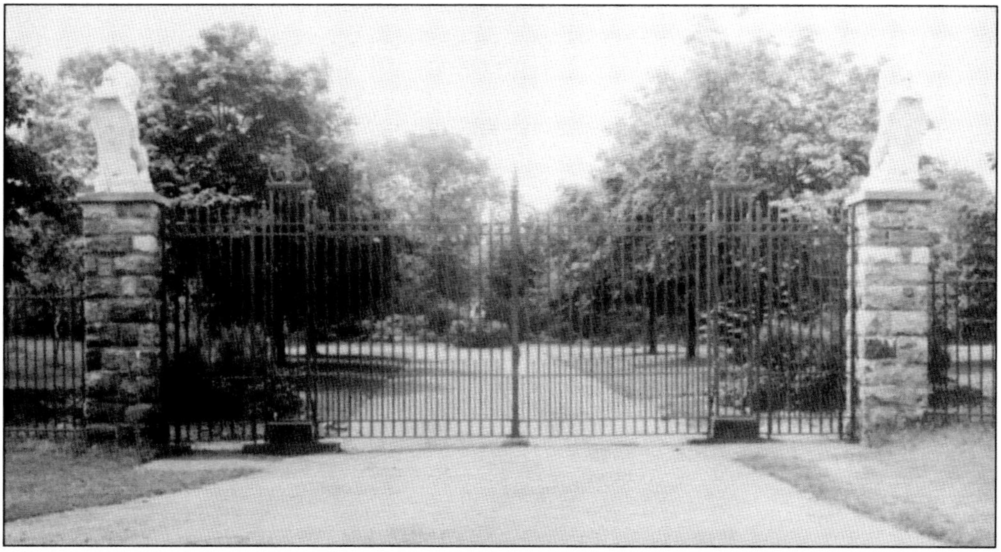

The entrance to the superintendent's cottage (above) is directly across the road from the entrance to Eagle's Nest. Iron fencing and gates surround the property, and two stone lions on pillars guard the front entrance. The manicured gardens (below) were filled with roses and other flowers, and vegetables were grown in neatly kept rows. This acreage and structure were an outgrowth of the main estate, and a great deal of effort was made to have it harmonize with the overall style of the other structures. The superintendent would close the estate down at the end of the summer and prepare it for Willie K.'s return the next year. In preparation for the museum opening, other employees worked on the exhibits year-round as well. They corresponded with Willie K. on a regular basis to keep him up to date on their progress.

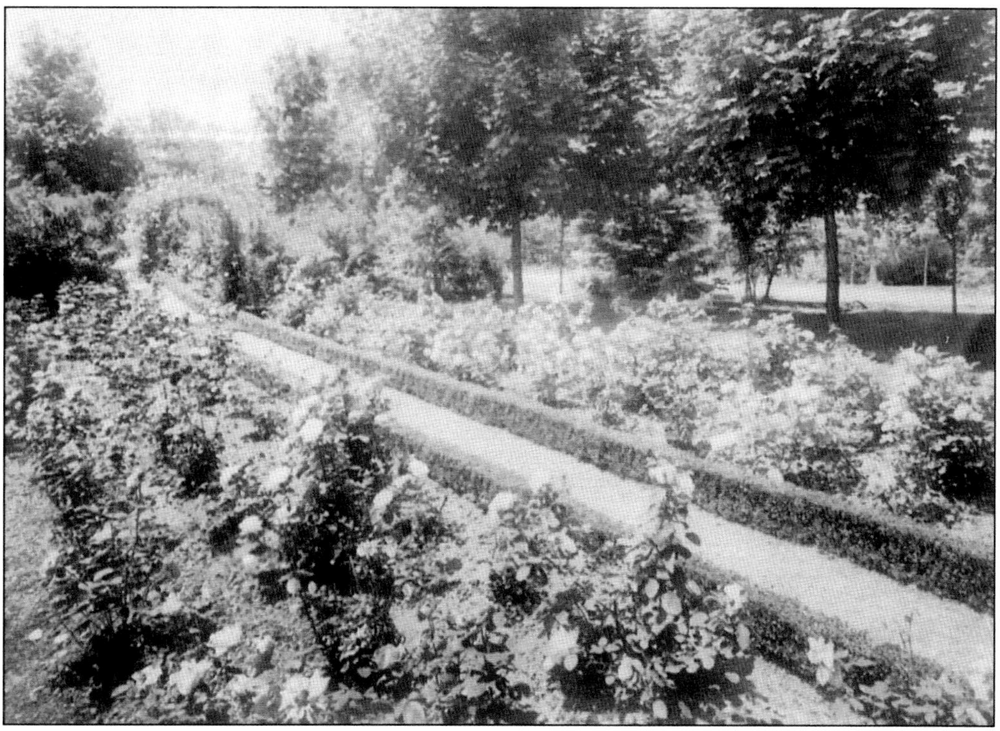

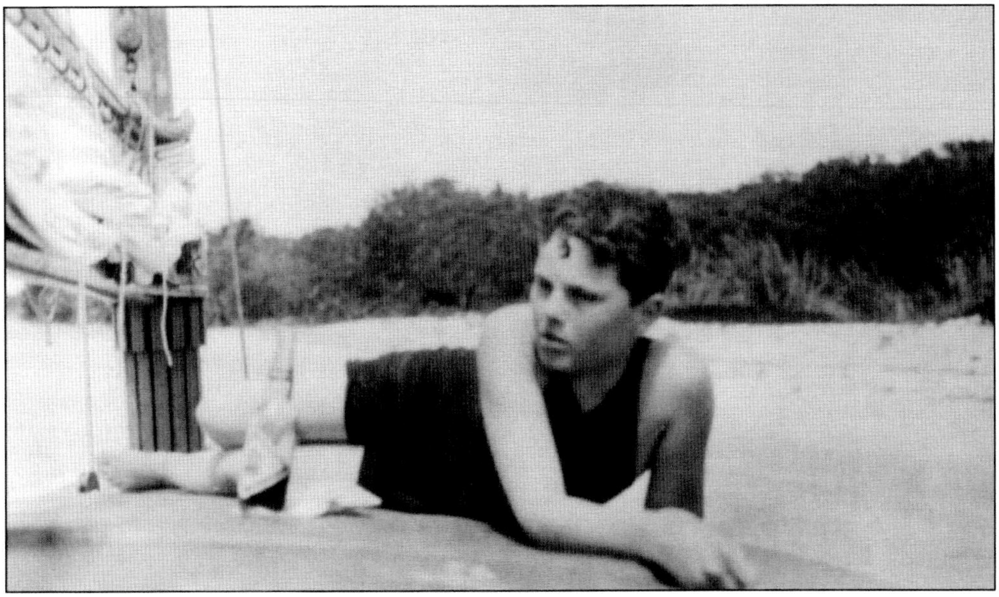

A young William K. Vanderbilt III is pictured here at summer camp in 1920 at 12 years of age. There are no indications that he spent much time at Eagle's Nest with his father until he was somewhat older. When he stayed there as a young man, he took up residence in the bedroom atop the estate's bell tower.

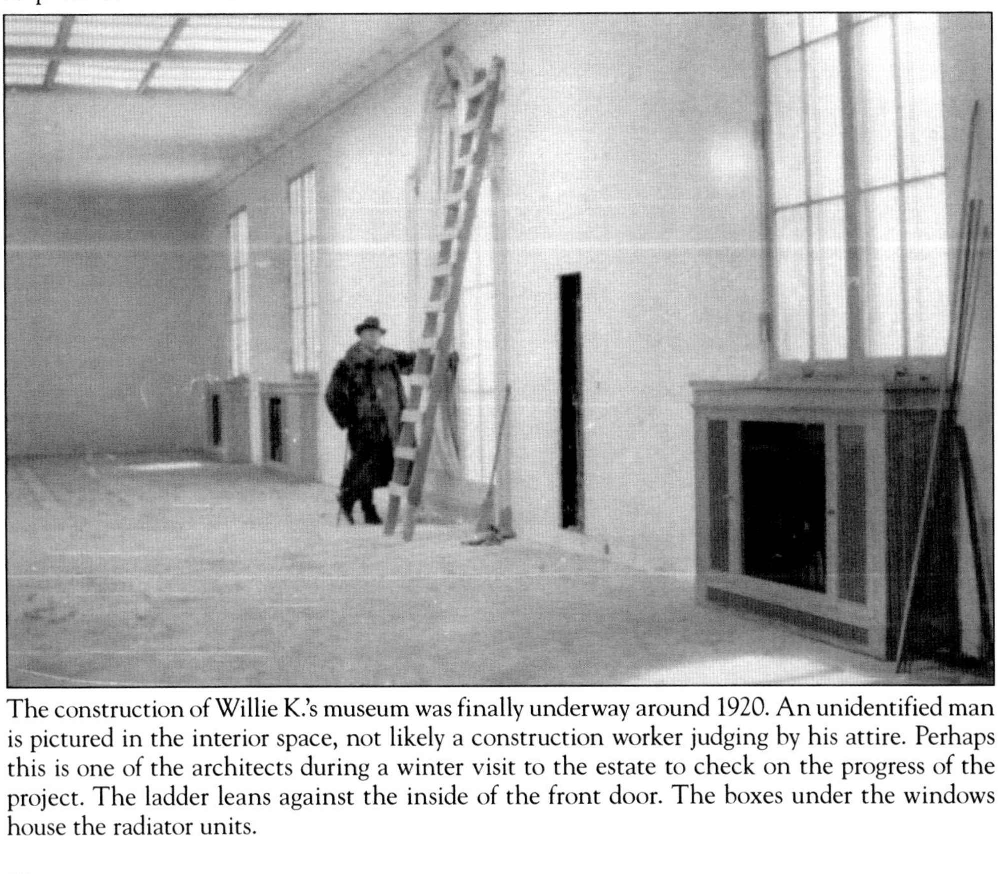

The construction of Willie K.'s museum was finally underway around 1920. An unidentified man is pictured in the interior space, not likely a construction worker judging by his attire. Perhaps this is one of the architects during a winter visit to the estate to check on the progress of the project. The ladder leans against the inside of the front door. The boxes under the windows house the radiator units.

The elaborate Baroque-style entrance design with twisted columns said to have been inspired by Willie K.'s travels to Spain, Portugal, and Central America would dominate the structure. This begins a new Spanish Revival aesthetic on the estate that matures and flourishes in the expansion of the residence.

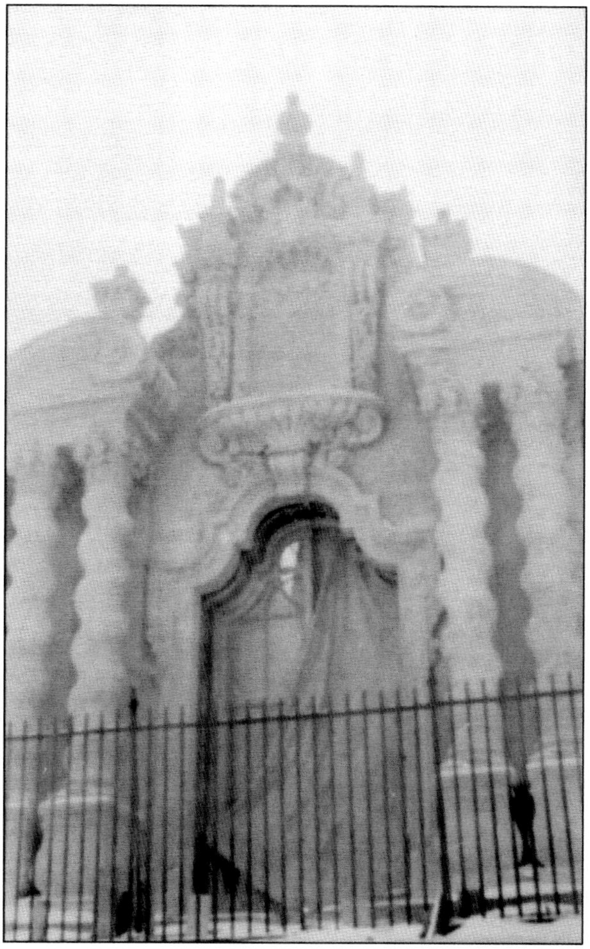

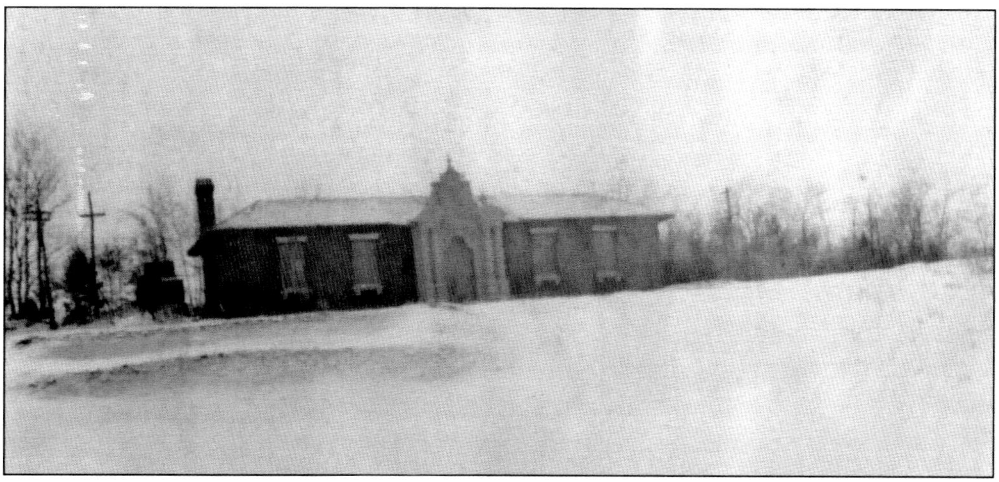

In a rare winter photograph of the early museum, the grounds are covered with snow. The surrounding whitewashed stucco wall is not yet visible up to this point on the property or has not yet been constructed. As can be seen from the position of the telephone poles, the road running down the peninsula is immediately behind this structure.

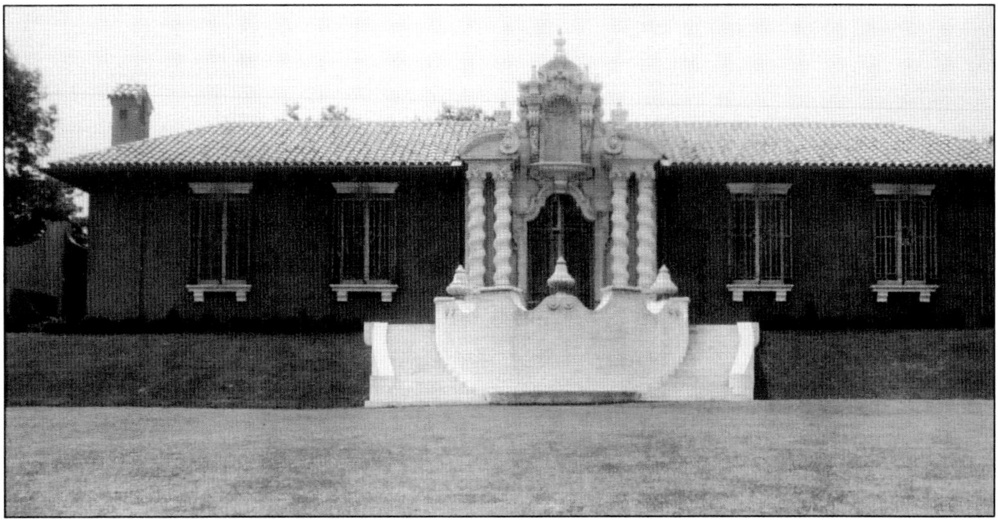

Both unique and impressive with a terra-cotta Spanish tile roof, iron window grilles, and twisted columns at the entrance, Willie K.'s museum was completed in 1922. The newly constructed white stucco wall surrounding Eagle's Nest meets with the structure to provide security and privacy, as the museum is located directly on the road. An access gate just visible to the left would be the entry point for museum visitors. In January of the same year, Willie K. purchased his next ship, a large yacht named *Ara*, to facilitate the collection of specimens to fill the exhibit cases inside. A niche over the entrance is empty at this point but will receive a Botticelli-like Venus statue at a later date.

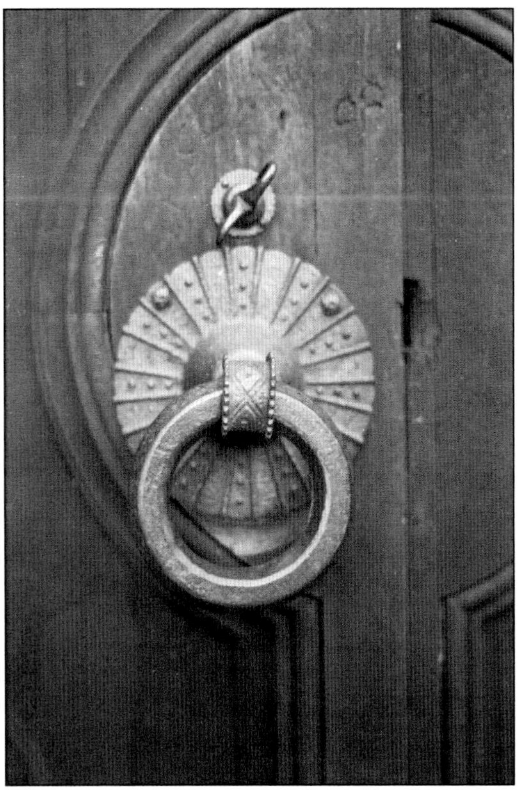

This is a detail view of the lock on the front door of the museum structure. In the early years of the estate, Samuel Yellin created custom-made metalwork for nearly every window, door, and lock. Many of the designs were in the form of sea serpents, shells, and other organic forms. He was regarded as the finest artist in metal and employed as many as 300 workers at his forges, one of which still operates in the state of Pennsylvania.

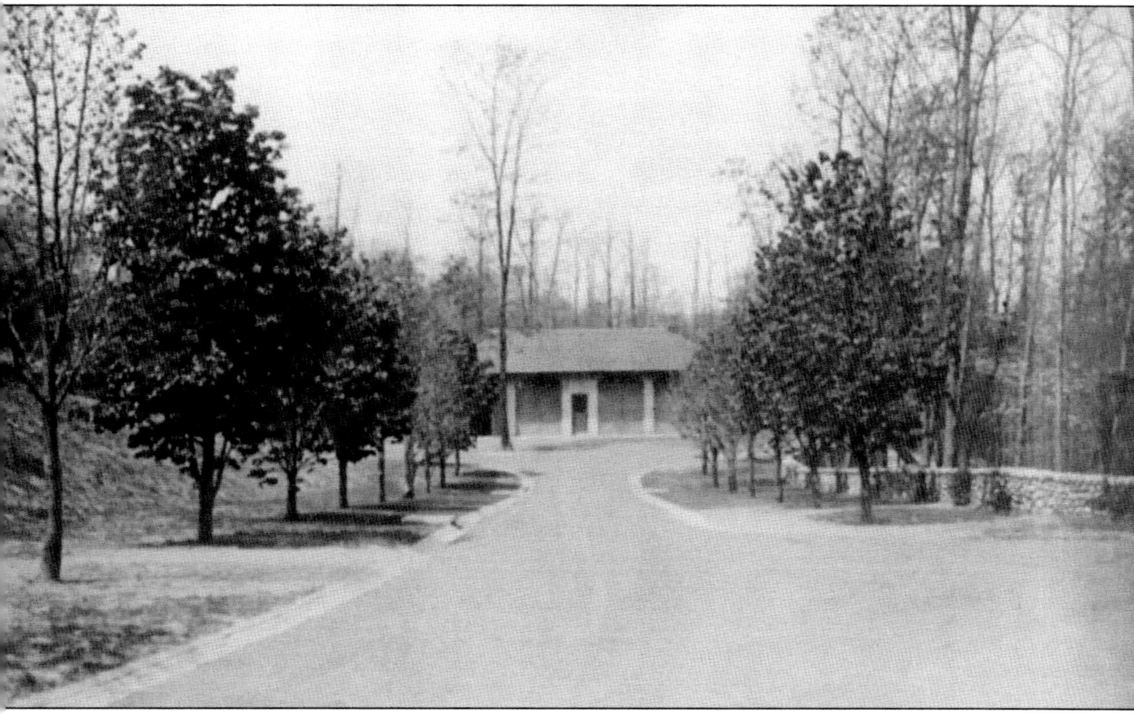

A linden tree allée leads to the four-bay garage located down the hill to the right of the museum. Due to its proximity to the museum building, its exterior matched some of its finishes. Like the museum, it was expanded to two stories in the next construction phase. The garage contained a gasoline pump and cabinets with tools, oil, and other fluids for the mechanics to keep the automobiles on the estate running in fine order.

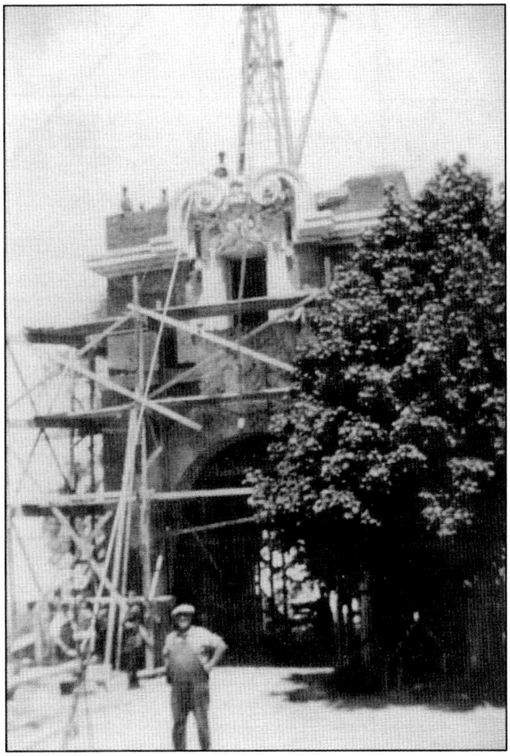

These undated photographs taken by Charles D. Wickers, an architect and mason, depict the bell tower at the entrance to the residence courtyard under construction. Surrounded by scaffolding, a crew of men is shown working on the upper levels. The lower level features a polychrome arch in a Spanish Moorish style, which is painted in a soft butter yellow, pink, and ecru. An applied wooden ornamental portcullis and wooden gate would be installed at a later date. The square fenestration is for one of the bedroom windows, and the round opening is for a clock and electric motors that will drive a large bell located above the clock to chime on the half hour and hour. Despite the loud and frequent knells, Willie K.'s son would use this bedroom during his stays at Eagle's Nest. (Both, courtesy of Frank Wickers.)

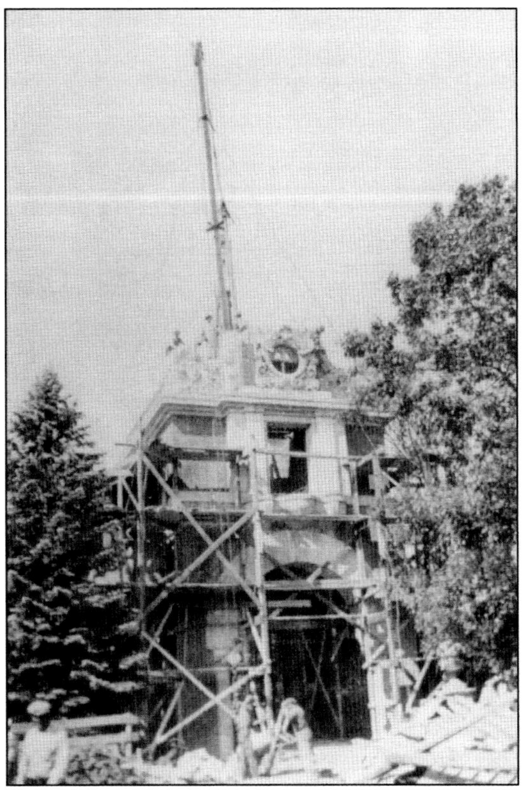

Three

Architects, Artists, and Craftsmen

In 1922, Willie K. realized his dream of having a museum of his own when the construction of the Hall of Fishes was completed. It was a one-story stucco structure with an elaborate entrance framed by twisted columns. Willie K. had it constructed directly on the road with an access gate to facilitate public visits. Warren and Wetmore were the architects of the estate, and there were many in their employ, or contracted by them (under Willie K.'s watchful eye), to carry out their plans. They were the same firm that built Grand Central Terminal in New York for his family. By 1924, the seven-room cottage was enlarged and transformed to Spanish-style stucco with terra-cotta tile roofs. To complete this architectural style, wrought-iron window grilles, lights, gates, and embellishments were made by Samuel Yellin. He won commissions to complete metalwork for some of the most important estates and edifices in the country. Willie K. retained only the most skilled artists to work on his estate. During the 1920s and early 1930s, architect Addison Mizner, who designed many estates in southern Florida and had a personal relationship with the Vanderbilts, no doubt influenced the Spanish style of this estate. During this time, the house was enlarged to enclose three sides of the central courtyard, and a bell tower was constructed. A saltwater swimming pool with two bathhouses was also added.

Despite its old-world appearance, the Eagle's Nest estate was a self-sufficient compound with every modern convenience. In addition to the main residence and the museum building, Vanderbilt constructed a cottage for the museum curator, a powerhouse to generate his own electricity, a boathouse, a four-bay garage, tennis courts, a saltwater pool, and eventually a seaplane hangar.

Changes to the estate began to evolve rapidly to meet various needs—one being the growth of Willie K.'s collections. By 1930, the Hall of Fishes had been expanded to two stories. There was also an exhibit hall at Eagle's Nest that he referred to as the lower museum, which was a private place for Willie K., his family, and closest friends. He retained staff from the American Museum of Natural History in New York to create a cavernous diorama hall underneath the mansion to showcase his most revered collections and commemorate his travels.

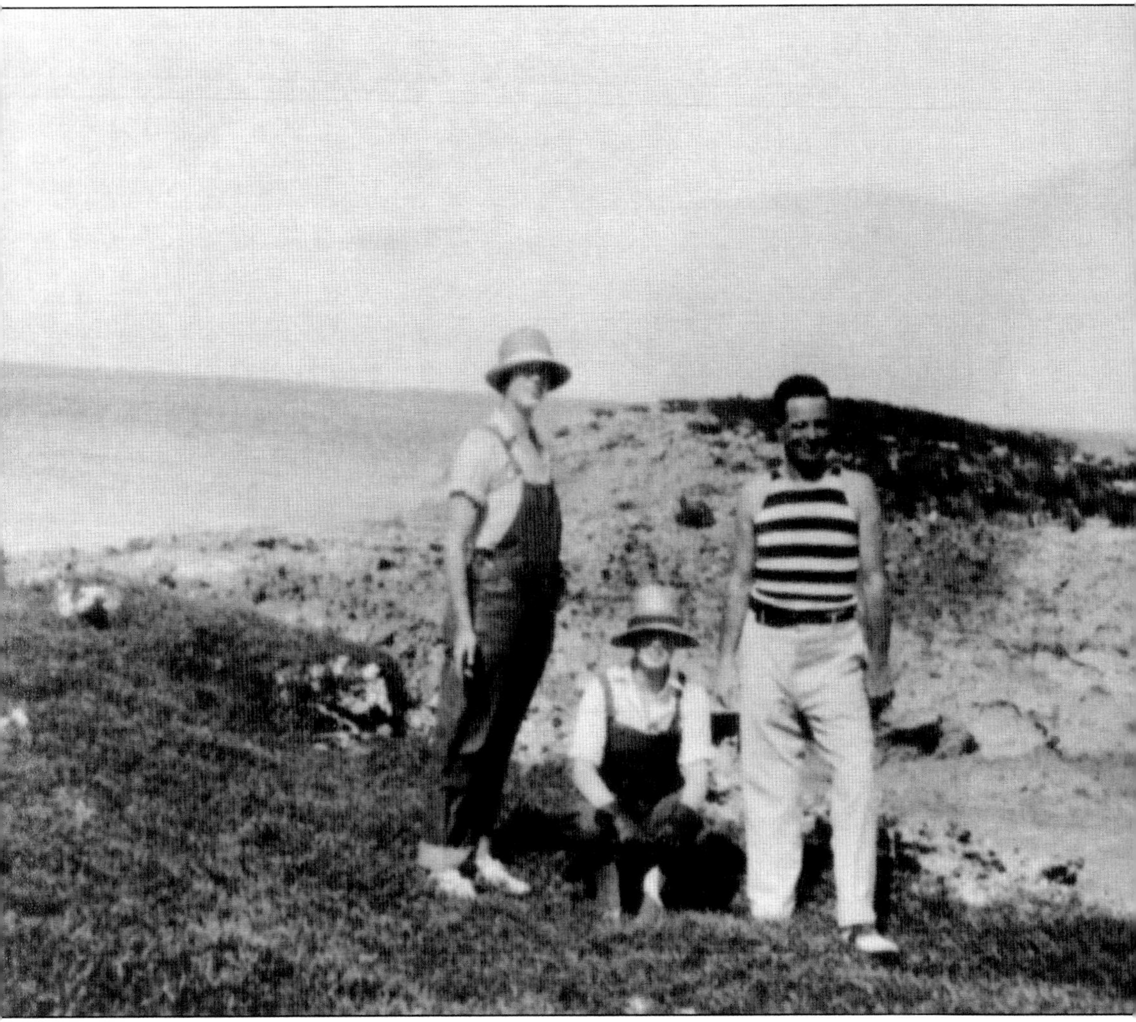

Willie K. is pictured with his daughters Muriel (left) and Consuelo, both in their 20s, on shore during their first trip to the Galapagos Islands off of South America. Like their father, they were adventurous and enjoyed traveling, fishing, and being outdoors. His son did not join them on this journey, perhaps having to attend school, as he was 18 at the time. Willie K. documented this trip in his book *To the Galapagos on the Ara* in 1926. This is his first publication to include full-color illustrations of the fish specimens rendered by artist and museum curator William E. Belanske, who was on the cruise as well. Vanderbilt's future wife, Rose, and her first husband, Barclay Warburton, were among the invited guests who accompanied them.

The front door to the mansion lies at the end of the arcade hallway, which connects the main residence with the annex known as the nursery wing. The door is coffered and embellished with a large iron doorknocker. Above the door are rocaille designs, and the designs at the bottom evoke ocean waves. The floor is slate, as the arcade was open to the elements at this time. The arcade was glazed in the 1930s during the final building phase.

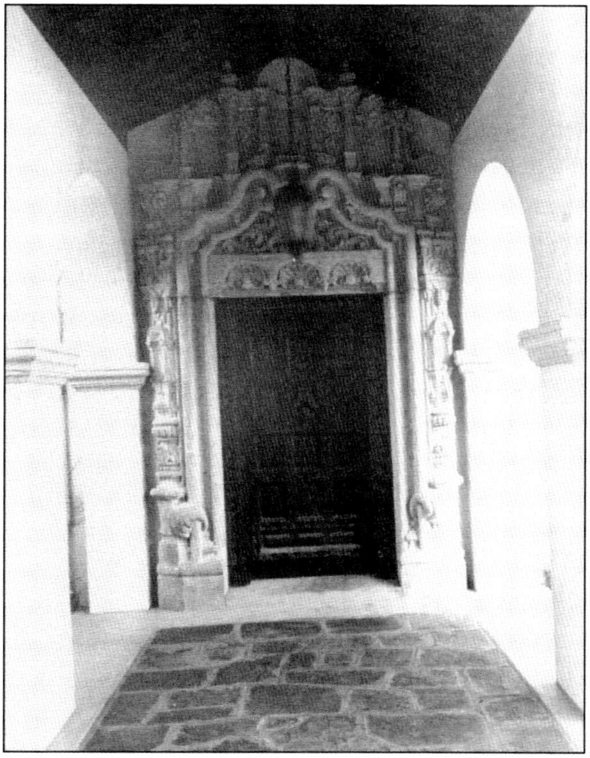

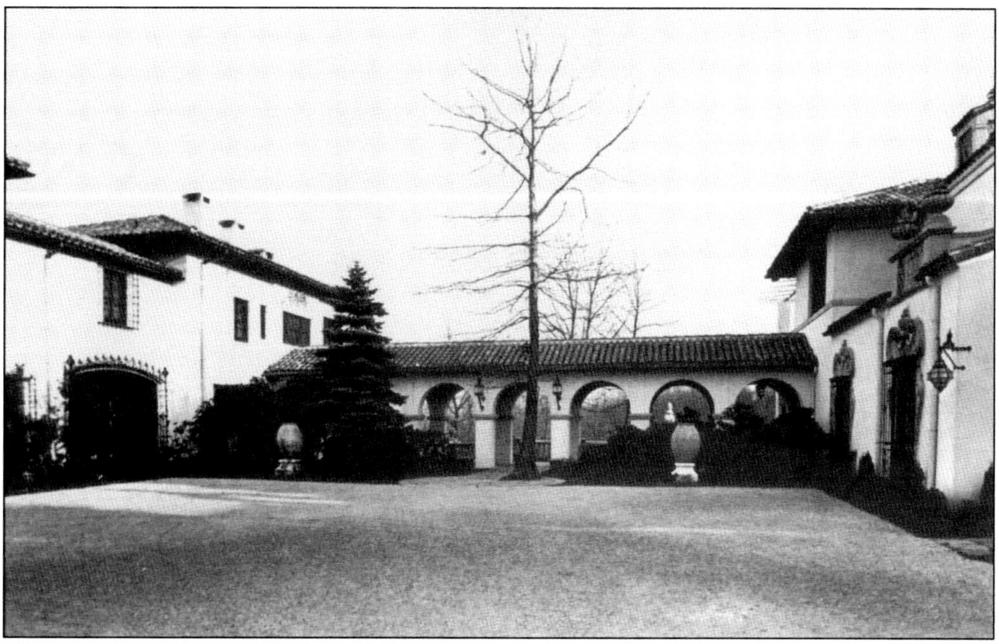

This is a view of the arcade from the courtyard in the 1920s during the expansion and stylistic change phase of the residence. This shows the sprawling structure that the mansion had become, with terra-cotta roof tiles like those of the museum and ornamental ironwork in the form of window grills and lanterns. The house begins to wrap around a central courtyard, completing the elements of the Spanish architectural style.

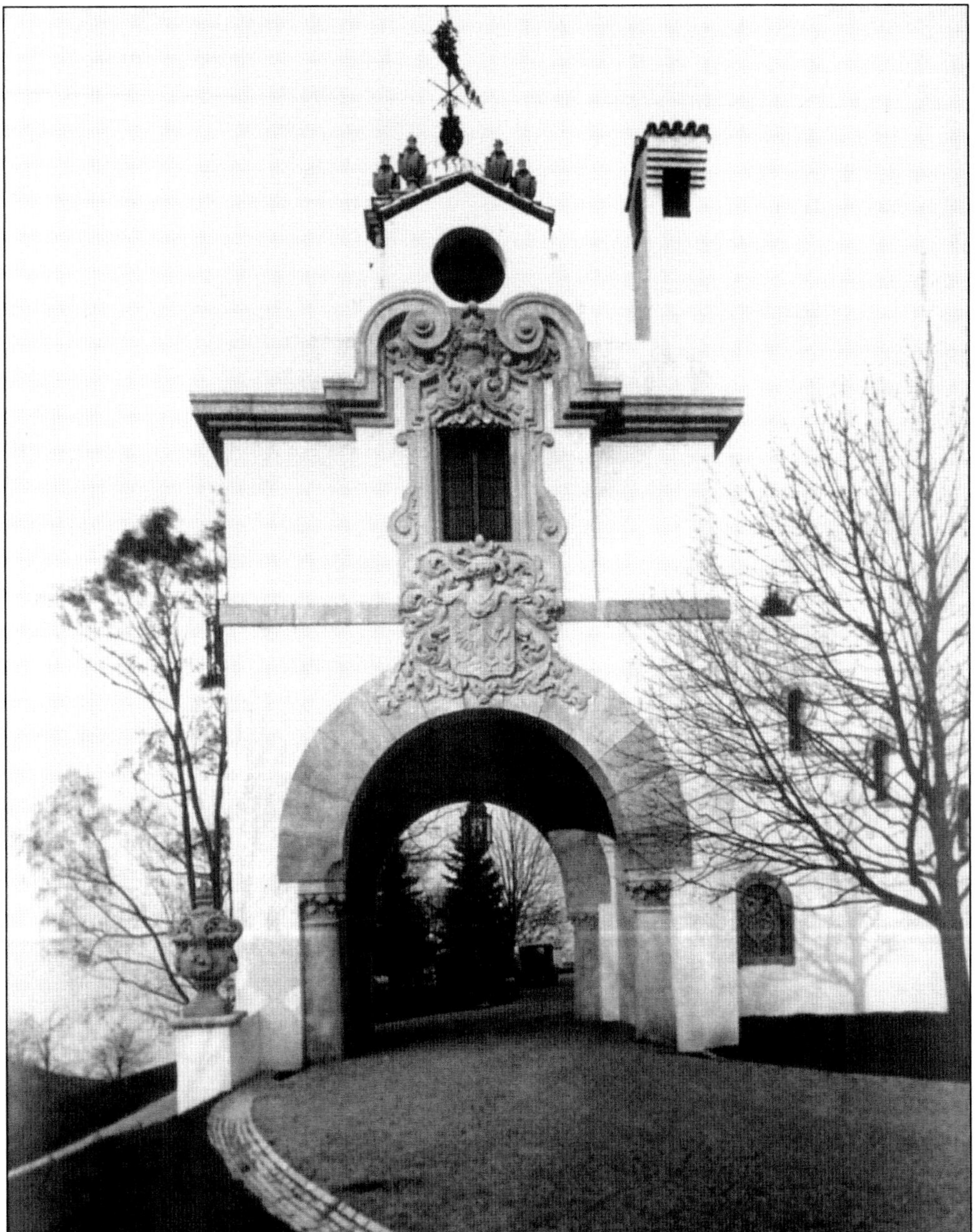

The main access road on the property winds down over the bridge and to a bell tower providing a dramatic entrance to the central courtyard. The structure is a clever harmonization of Spanish, Moorish, and Medieval styles. A family crest in a somewhat exaggerated size applied over the arched opening is a Medieval element that would be restated by the addition of a large wooden gate and an applied portcullis. From a distance, the eight chunky urns that sit atop the roof look like fat birds. The window above is for the bedroom located there that was accessed by a steep, narrow staircase hidden behind the wall to the right of the tower. The interior of the room reflects the exterior, creating a masculine space with Spanish-tile floors and the same playful mixture of elements. Willie K.'s son, William, stayed there during his visits.

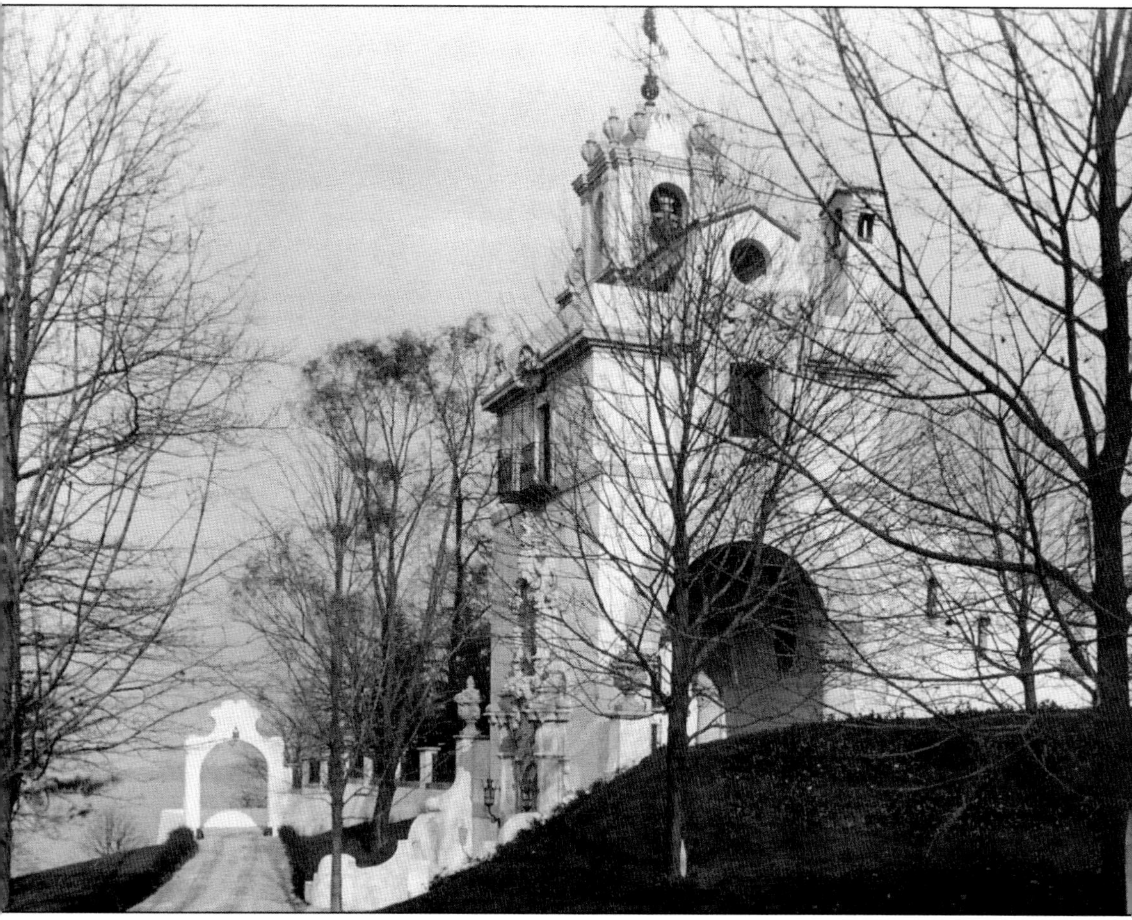

This view of the tower structure reveals the lower western side of the mansion. A wave-like wall splays out from the ground level, like two supporting arms, surrounding the utility area and laundry room, cleverly easing the transition in grade. The large decorative urns serve to transition the eye down in small steps. This situates the structure in a remarkably graceful manner considering the acute slope of the property. The talent and experience of the Eagle's Nest architects are evident in problem-solving features such as these. The simple landscaping consisting of several tall trees also relieves the transition in height from the tower to the ground. The road leading to the mansion splits at a grassy knoll, leading down to the left and terminating at a decorative arch.

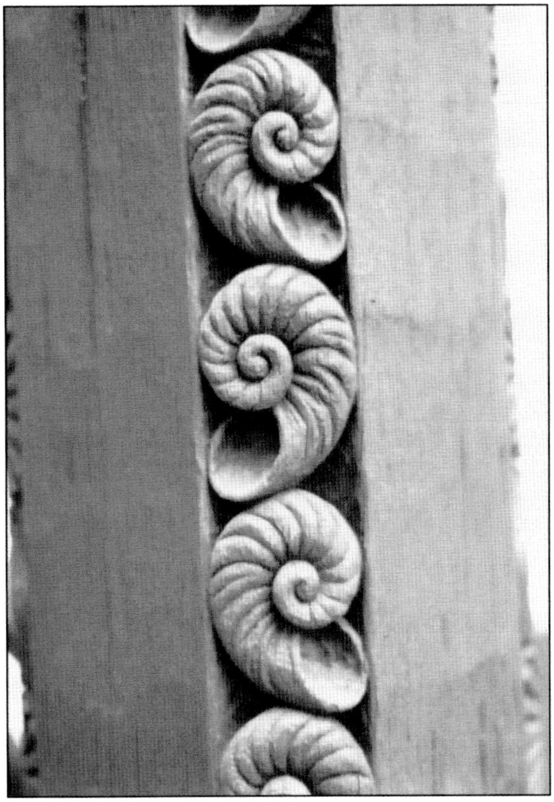

The extremely flat light stucco exteriors of the residence allow for a plethora of embellishments and detail work to be tolerated. The use of wood trim work provides an agreeable medium for carvings. The shell detail carved in wood can be found on the staircase leading to the bell tower bedroom. Marine forms are used in unexpected ways throughout the estate to reflect Willie K.'s personality and to add whimsy. In a small fenestration located near the tower staircase, the chain or rope-like detail seems impossibly carved in stone. There is brilliance in using the conflict of the material and treatment to create a fun, trompe l'oeil effect.

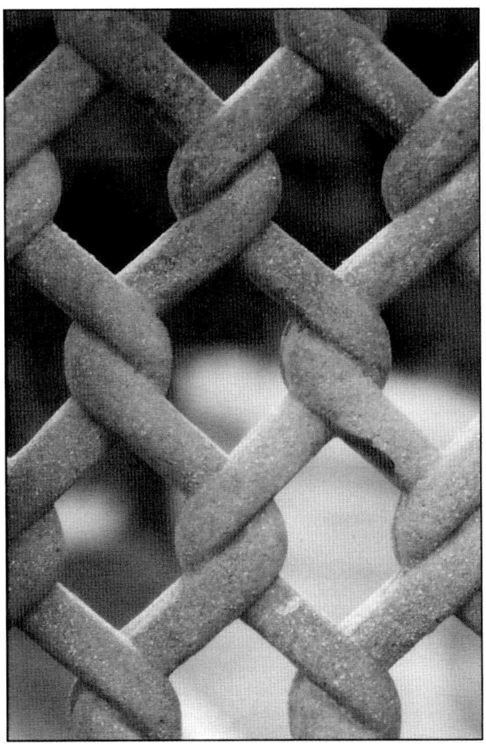

This view from the courtyard reveals the staircase, protected by a tiled overhang, leading up to the bell tower bedroom. The tower clock driven by small General Electric motors is visible, as is the door opening to a trefoil balconet. The rocaille treatments at the corners soften the transition between the vertical and horizontal elements. The courtyard is paved in ordinary macadam.

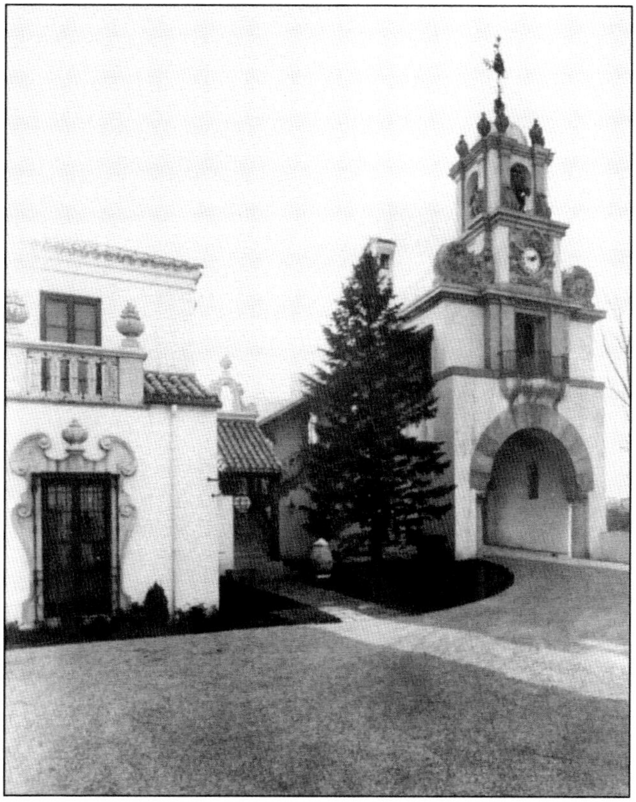

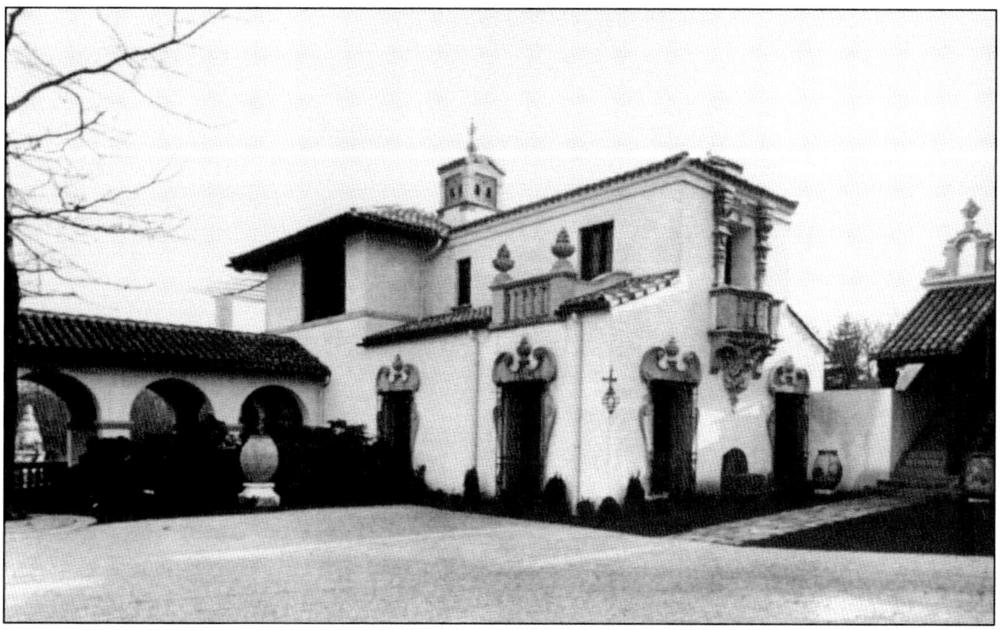

The bell tower access staircase attaches to the nursery wing. The upper level of the wing has an outdoor sun porch off of the back, bedrooms, and bathrooms. On the lower level, there are two bedrooms, three baths, and a sitting room. The nursery wing was used for young visitors as the name implies, and it was located at a comfortable distance from Willie K.'s bedroom.

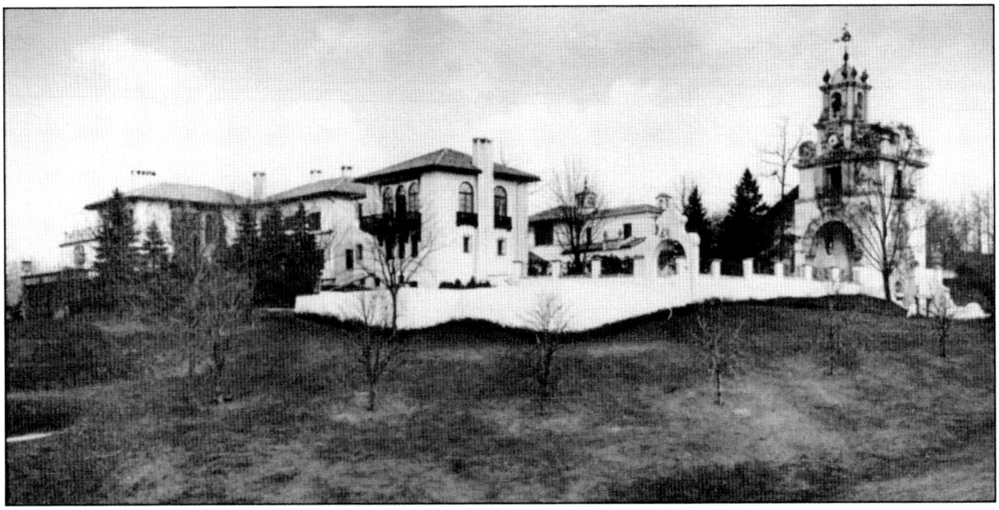

This photograph shows the now sprawling residence as viewed from the waterside of the property at the end of the golf course. Sitting comfortably on the site, the estate is a good example of architecture that does not resist its environment. In the square building to the left of the decorative arch are Willie K.'s bedroom, a passage hallway containing closets and back stairs, and the outdoor porch off of the organ room (to the far left).

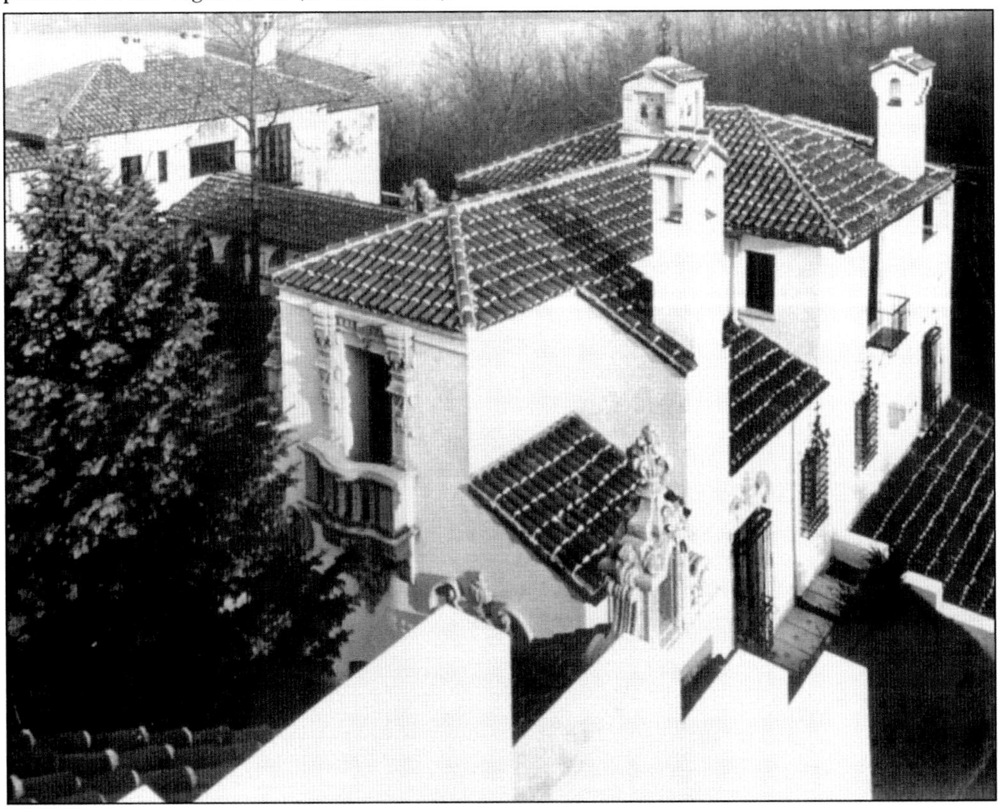

A photograph taken from high atop the bell tower stairs gives a rooftop view of the nursery wing, the arcade, and the mansion entrance to the far left. Northport Harbor is visible just over the rooftop. From this vantage point, Eagle's Nest is reminiscent of a holiday gingerbread house.

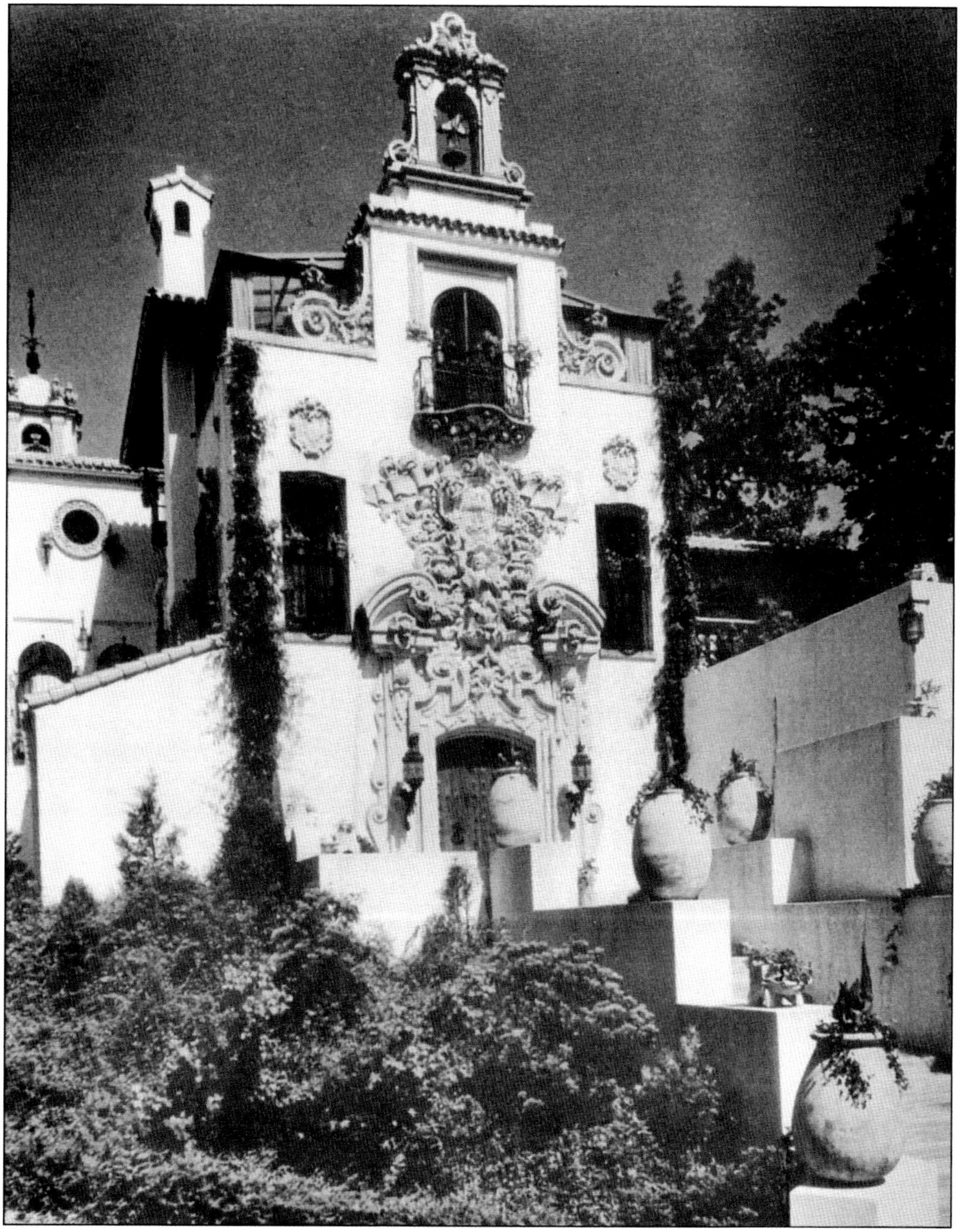

At the eastern side of the residence, just behind the nursery wing, the property slopes down sharply. Underneath the nursery wing, a subterranean exhibit hall that Willie K. called the lower museum was built into the side of the hill. Created by artists from the American Museum of Natural History in New York, it showcased specimens from his earlier collecting days in the Galapagos Islands, the Caribbean waters, Canada, Cuba, Long Island, and the West Indies. Unlike the museum on the road, he made this one for himself and his friends and family, not for public viewing. Like the other areas of the museum, the entrance is embellished with sea forms, carved wooden doors, and ornamental iron pendant lights. The angles of the tiered walls are softened by large, well-placed urns and plants.

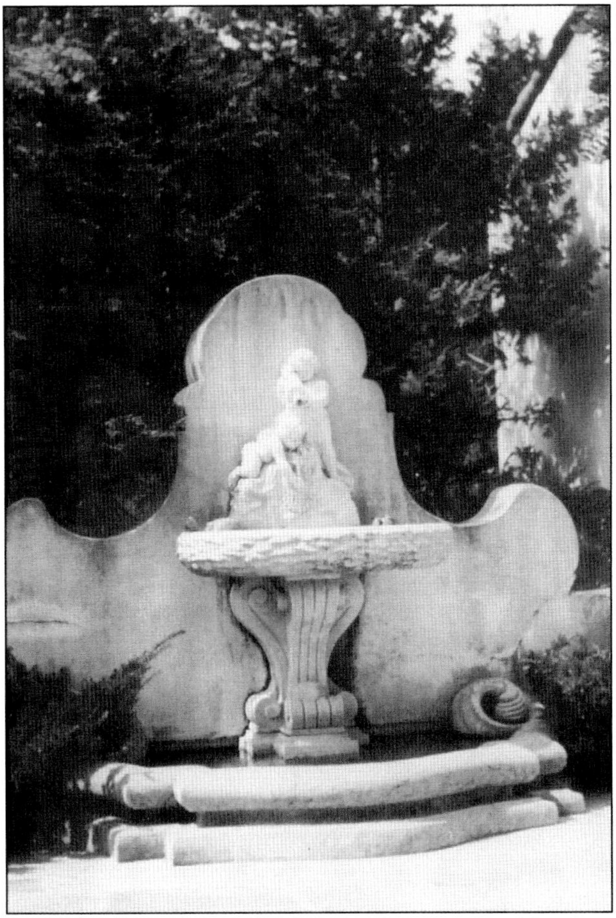

Just outside the entrance to the lower museum was a grotto-like sitting area with a slate patio, cherub fountain, and stone bench (at left). In an unbelievably clever ruse, entering the lower museum from here is like entering another world. In contrast to the serenity of the patio area, the room is cavernous, ominous, and dark, with a glass floor illuminated in blue to give the effect of being underwater (below). The custom plaster moldings around the ceiling are dripping with sea creatures. Nine natural history dioramas, each framed in bronze and embellished with more sea creatures, surround the room. The lights within each one are controlled by stepping on a floor switch in front of it, revealing the dramatic scene inside. The first diorama on the left is a West Indian shark group, swimming from a shipwreck with rows of teeth pointing out. This is a sight that only a handful of divers may encounter, and Willie K. made it possible for everyone to experience.

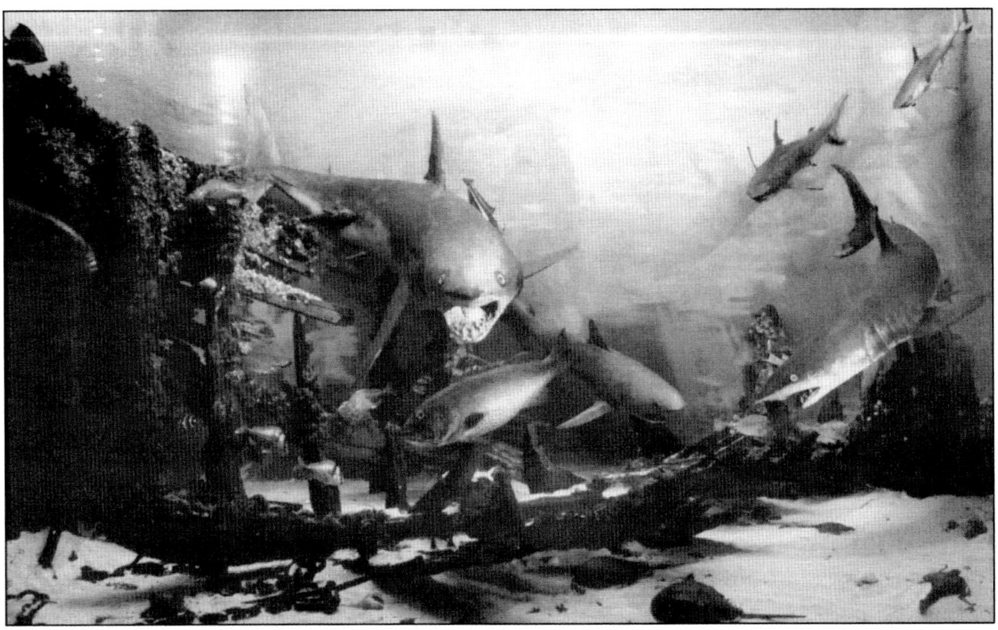

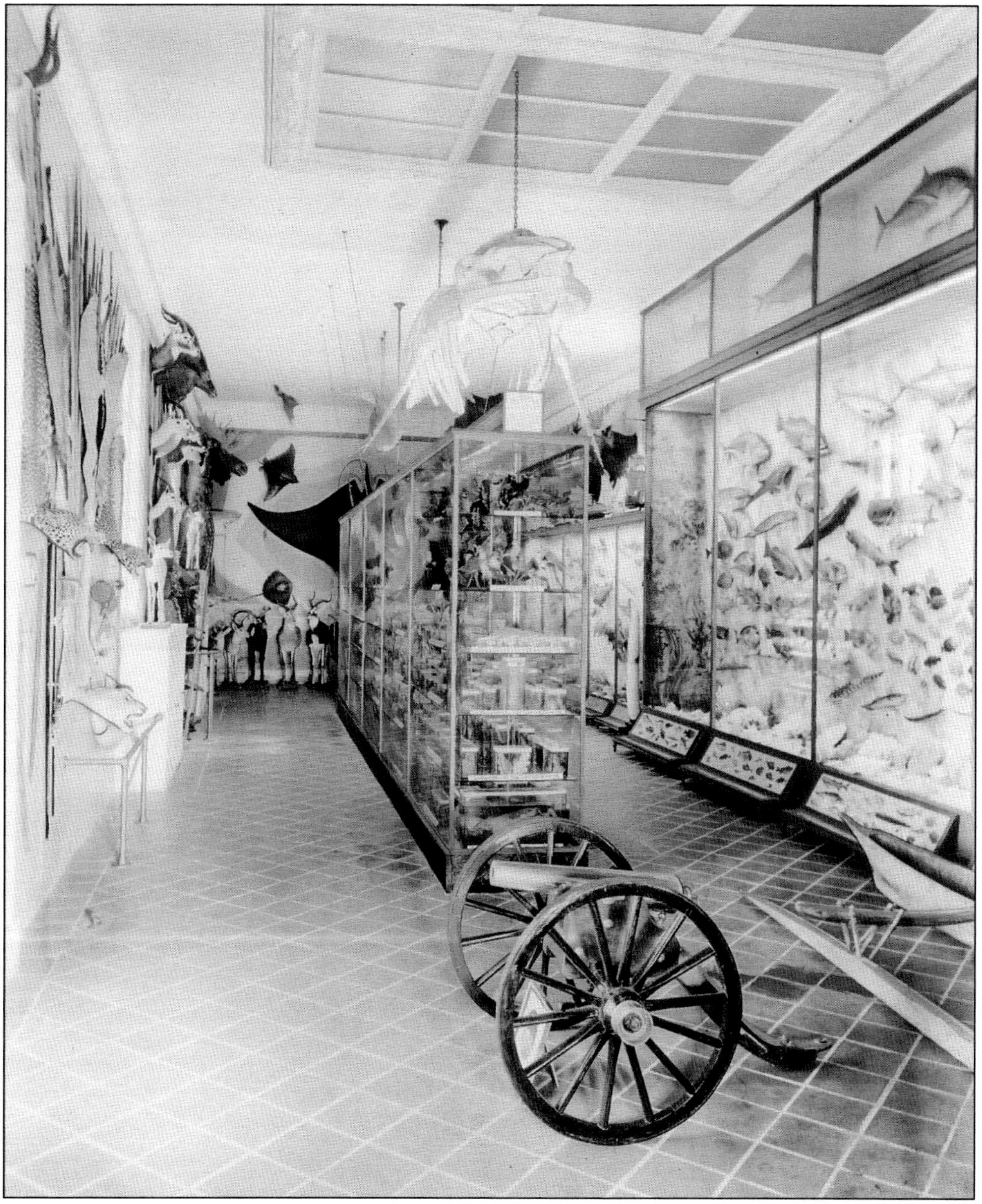

The museum that Willie K. made for the public is filled with every possible natural history specimen and ethnographic artifact imaginable, from old war cannons and outrigger canoes from the South Pacific to sea rays, big game, and little fish. Willie K. had glass cases and hand-designed labels made to display and interpret his collections. This building and its contents became his passion, and by now he had the *Ara*, a ship large enough to support serious collecting. His efforts to fill his museum had been so successful that within a few years his collections had outgrown the space. He began to make plans to expand the museum and by 1930 had added a second floor, just in time for his next big cruise on his last and largest new yacht, *Alva*.

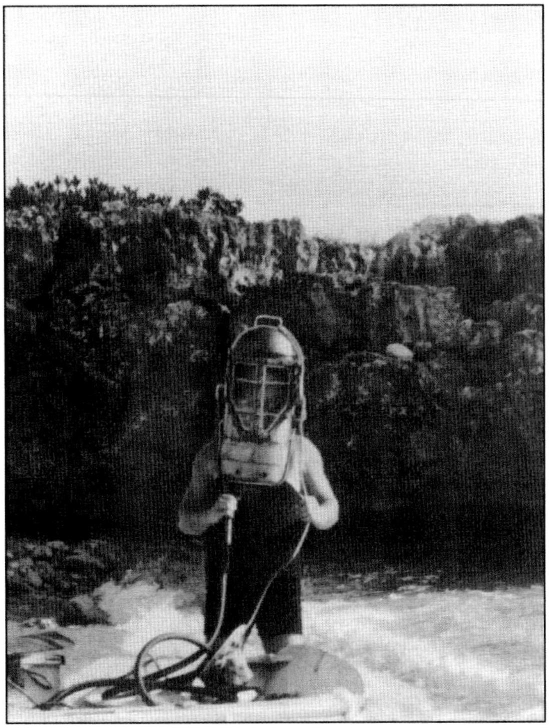

Willie K. used this portable diving helmet to facilitate the collection of marine specimens for his museum. Pictured wearing the helmet in his book *To Galapagos on the Ara*, he asserts that by merely placing it on the shoulders one can go down as far as 40 feet. Some of his crew also tried out the helmet.

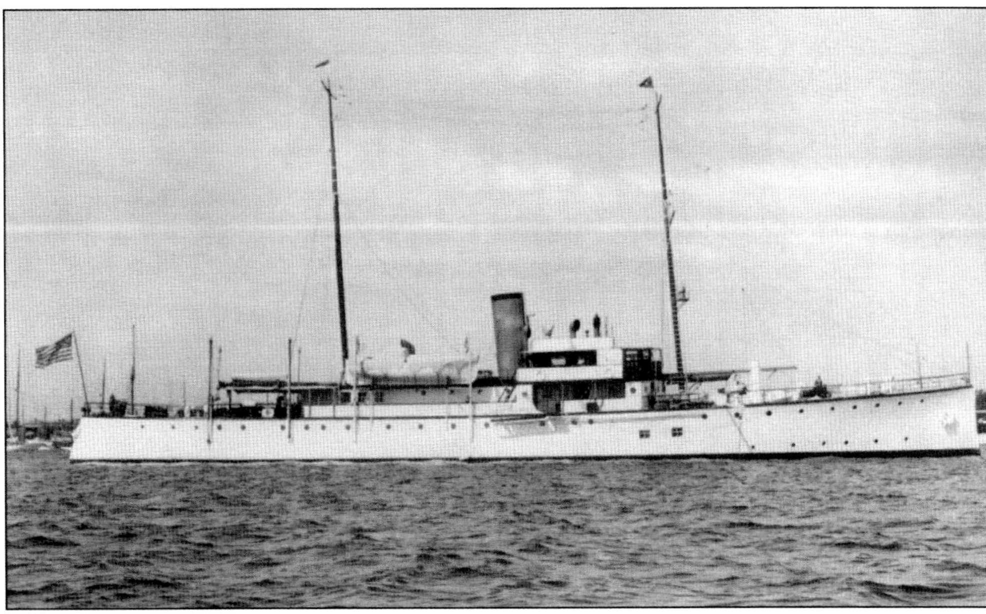

Willie K. purchased the diesel yacht *Ara* in 1922, a ship that formerly served the French navy. He described her as resembling a small British cruiser, 213 feet in length, with three decks and propelled by two Polar diesel motors. On it he had the latest equipment, including a "Metal Mike" to steer the boat automatically and truer to course than any quartermaster. Willie K. describes having a museum on board between the ship's library and the staterooms containing ship models and mounted birds and fish. There was also an Aeolian Duo-Art Steinway grand piano and Brunswick Panatrope phonograph on board to help occupy passengers on an extended voyage.

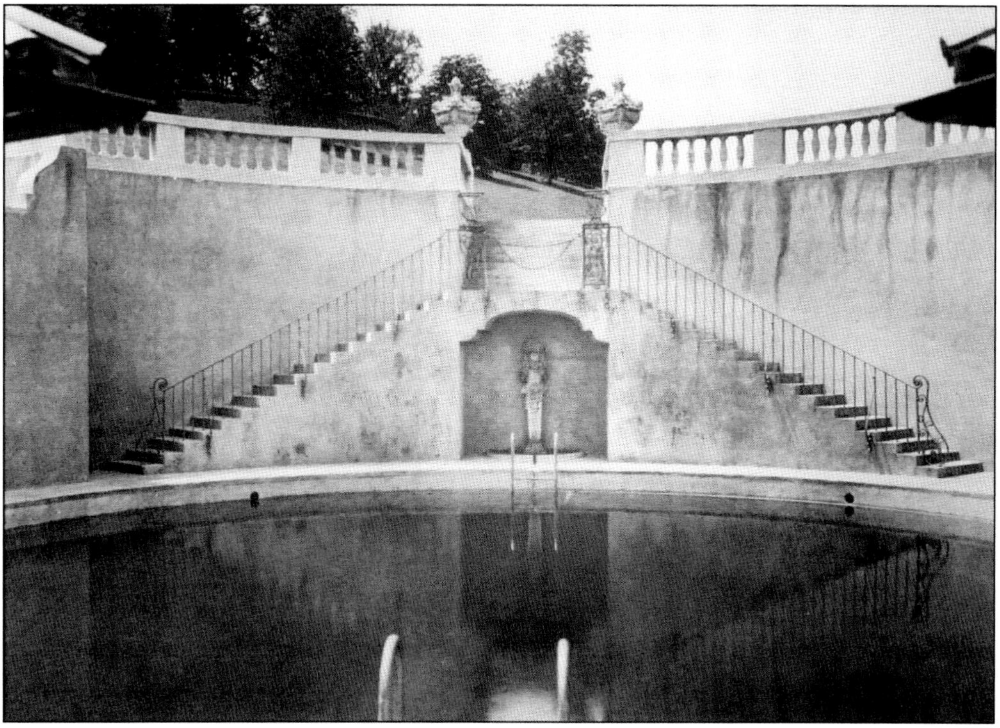

The round saltwater pool (above) and adjacent cabanas (below) were added to the estate near to the water's edge in the mid-1920s. The extreme grade change in the property may have been considered a problem, but instead it was effectively incorporated into the design. Creating Hollywood-like drama, the descent down to the pool has dual staircases, flanked by delicate iron railings dotted with square-shaped iron planters. With fewer decorative elements, there is a quiet classicism to the design. Dual 36-square-foot cabana structures with tile roofs located on the opposite side provide private male and female dressing areas. The water view from the pool area gave the impression of teetering at the edge of the shore. The producers of the movie *The Great Gatsby* sent location scouts to Eagle's Nest in 2013 to view the saltwater pool as a stylistic reference for their production.

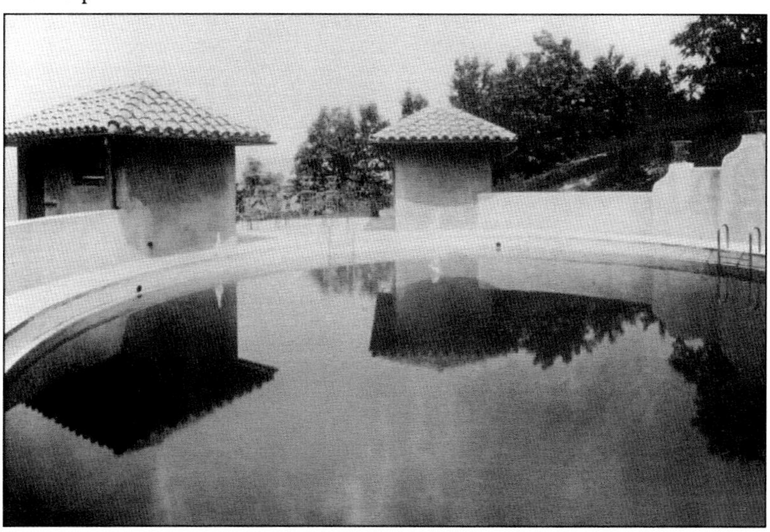

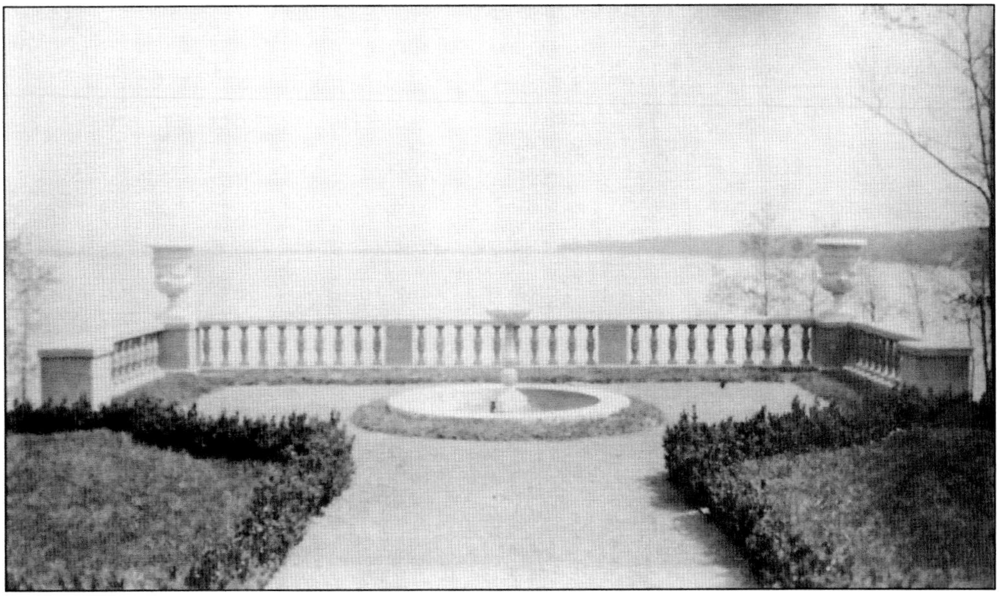

Off of the back porch of the house, a *T*-shaped garden path culminates in a circular fountain, surrounded by classical balustrades topped at the corner by two graceful urns. The style is simple in comparison with the other areas of the estate, and it is not adequate to complement the spectacular water view. The architects would change this to a larger reflecting pool at a later date.

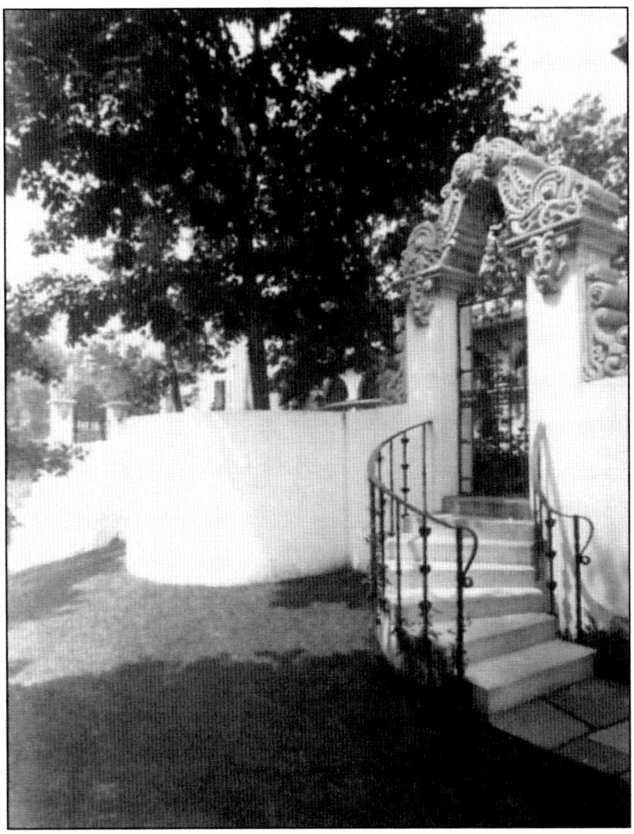

Behind the east side of the arcade and below the boxwood garden are rounded stucco walls and curved stairs used in favor of tiered gardens to compensate for the grade of the property. This type of architectural device works remarkably well on this site and with this style of architecture.

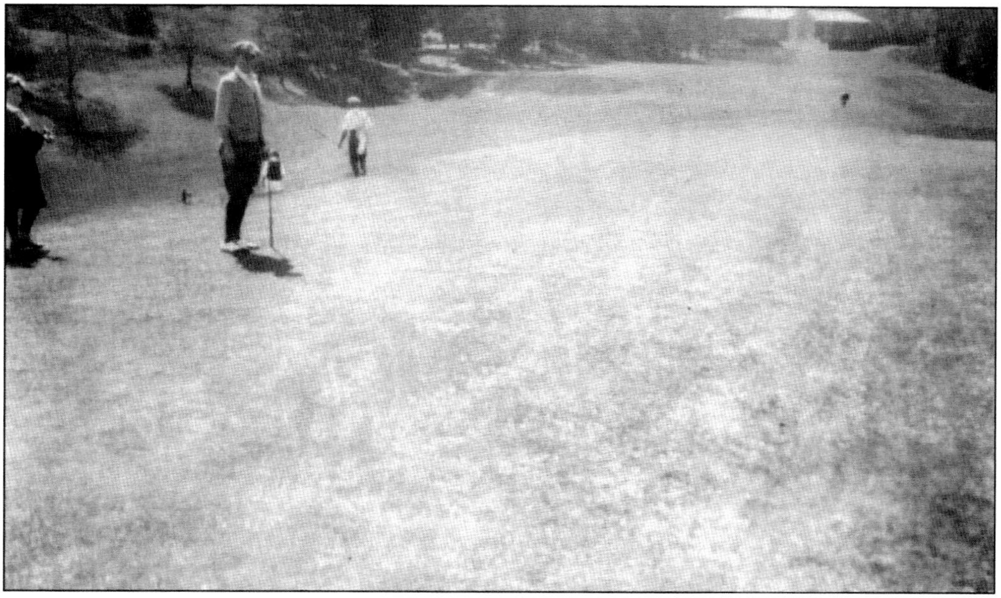

Willie K. plays the golf course at Eagle's Nest with unidentified golfers in the 1920s. Above, a view of the museum is in the distance. The shadow of the museum structure is seen to the left in the image below. The original design of the par-60 course is credited to Devereux Emmet, who designed many courses on the East Coast and locally on Long Island. Emmet designed the courses for the nearby Garden City and Huntington, New York, country clubs. Typical of Willie K.'s playful personality and humorous nature, he named each of the holes for his ships, renaming them per time played, with six holes played three times for an 18-hole round. For example, *Carmita* was the name given to the first hole in the first round, and again to hole 13 in the third round.

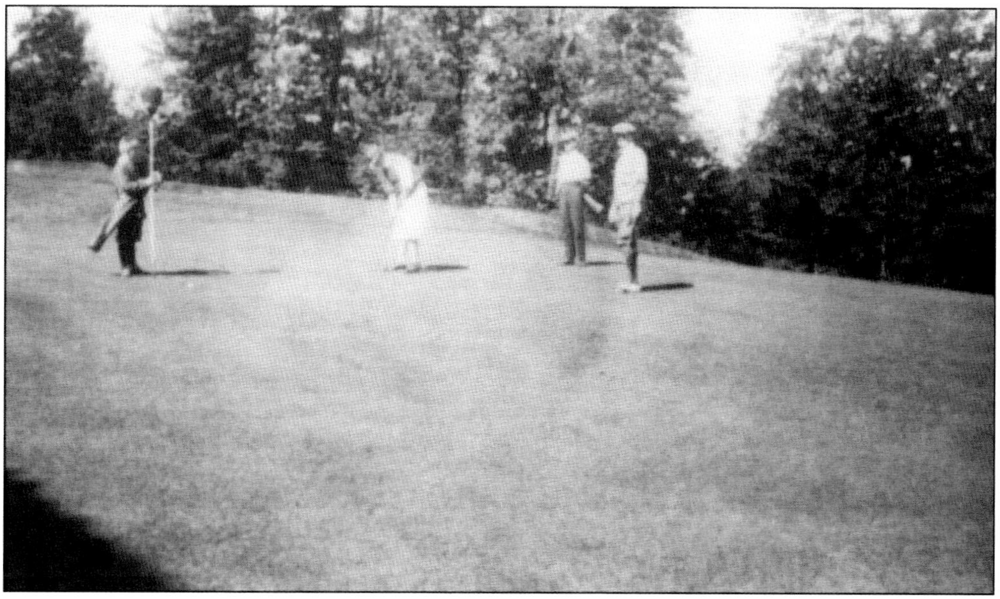

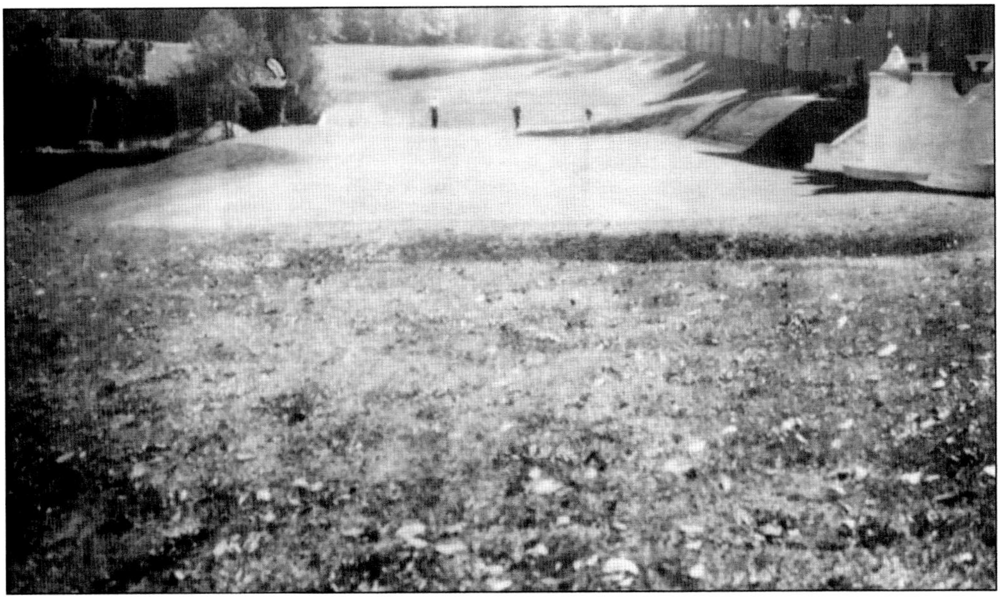

These views show the golf course in front of the entrance staircases to the museum and the water view at the other end of the course. The course ran from the water's edge to the road at the west side of the property, took a dogleg turn in front of the museum, and extended to the estate entrance. Willie K. employed a grounds-keeping staff to keep the course finely manicured. Over the years, he played the course with various friends and celebrities. Estate architect Ronald Pearce played golf with Willie K., as did professional golfer Sam Snead, who signed the day's scorecard for him as a souvenir. Apparently impressed with Snead, Willie K. kept the card with his records (see page 102).

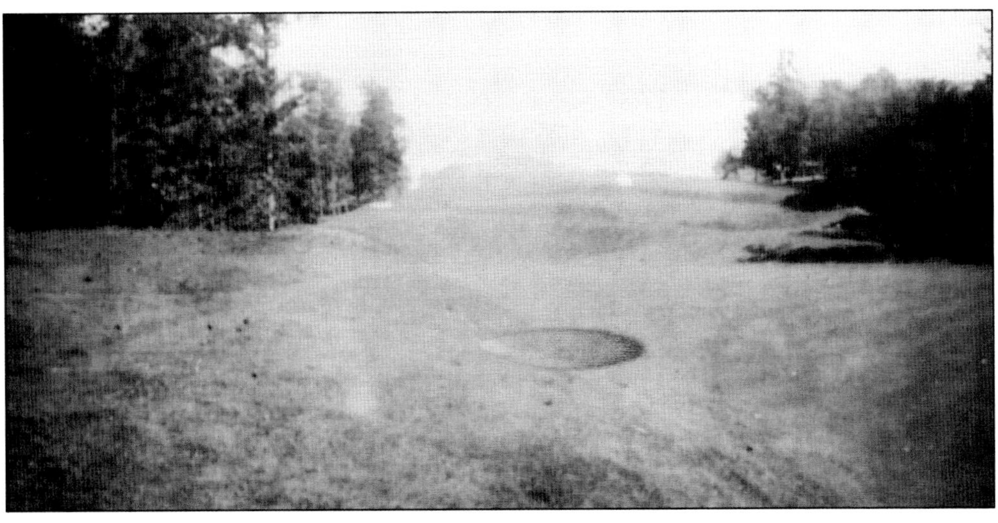

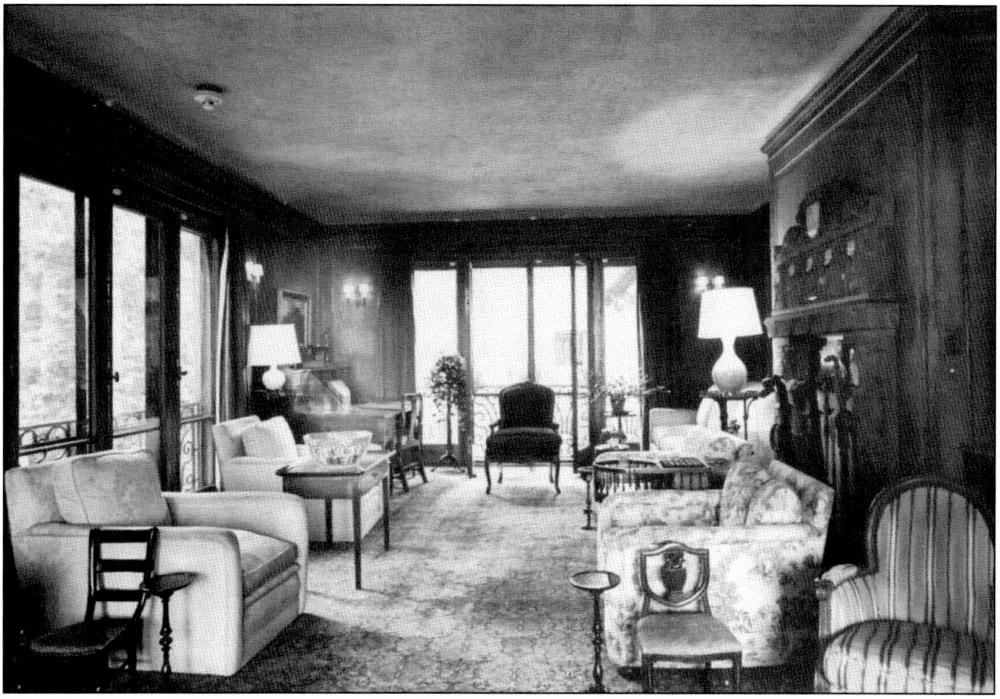

These are two views of the sitting room off of the entrance foyer. The furnishings appear to be crowded and are arranged differently in photographs obviously taken during different years. It is uncertain exactly how the room was arranged when the Vanderbilts lived there. There were chairs and possibly other pieces added to this room in the early 1940s that were removed from the ship *Alva* in preparation for turning her over to the Navy. The mantel contains carved faces that represent figures from the Crusades, which is the source for the name Portuguese Sitting Room, as it is sometimes called. The room has dark, wood paneling, and a silk Sharistan carpet in beautiful shades of green and blue fills the floor. This was the room used by Willie K. to conduct business and write correspondences prior to the construction of his library in the late 1930s.

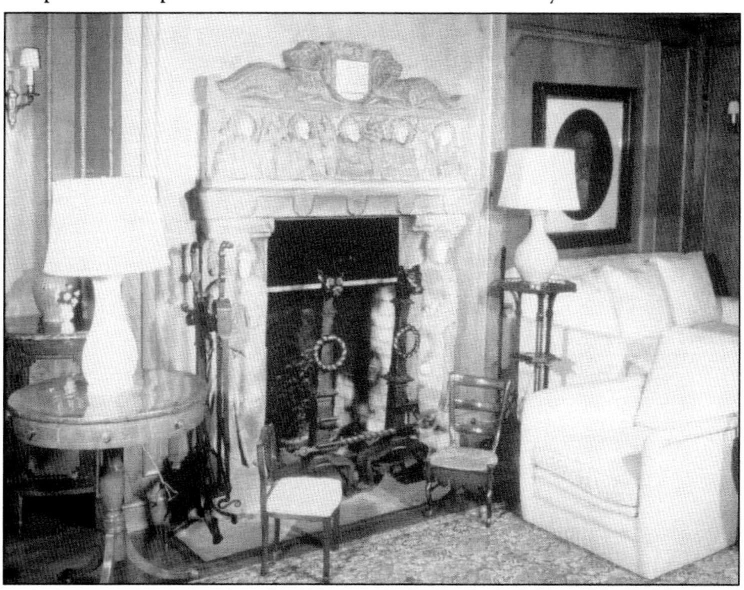

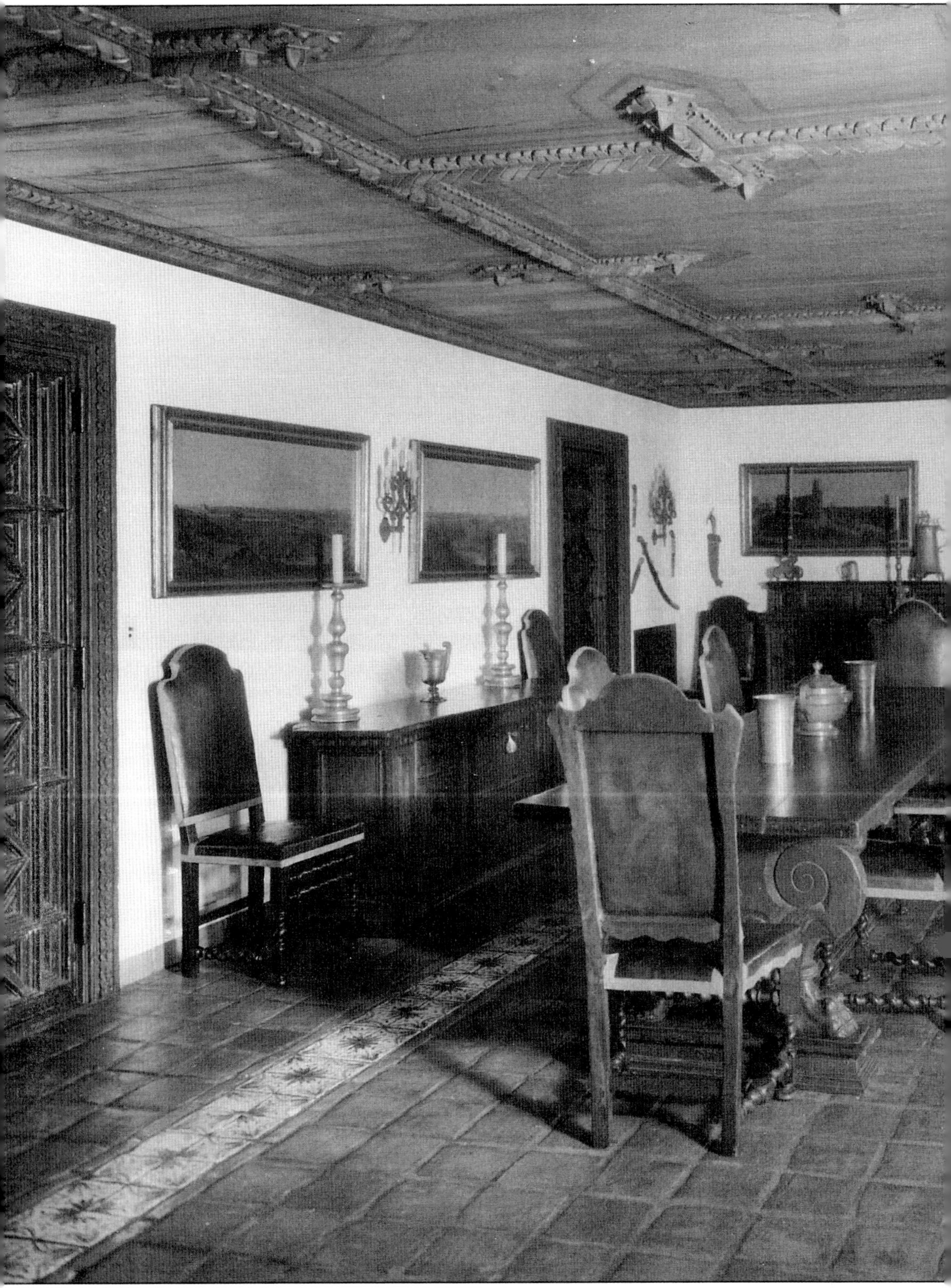

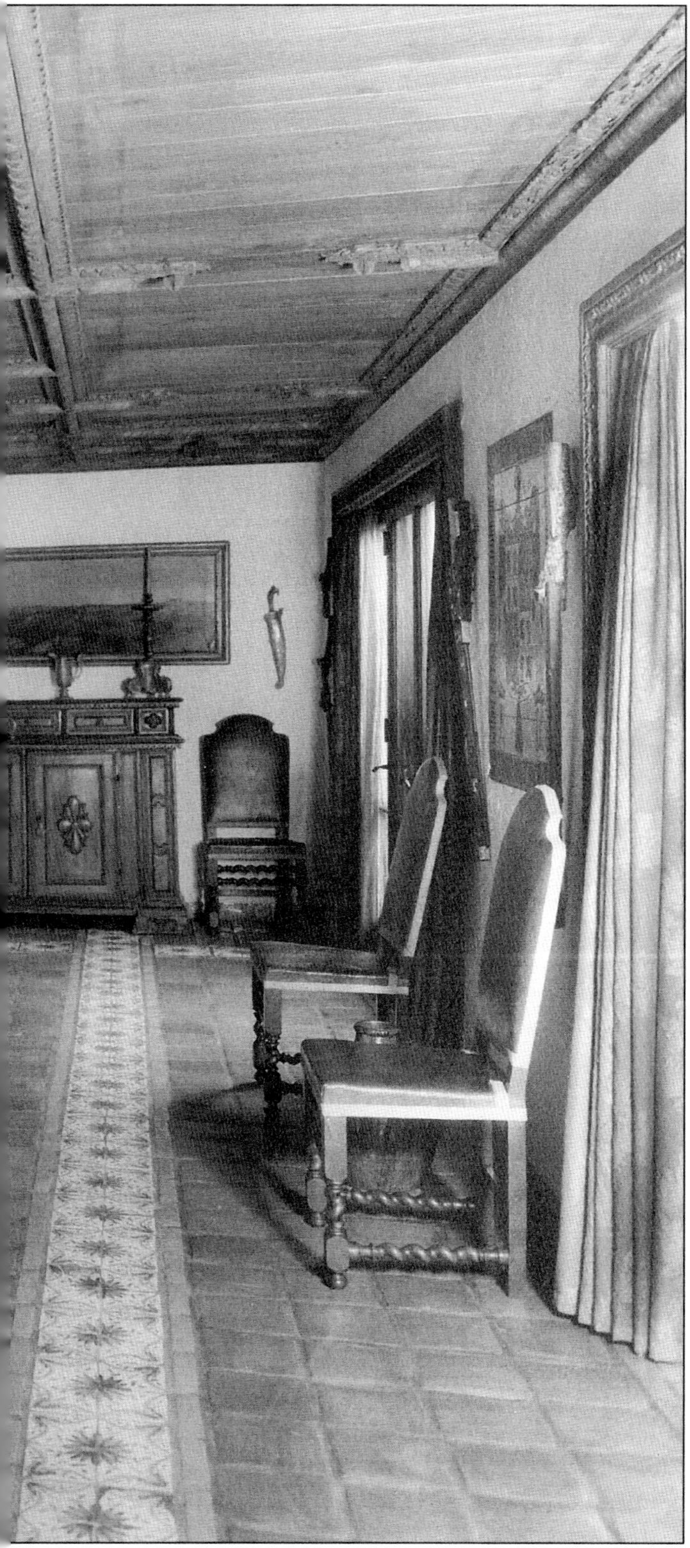

The style of the dining room most closely matches the style of the exterior of the estate. The long, thin refectory table and alms cabinet with felt-lined drawers are in the style of Spanish monastery furnishings. The four landscape paintings depict scenes from a town in Spain. The floors are tiled in terra-cotta, with a multicolor border design. The ceiling is planked in hand-carved Florida cypress, with brightly painted accents. Former staff members recall that the Vanderbilts dined in formal dress, with Willie K. at one end of the table and Rose at the other. They hosted intimate dinner parties for friends or had visits from family members. This was not a place where large, loud parties were held.

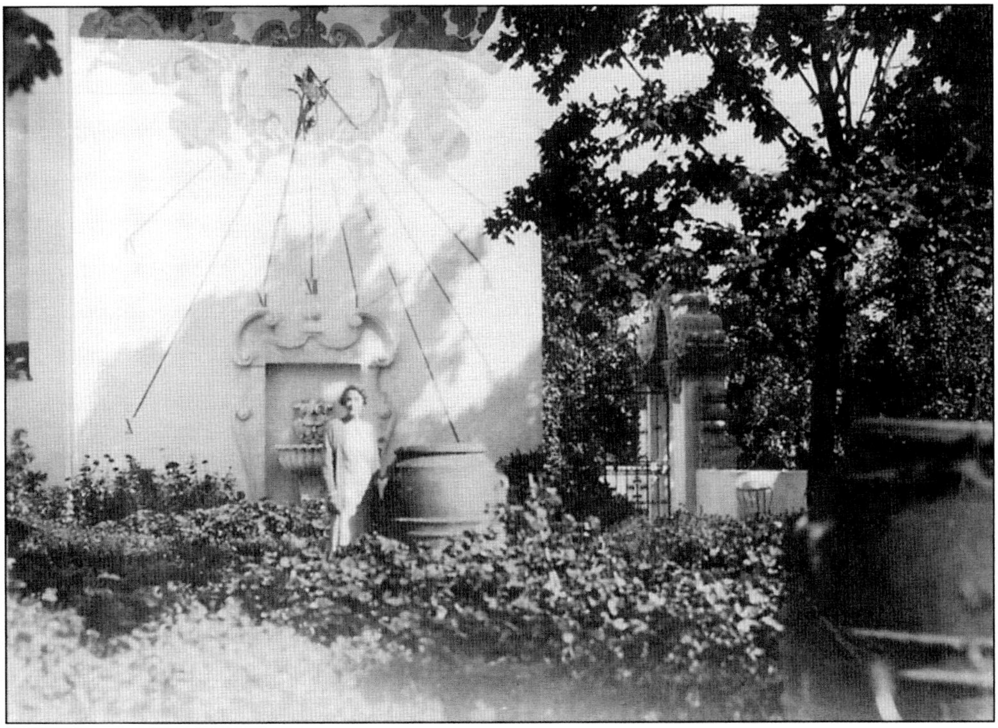

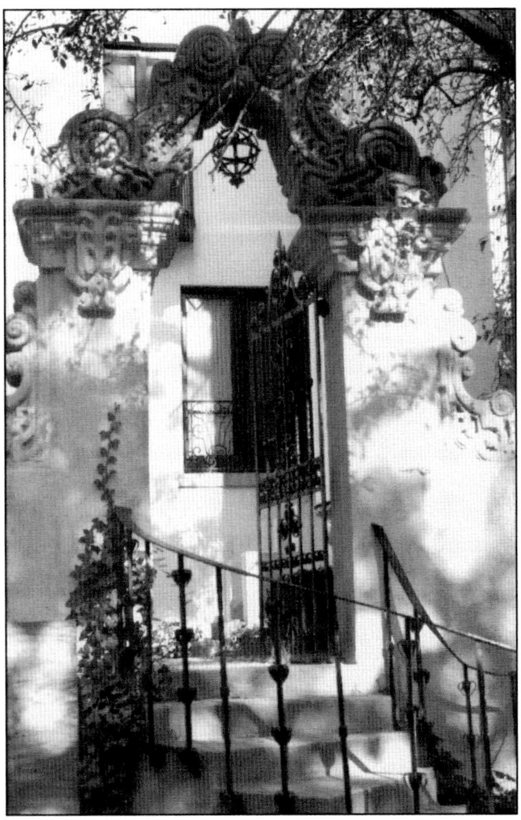

Rose is pictured under the sundial in the boxwood garden behind the arcade at the estate in the late 1920s. Just a year after cruising on Willie K.'s yacht with her husband, Barclay Warburton, she became Vanderbilt's second wife during a stop in Paris, France, on a 1927 voyage. The circumstances surrounding this life event were never shared with the public. This is a rare photograph of a Vanderbilt family member at Eagle's Nest contained in the museum records. If there were any photographs of the interior spaces during the years that Willie K. and Rose lived at the estate, none remain.

This staircase and gate lead up to the boxwood garden where Rose is standing in the previous image. Each area of the estate and its gardens received consistent attention to detail and treatments, with custom-designed ironwork and embellished details that evoke organic forms such as seashells.

A beautifully rendered Madeira stone walkway lines the roadside crossing the bridge and entering Eagle's Nest courtyard. These walks were a somewhat later addition in the 1930s. The stones were brought back from Spain and reassembled in situ.

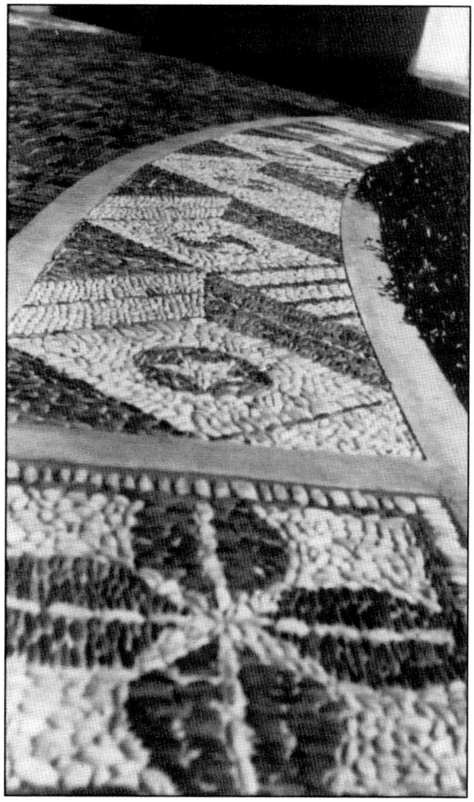

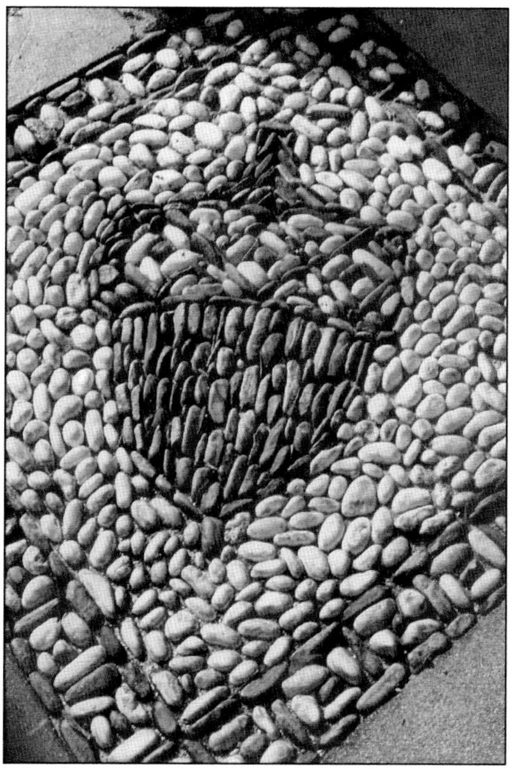

A close-up of the Madeira detail shows an acorn that was a personal symbol of the Vanderbilt family through the generations, signifying strength. This symbol appears on their family crest in the dining room and in other places on the estate as well. References to Willie K.'s heritage are a repeated theme at Eagle's Nest.

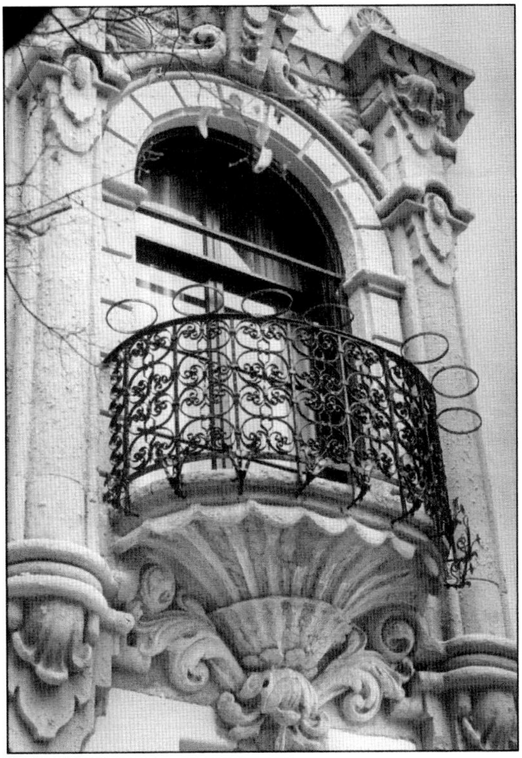

A closer view of the ironwork on a balcony off of the library shows rings jutting out to receive potted plants. The balconies throughout the estate best illustrate the harmony between the cast stone treatments and iron motifs and the skill of the artisans.

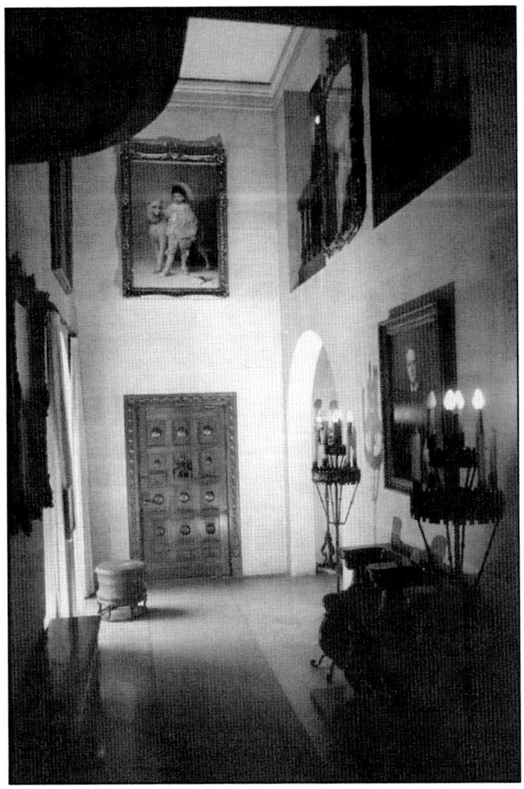

This interior view looks toward the main entrance to the mansion from the entrance foyer. The door is dotted with seashells rendered in iron and, oddly, a door knocker, which would not customarily be found in an interior side. Perhaps this is another example of Willie K.'s humor. The limestone walls are imprinted with ancient fossil reliefs. Use of this material brings yet more organic forms into the design.

Four

Creating a Public Museum on a Private Estate

The correspondence left behind at Eagle's Nest between Willie K. and Warren and Wetmore's New York office discussed endless decisions about the execution of the museum displays. From the color of the glass to the size of the lettering, no detail escaped Willie K.'s attention. The massive exhibit cases were custom made by the Library Bureau to his specifications. Willie K.'s initials and red checkmarks can be found on copies of nearly every invoice and letter in the estate archives.

As fastidious as Willie K. was in his documentation of his journeys, he was even more so in the preparation of his museum and its catalogs. He retained scientists Lee Boone and Nicholas Borodin to identify each marine specimen. This collection is published in eight volumes, accompanied by detailed scientific illustrations. He hired anthropologist Gene Weltfish to produce a catalog of his ethnographic collection.

Determined to have the finest private marine museum, Willie K. became a voracious collector of specimens. He hired Charles Thompson, a famous charter fisherman from southern Florida, to help him. Thompson had the credentials and a reputation for being highly skilled, fearless, and knowledgeable about specimen identification. He accompanied not only the Vanderbilts, but other prominent families such as the Astors on their fishing expeditions.

When Willie K. sailed on his largest expeditions to the Galapagos Islands and during his circumnavigation of the globe, he was accompanied by a large crew that included an artist, photographer, and cinematographer to document everything. These journeys are published in the largest and most elaborate of his books: *To the Galapagos on the Ara*, *Taking One's Own Ship around the World*, and *West Made East with the Loss of a Day*.

To facilitate the execution of his exhibits, he provided a modest, comfortable cottage at the southwest corner of the property for his museum curator, William E. Belanske, a talented artist who lived there year-round with his wife and son. There was a large studio space in the cottage where he worked on exhibits and specimens. He corresponded with Willie K. regularly to keep him abreast of his progress.

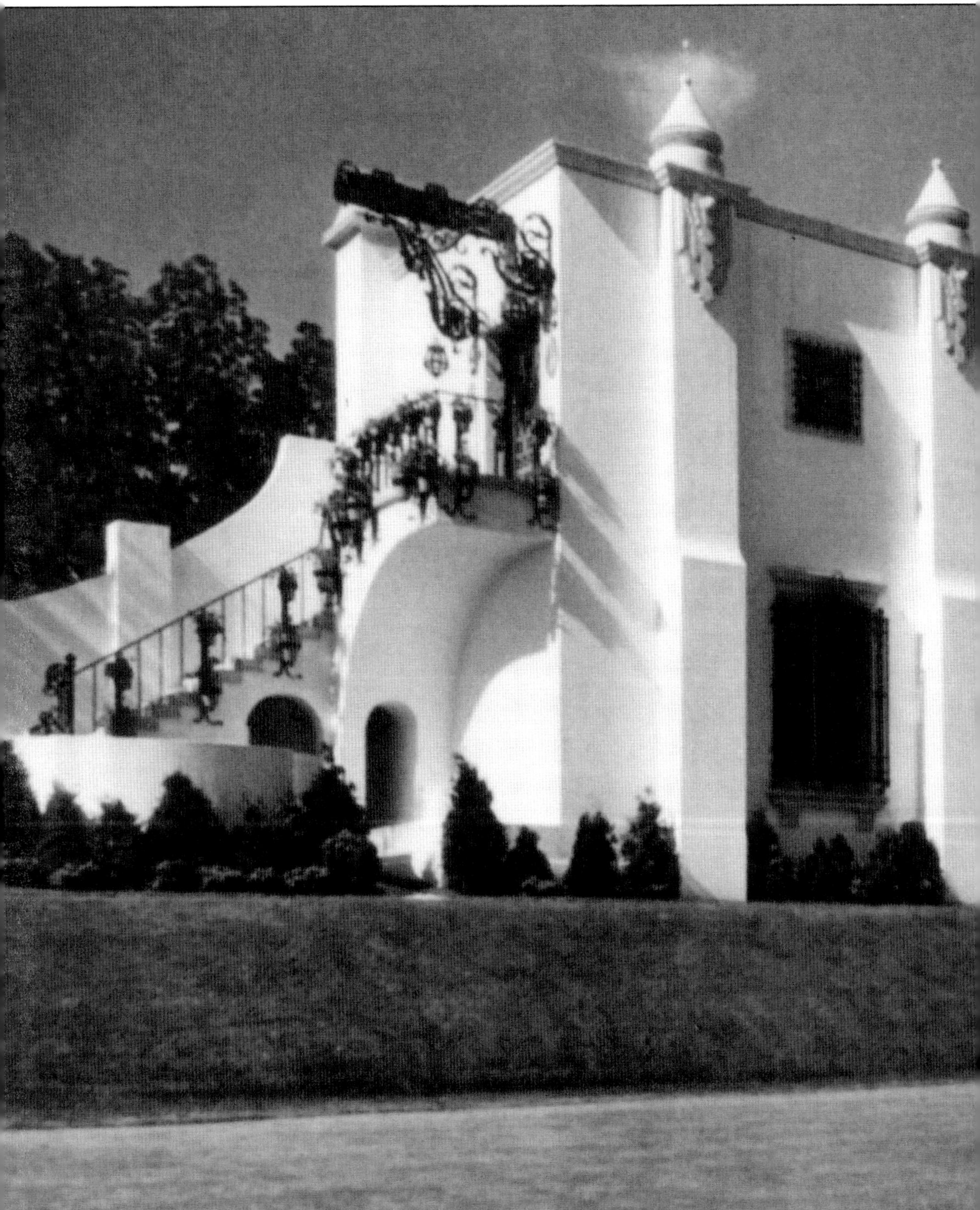

By 1930, the one-story Hall of Fishes was expanded to two floors and changed to correspond with the style of the residence. While the entrance door and treatments were left intact, the remainder of the building was changed. The exterior surfaces, formerly dark brown, were whitewashed, more closely matching the residence. Six applied vertical pilasters spanning both floors were

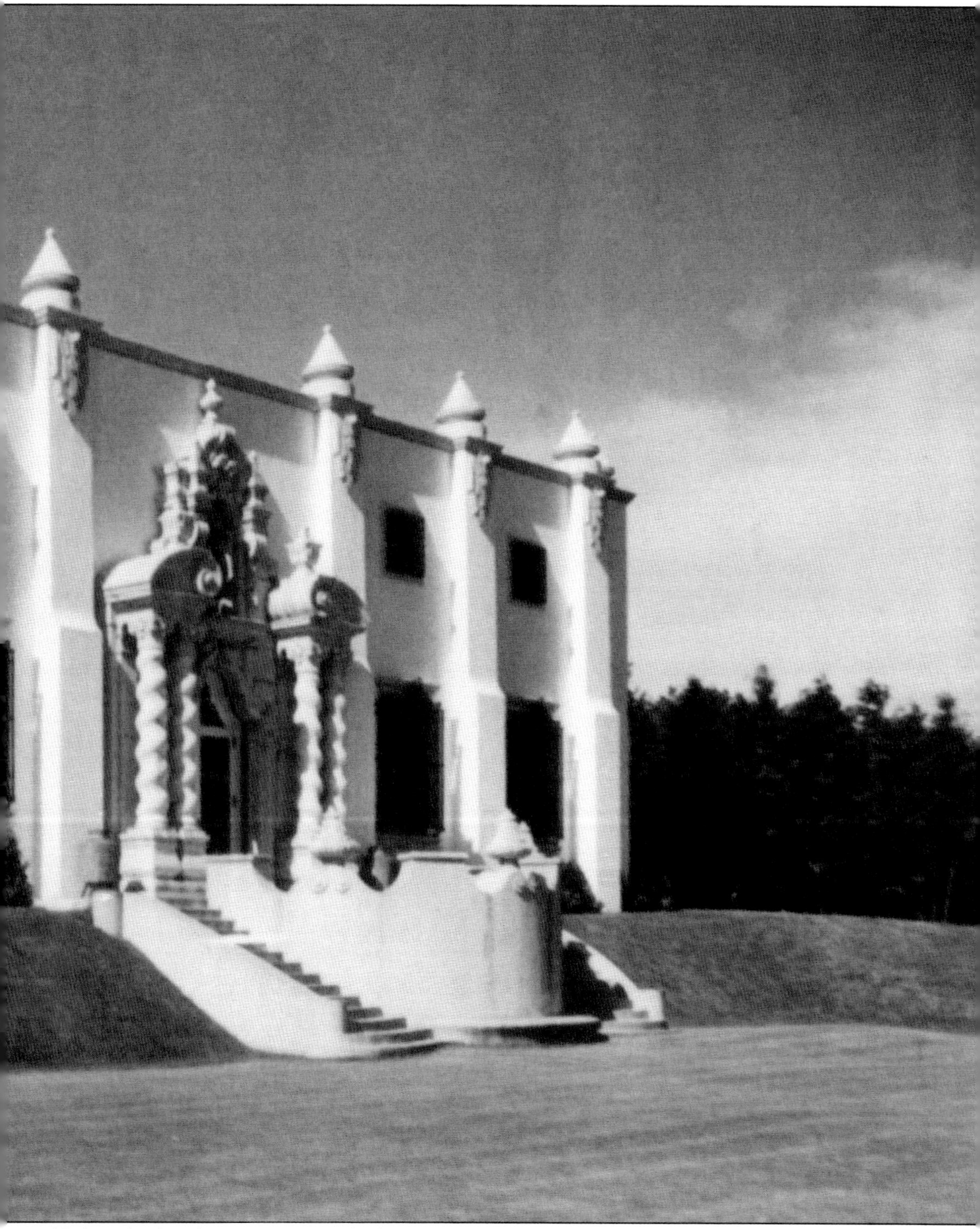

added to the facade to counteract the horizontality of the large structure. An exterior staircase was added to access the second floor and a decorative iron winch above the top landing to haul heavy, fluid-filled specimen jars.

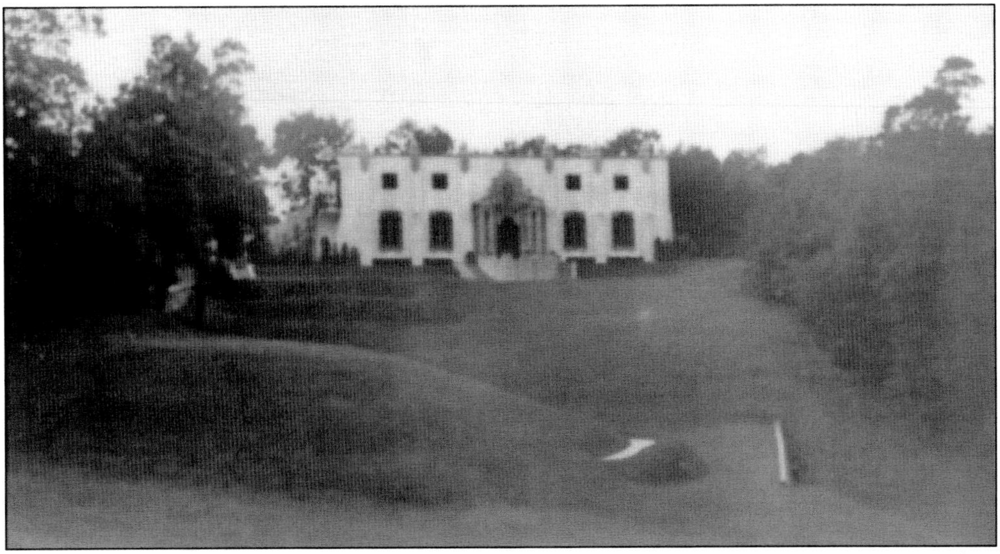

In a distant view from the golf course, the new two-story Hall of Fishes appears substantial as compared with the older structure. The flat rooftop, accessible by a staircase on the north side of the building, provided one of the tees for Willie K.'s golf course to the astonishment and amusement of his golfing partners. The lawn of the course seems to be as lush as a carpet, and some of the sand traps are visible.

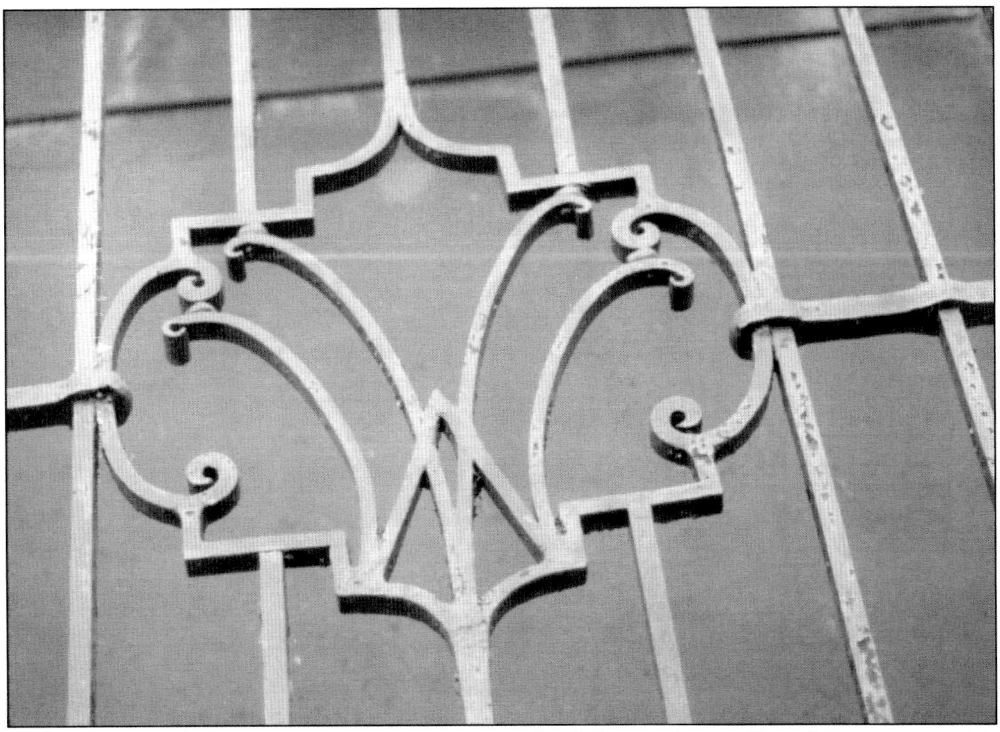

The original ironwork monogram remains on each of the window grilles of the museum. No longer glazed, the fenestrations were covered to provide more interior wall space for exhibits. The frequent inclusion of Willie K.'s initials, portraits, and family crests throughout the estate indicates reverence for his ancestry.

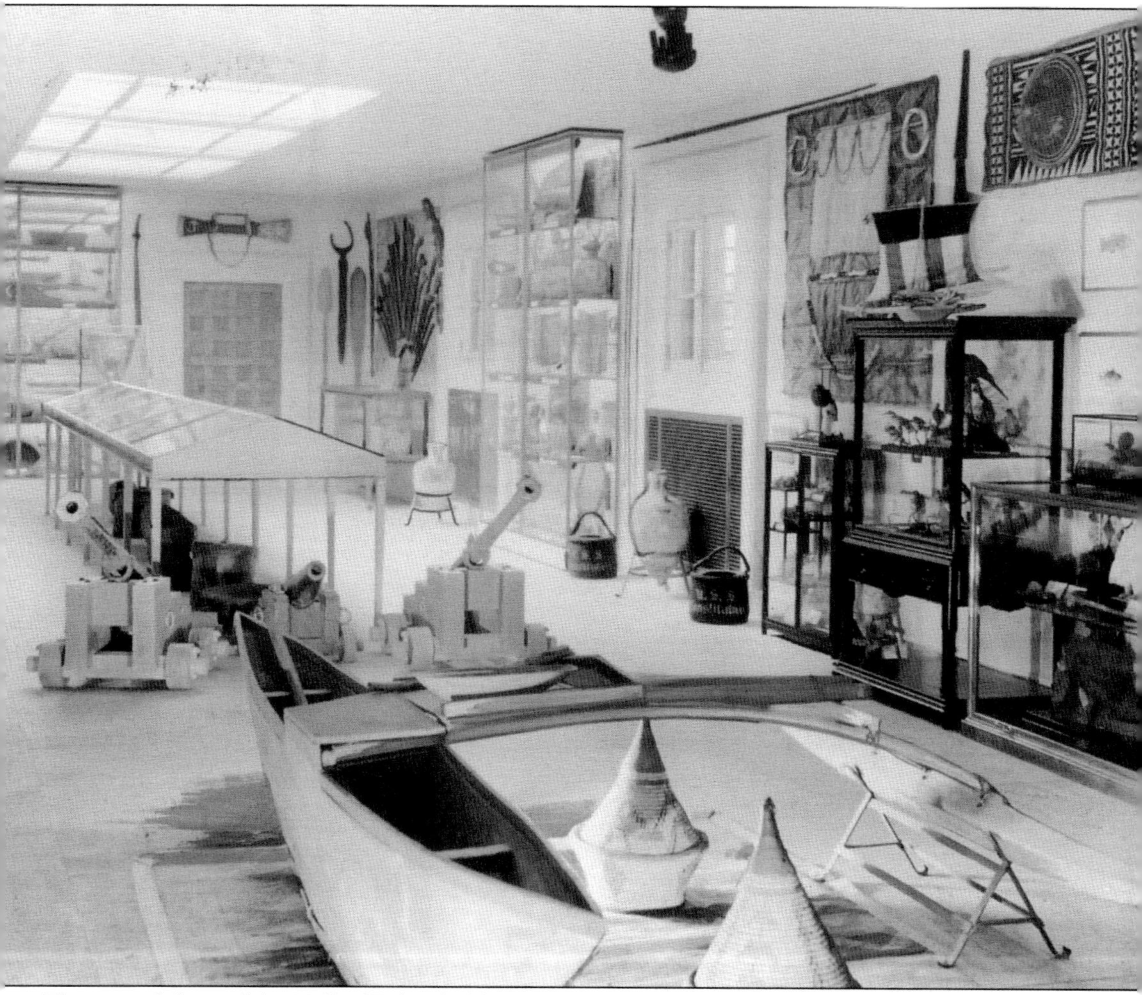

The second floor of the Hall of Fishes holds jars of specimens in fluid, a variety of ethnographic artifacts, and at the far end of the room the Vanderbilt Cup Trophy was displayed inside of a glass case. This dates the photograph to pre-1934, when Willie K. donated the cup to the Smithsonian Museum in Washington, DC. Objects were prepared and arranged by Willie K.'s full-time museum curator and artist, William Belanske, who resided on the property with his family. The door at the far end of the room opens to an iron staircase leading to the roof. The upper floor would eventually be filled with over 1,000 glass specimen jars displayed in exhibit cases wrapped around the circumference of the room. An access panel hidden under a slab in the floor at the far end of the room, just in front of the door, conceals a small iron ladder to access the exhibits on the floor below.

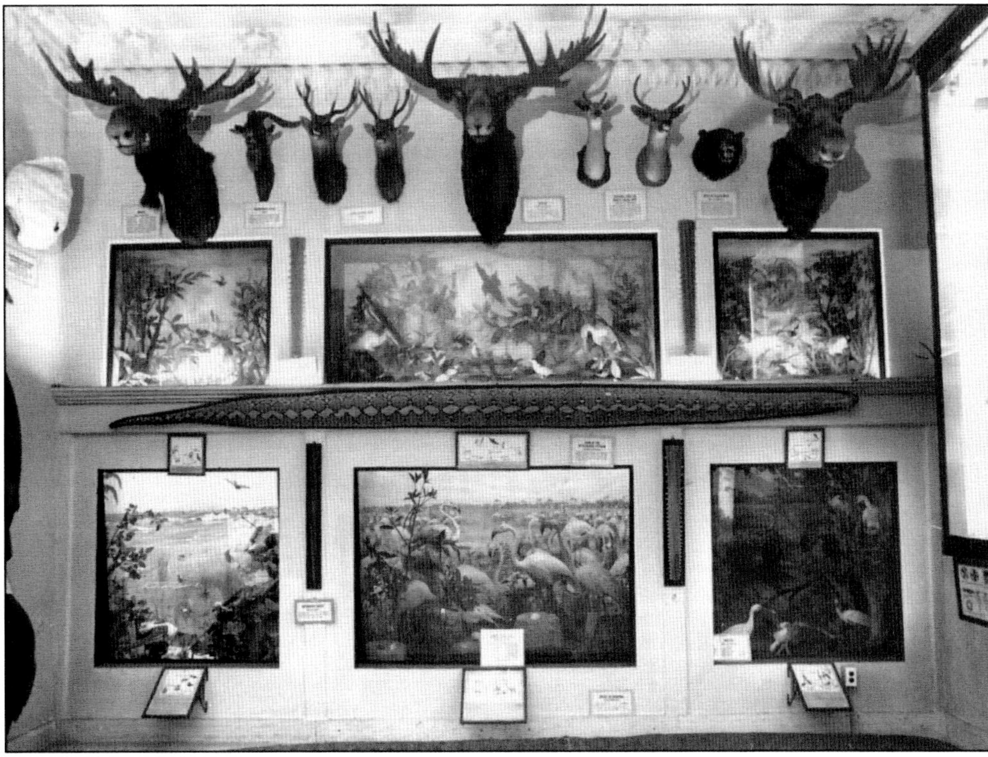

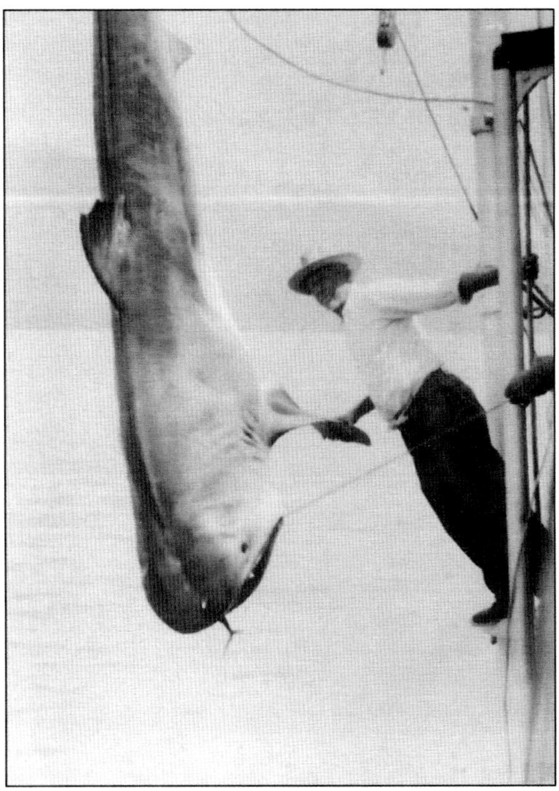

At one end of the first floor, to the right upon entering, is a wall containing six bird dioramas, and big-game trophy heads hang above. Hunting was a youthful pastime shared with his family at their lodge in Quebec, Canada. Willie K.'s focus turned to marine life, which he found to be far more fascinating for their endless varieties and more challenging for their underwater location.

Charter fisherman Charles Thompson of Florida is pictured with a large shark he hauled up. Thompson accompanied Willie K. on many expeditions. He was known for his fearless pursuit of marine specimens. A story related by Willie K. in *West Made East with the Loss of a Day* recounts how Thompson wrestled a large sea turtle while on the *Ara* world cruise in 1928.

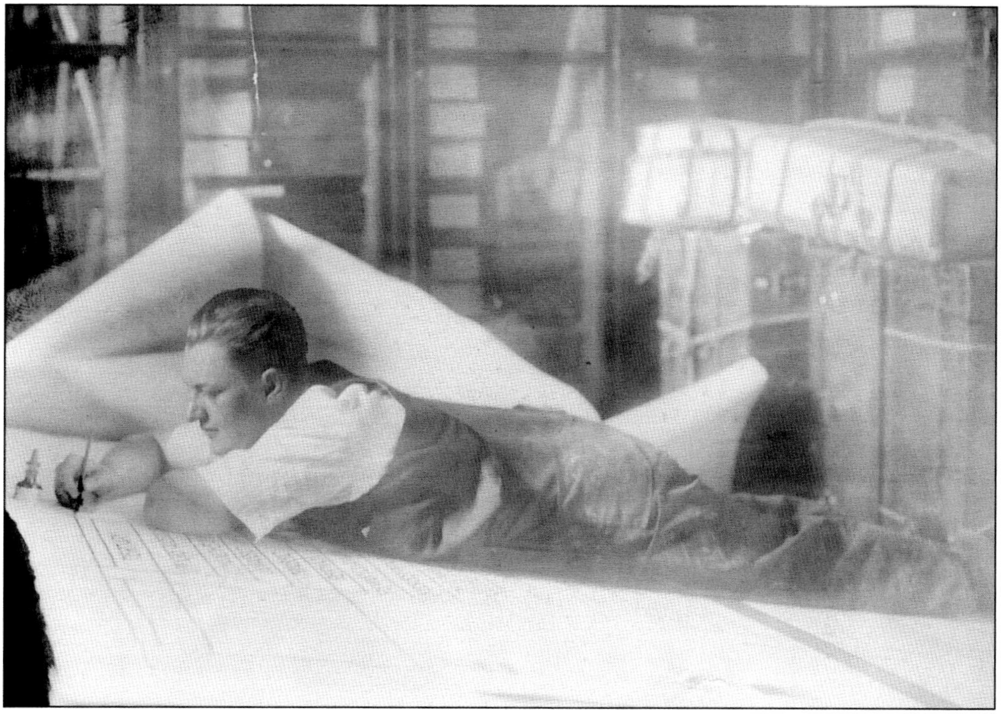

William Belanske, museum curator and artist, is working on drawings while waiting to embark on a long voyage with Willie K., judging by the large pile of luggage behind him. Willie K. borrowed Belanske from his employ at the American Museum of Natural History in New York to accompany him on a collecting voyage. He was hired as the resident curator of Willie K.'s museum collections in 1926. (Courtesy of J.A. Stimatz and the Capt. Sidney Hay Collection.)

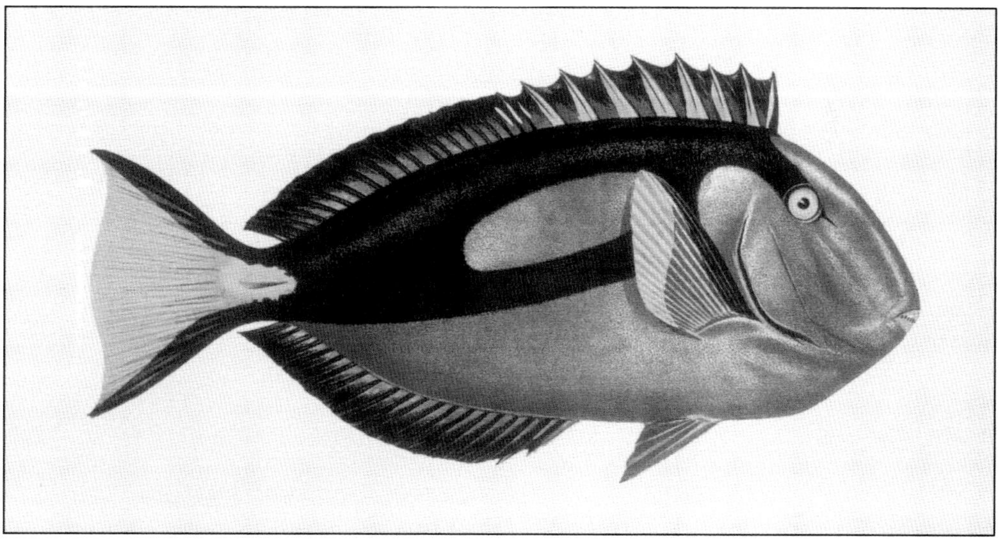

This rendering of a camouflaged surgeonfish (*Acanthurus hepatus*) was one of the many paintings made by Belanske for the museum displays. Willie K. installed holding tanks on his ships so the colors of the live fish could be captured in the paintings Belanske made as they swam. This image of the bright blue fish is reproduced in full color in Willie K.'s publication of his 1928 *Ara* voyage, *Taking One's Own Ship around the World*.

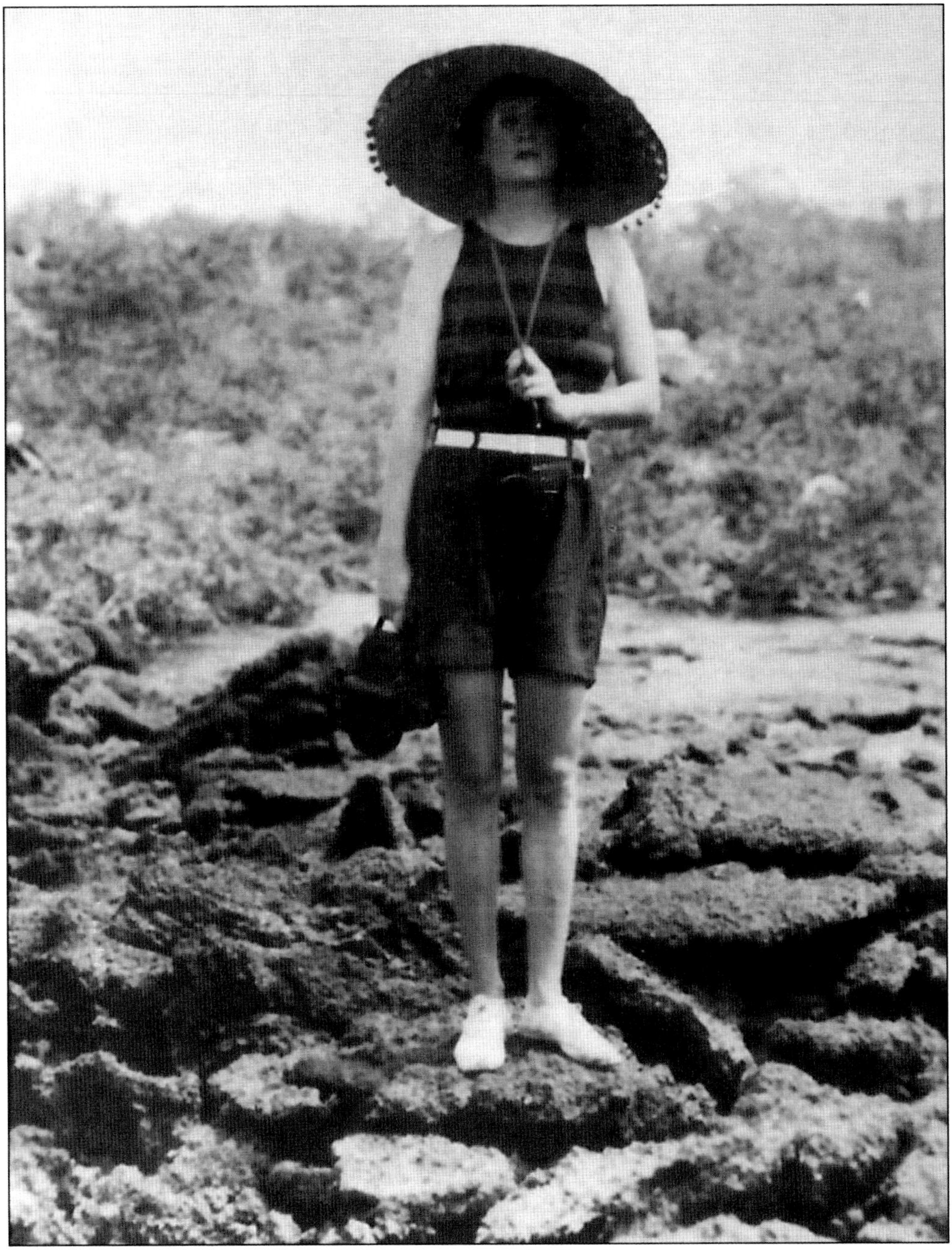

This photograph of Rose is from the *Ara* voyage of 1926. Even on a long voyage and in the sweltering heat of a tropical island, it is evident why she was regarded as one of the world's most fashionable women. Her solemn deportment provides a clue that something is not quite right. She and her husband, Barclay Warburton, with whom she had two children, would part ways shortly after making this trip together. The next year, she and Willie K. were married in France during his next voyage. Whatever transpired between 1926 and 1927 is not known outside of the family. Rose was about 15 years Willie K.'s junior, and her relatively young children, Rosemary and Barclay III, would make frequent visits to Eagle's Nest.

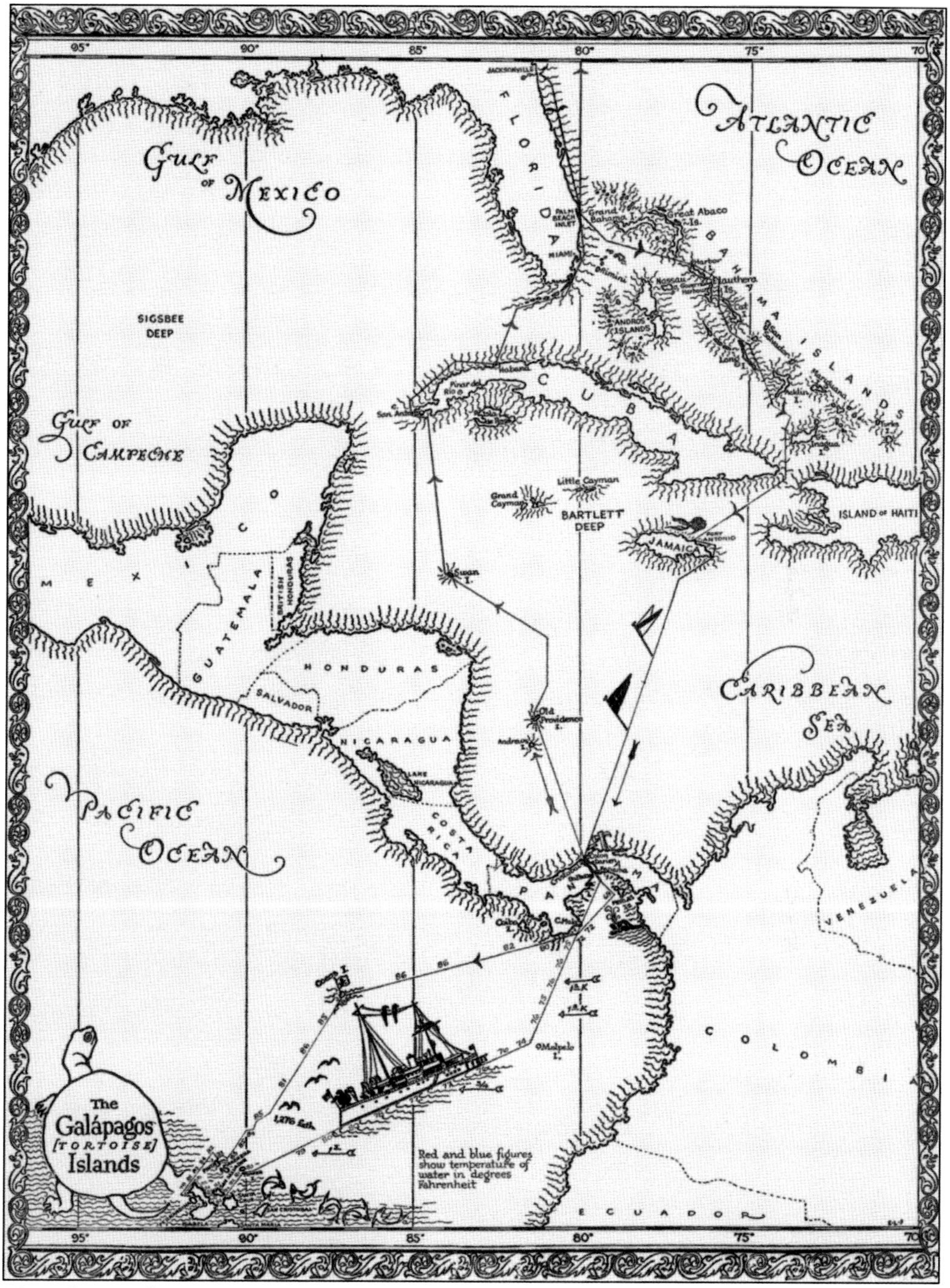

This whimsical map appears in Willie K.'s privately printed publication *To the Galapagos on the Ara*. The round-trip route of the voyage is outlined, showing the trip south rounding the east side of Cuba and on the route back the west side. The burgees flown on the *Ara* are drawn in on the line of the southern leg of the voyage. The tiny initials "ELF" appear at the bottom right, perhaps those of the artist.

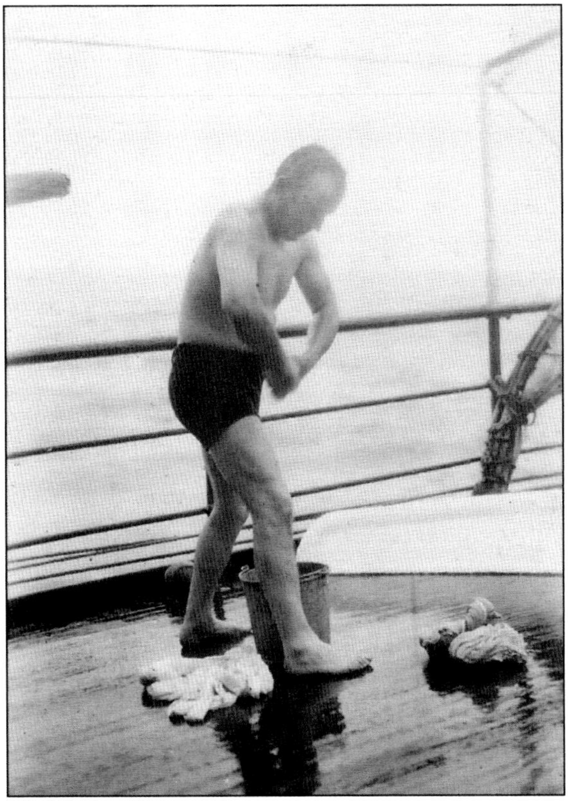

In a photograph taken by one of his fellow crew members, quartermaster Sidney M. Hay, William Belanske is washing his clothes in the rain on the deck of the *Ara* during a world voyage in 1928. (Courtesy of J.A. Stimatz and the Capt. Sidney Hay Collection.)

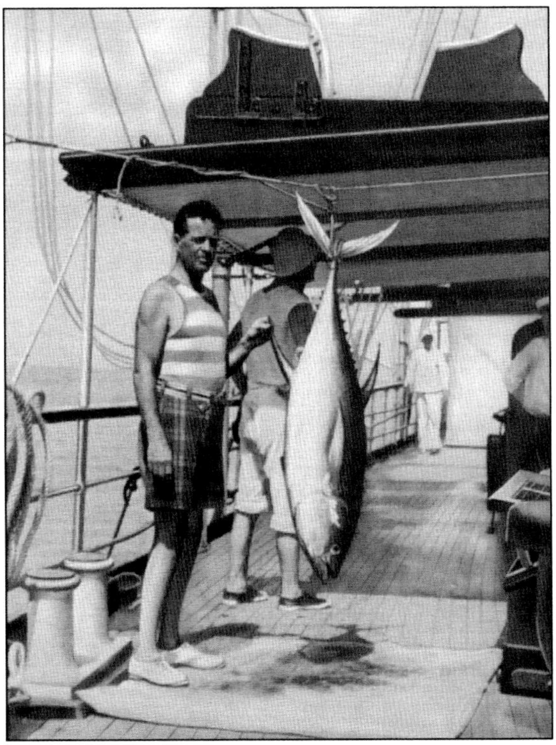

Pictured aboard *Ara*'s deck, Willie K. shows off a tuna weighing over 100 pounds, taken with rod and reel at Tagus Cove in the Galapagos Islands in 1926. He describes the surface of the fish-filled water as alive. It is no wonder that these islands were one of his favorite destinations, and he would return to fish again.

This invoice for a special glass product for his lower museum is just one example of the thousands of pieces of correspondence left behind by Willie K. He personally selected every material for the fabrication of the exhibits to achieve the desired effects.

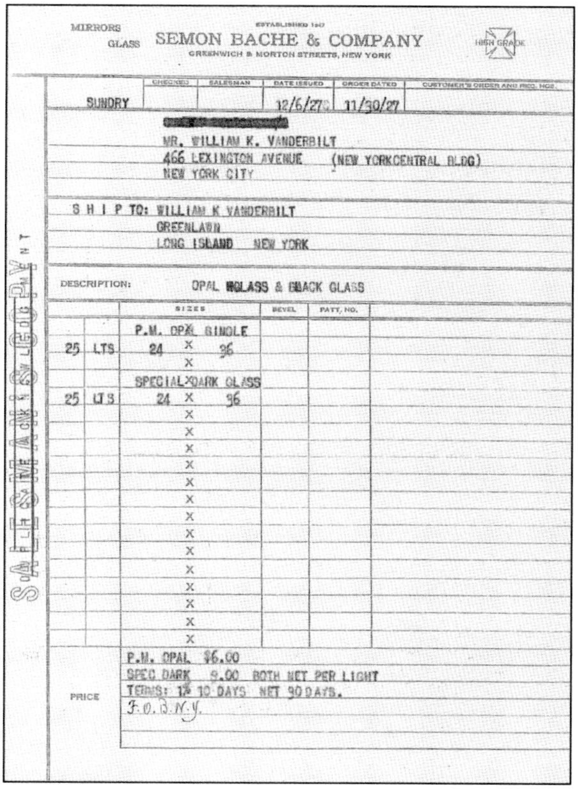

MIRRORS GLASS SEMON BACHE & COMPANY
GREENWICH & MORTON STREETS, NEW YORK

	CHECKED	SALESMAN	DATE ISSUED	ORDER DATED	CUSTOMER'S ORDER AND REQ. NOS.
SUNDRY			12/6/27	11/30/27	

MR. WILLIAM K. VANDERBILT
466 LEXINGTON AVENUE (NEW YORK CENTRAL BLDG)
NEW YORK CITY

SHIP TO: WILLIAM K VANDERBILT
GREENLAWN
LONG ISLAND NEW YORK

DESCRIPTION: OPAL GLASS & BLACK GLASS

		SIZES	BEVEL	PATT. NO.
		P.M. OPAL SINGLE		
25	LTS	24 X 36		
		SPECIAL DARK GLASS		
25	LTS	24 X 36		

PRICE
P.M. OPAL $6.00
SPEC DARK 9.00 BOTH NET PER LIGHT
TERMS: 1% 10 DAYS NET 30 DAYS.
F.O.B. N.Y.

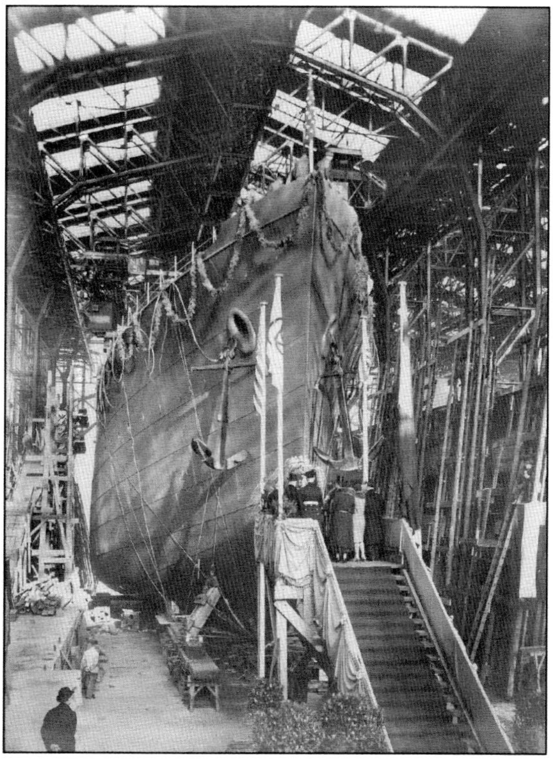

Willie K.'s next major undertaking was the commission of a custom luxury yacht. This photograph was taken at the shipyard in Kiel, Germany, where the yacht was built by Krupp-Germaniawerft, based on a model made by Cox and Stevens. In his book *West Made East with the Loss of a Day*, Willie K. said that he found the cost to build this ship in the United States "prohibitive." On November 18, 1930, *Alva* was christened by Mrs. Jessie N. Castleman, wife of Capt. Kenneth G. Castleman of the US Navy, who broke a bottle of champagne across the prow. The ship was named in honor of Willie K.'s mother.

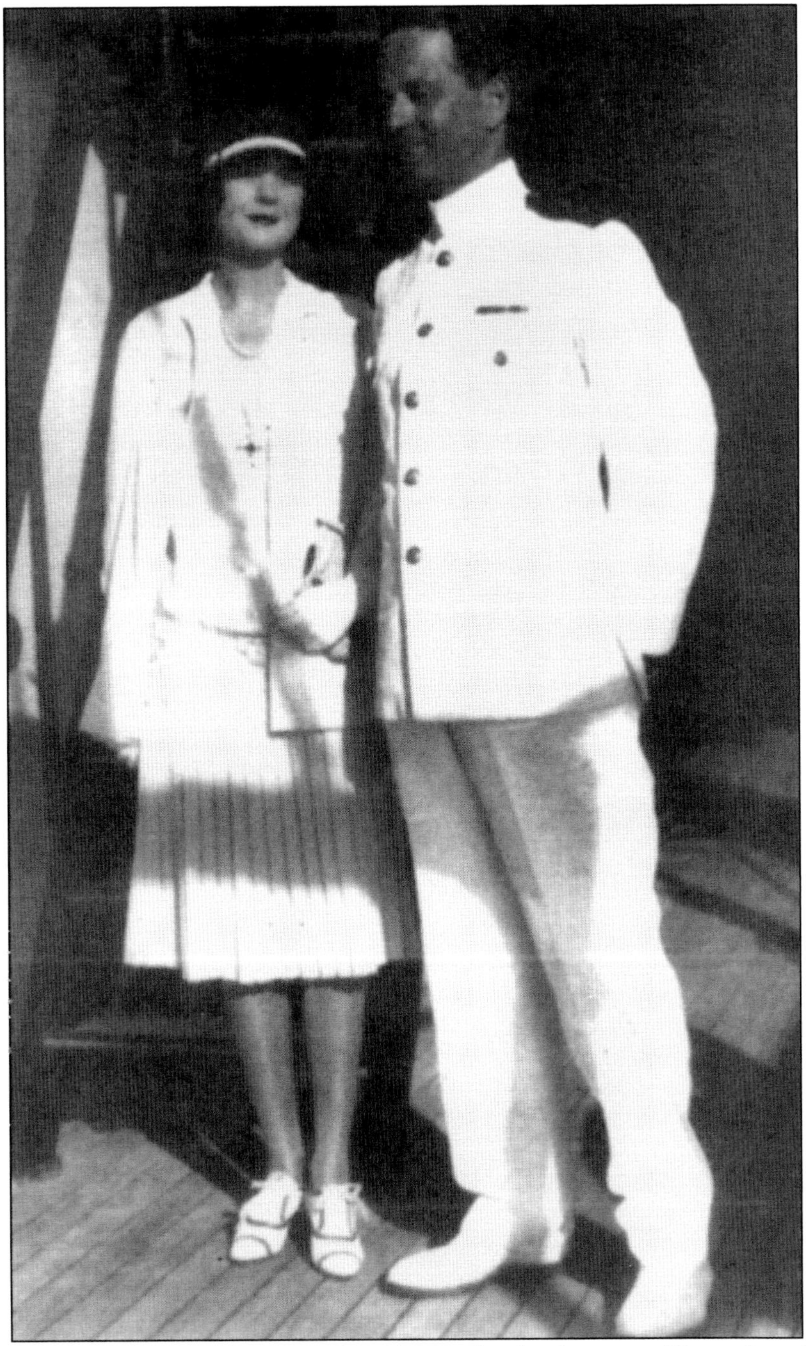

Willie K. is pictured his formal Navy uniform, known by the slang term "dress whites." In 1918, he earned the rank of commander in the US Naval Reserve and became qualified to sail a ship of any size. Because of his rank, he was permitted to fly the official Navy pennant on his private ship. Rose is pictured by his side in a white nautical summer ensemble to match his. The activities of the attractive couple had become a favorite topic for the public. They were photographed everywhere they went, and these images appeared in countless newspapers in New York and Miami, Florida.

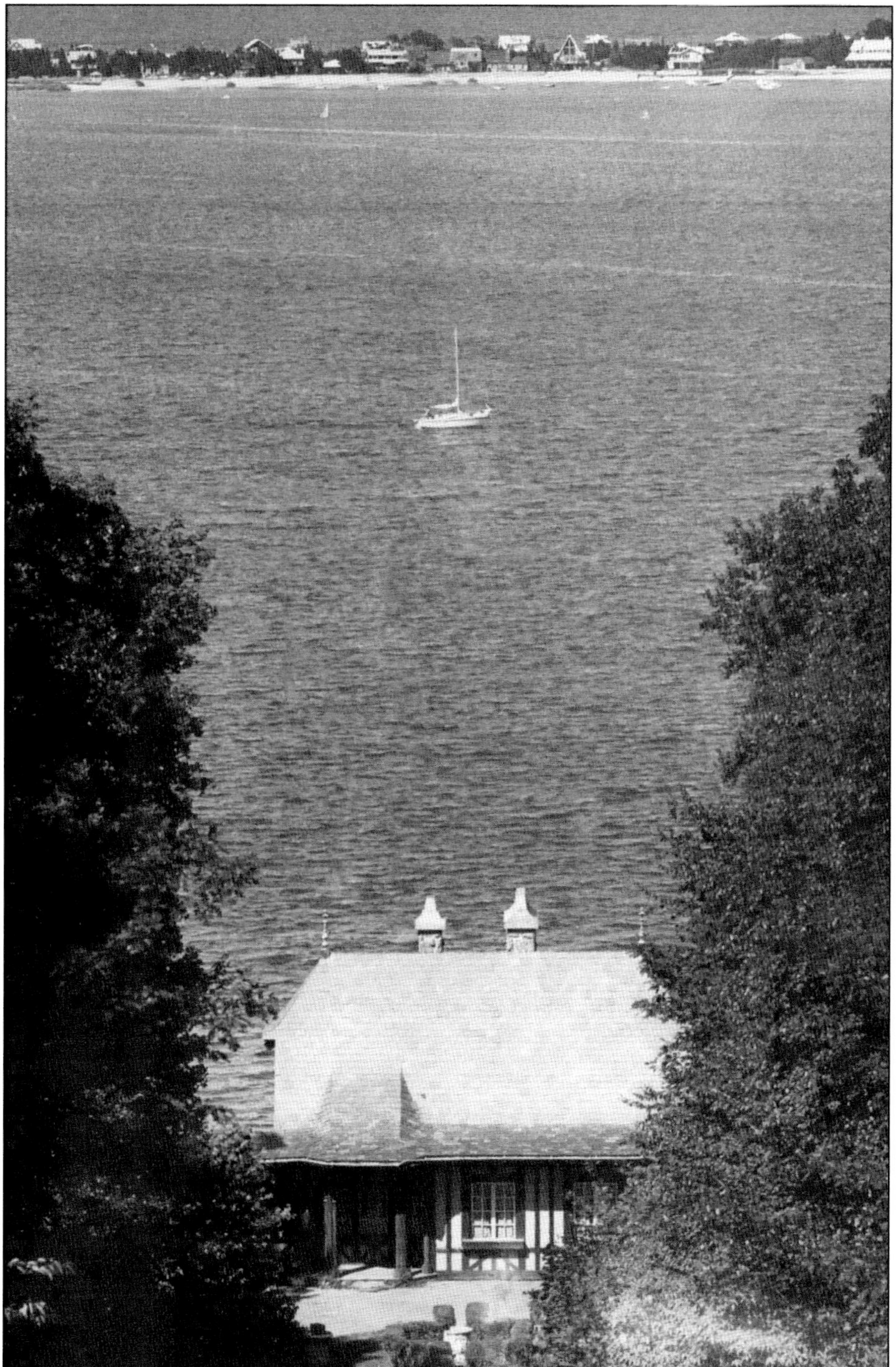

The boathouse is pictured with a boat sailing in the bay. Willie K. used a smaller craft to reach the *Alva*, moored out in deeper water in the Long Island Sound. The narrow strip of land pictured behind the boat is the village of Asharoken, where many summer homes of a more modest size than Willie K.'s were built.

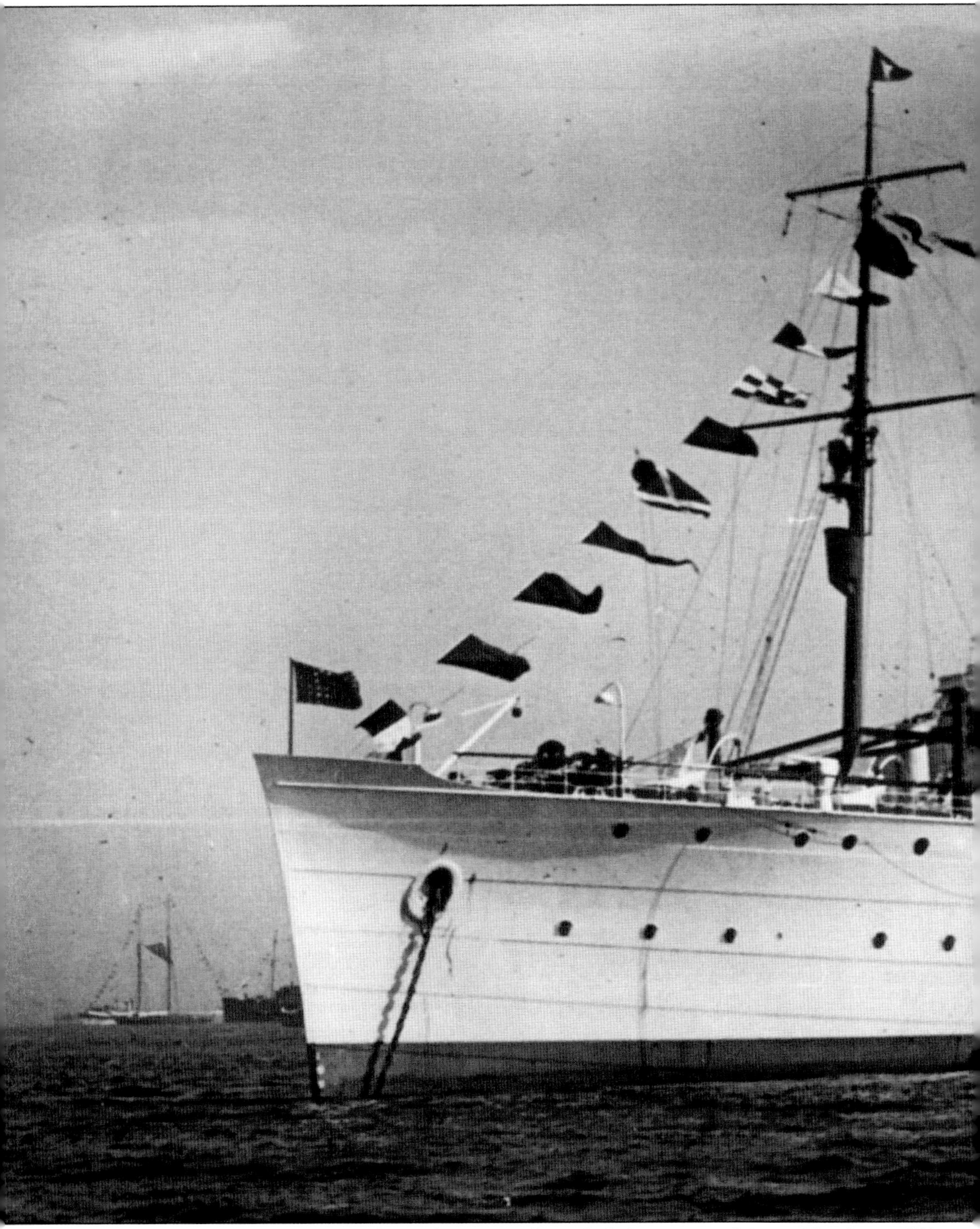

The ship *Alva* made her 6,731-mile maiden voyage from Kiel, Germany, to Miami, Florida, in 1931, and Willie K. immediately began to plan his next circumnavigation of the globe. At 265 feet in length, it would be his largest ship. With two Krupp diesel engines, the ship could sustain a sea speed of 17 knots. Luxuriously outfitted, no doubt with Rose's influence, it was furnished like a

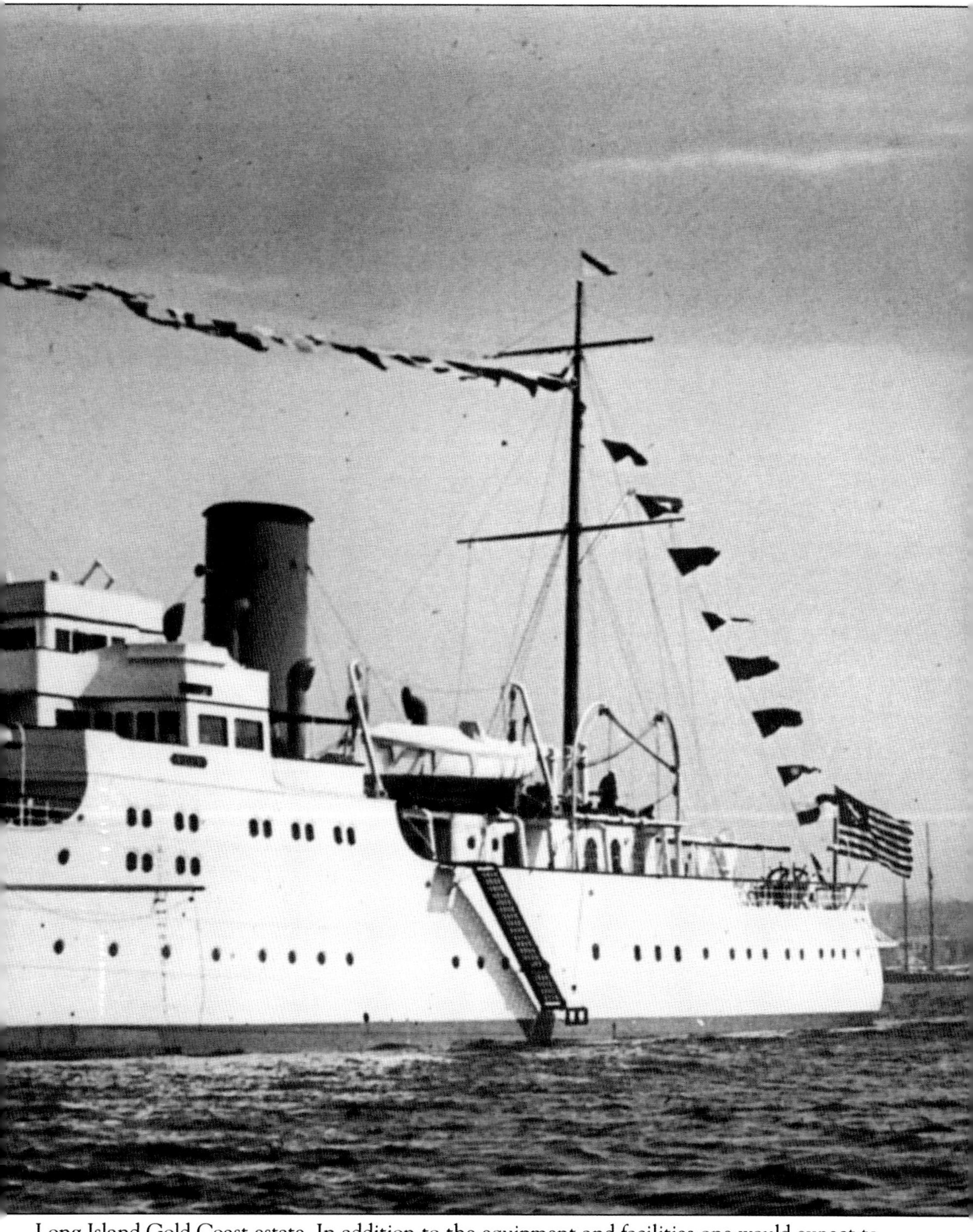

Long Island Gold Coast estate. In addition to the equipment and facilities one would expect to find on a luxury yacht, there was also a darkroom laboratory to develop film and facilities for the collection and documentation of specimens.

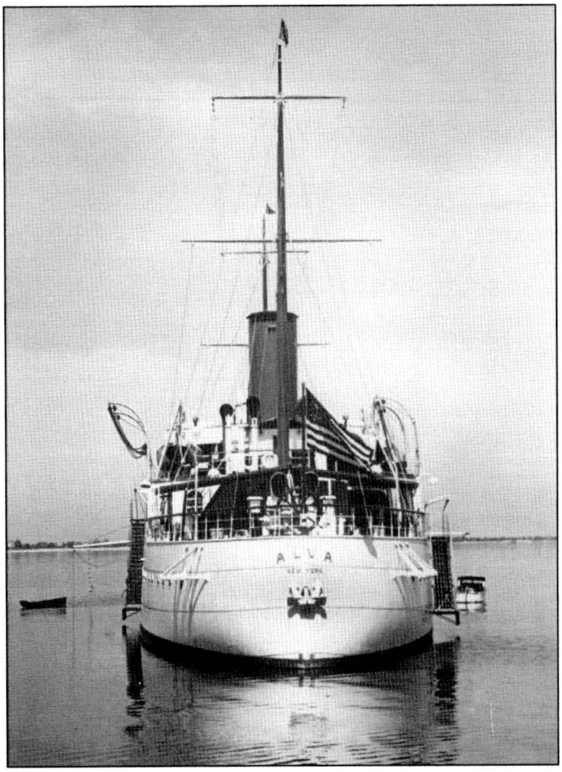

This is a view of *Alva* from the aft. Willie K. had the ship stocked with the finest products for his guests and crew to enjoy during their voyages. He provided them with fresh produce, fine cuts of meat, and Walker-Gordon milk, a superior low-bacteria product that would keep for months on the ship. When the ports of call were distant from one another, they had to wisely conserve supplies.

Willie K. is pictured at the helm aboard the *Alva* in 1931. The sky appears ominous behind him, and perhaps he is concerned with the weather conditions. In his published journeys, Willie K. often describes taking command of the ship during storms, sometimes staying awake through the night to ensure the safety of his passengers.

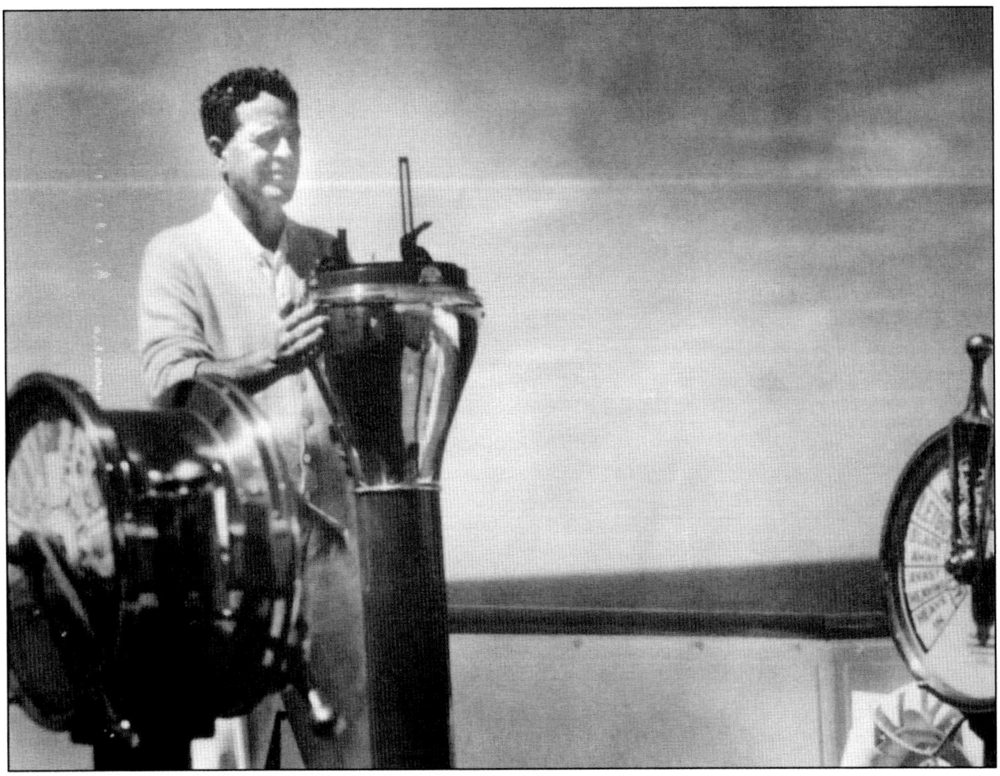

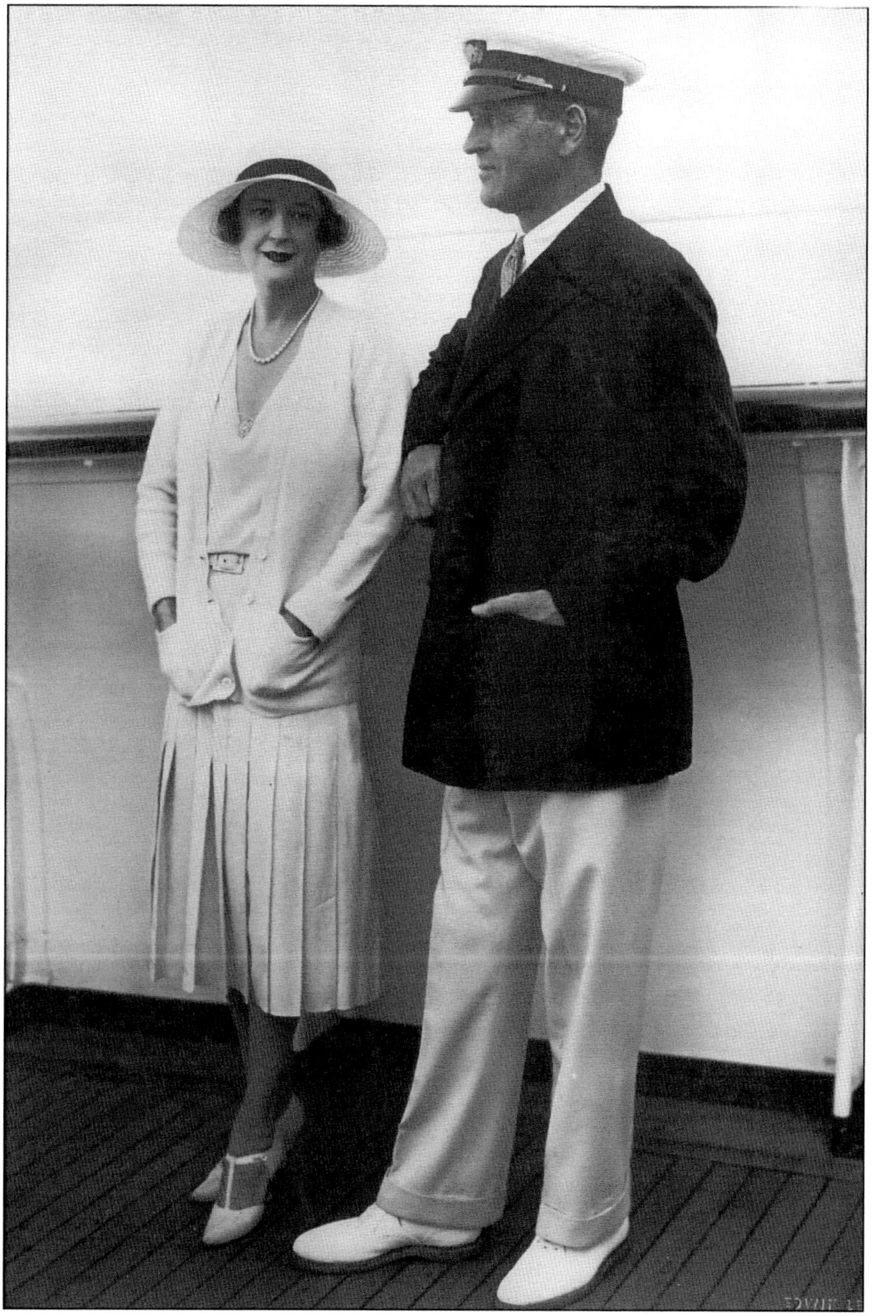

Willie K. and Rose pose aboard the *Alva* in 1931. Although Rose was a diminutive woman, Willie K. describes her as a hearty traveler and good sport. She would bring volumes of research materials and a typewriter along on their journeys to help her husband document every aspect of the trip for his next publication. Rose and Willie K. surprised the crew and passengers on this voyage with movies to help pass the time. This journey was, perhaps, one of the happiest times of Willie K.'s life. He had a new ship, a new wife, and his daughter Consuelo and her husband, Earl Smith, would join them for part of this voyage from Panama to Pago Pago, Samoa. Once again, his son, William, is not present for the voyage.

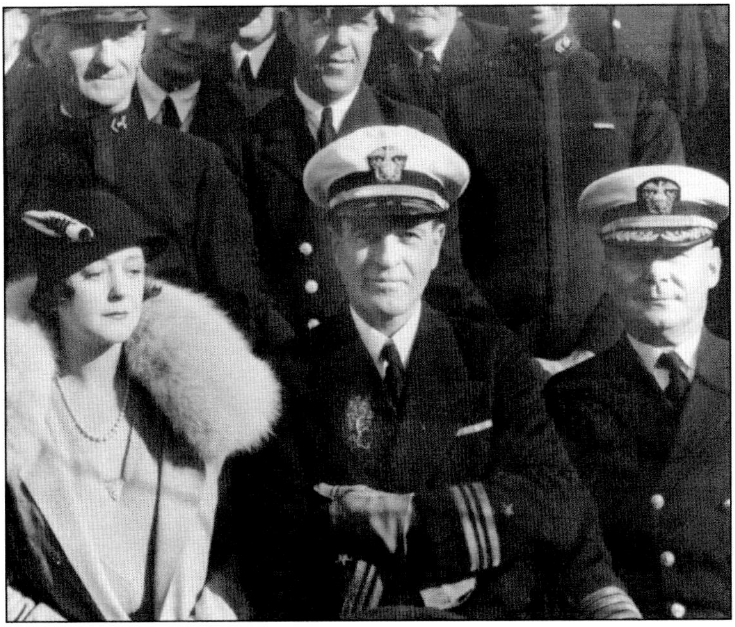

Willie K. and Rose are pictured seated among the crew of the *Alva*. Dr. Harry Hamilton Lane, a captain in the US Navy Medical Corps, the ship's physician, is pictured to the right. The ship included full medical facilities for the well-being of all on board. Willie K. speaks fondly of his crew in his publications, providing biographical information for those who were with him for many years.

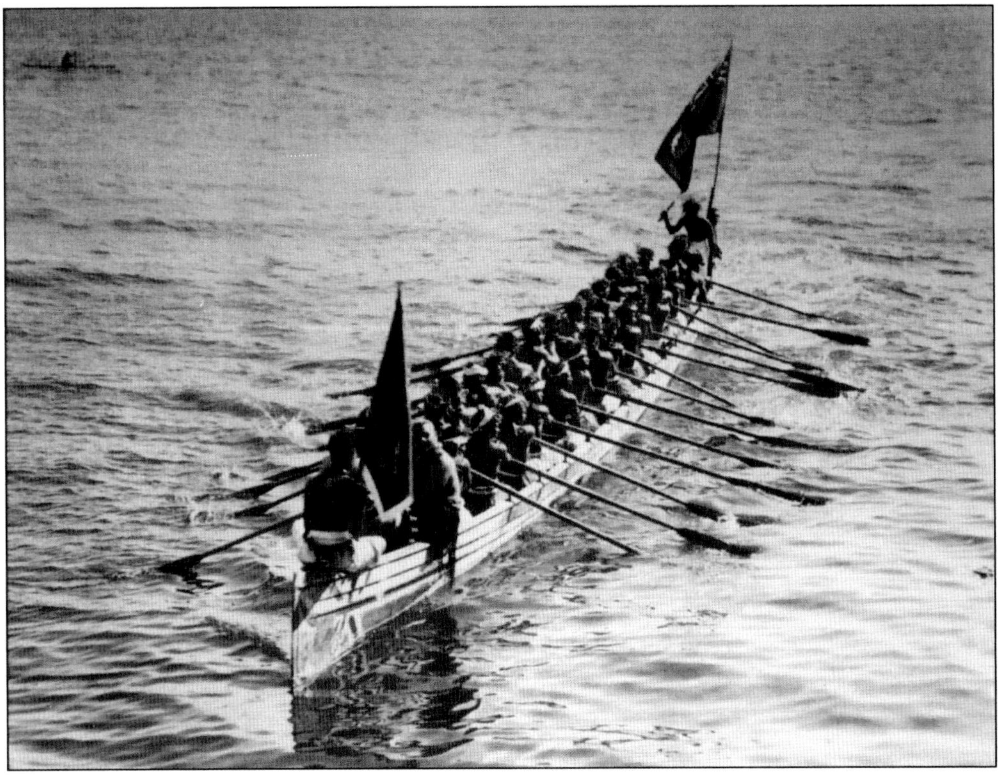

A 28-oared wooden cutter with men that Willie K. described as Samoan chiefs paddled out to greet the *Alva*. Willie K. enjoyed learning about other cultures and their practices; in particular, he was interested in their fishing methods. He learned that when fish were caught, they would be kept alive until the end of the day in baskets that hung from the fishing boats into the water. He brought some of the baskets back for his museum display.

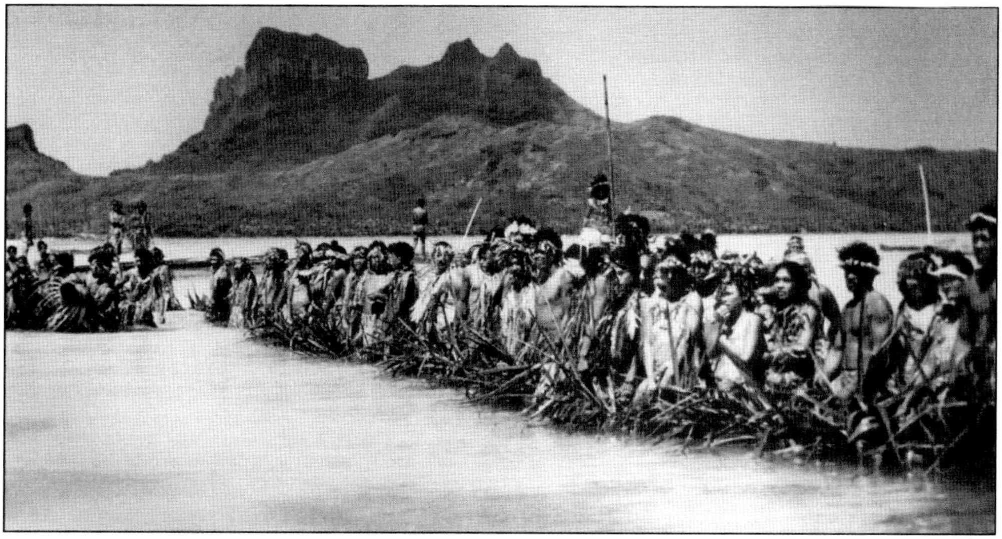

This scene pictures stone fishing in Bora Bora and provides another fishing lesson for Willie K. He said that 400 locals assemble in the water, while another 200 watch from shore. They use stones and loud shouting to drive fish into a circle and then surround them, using strips of palms leaves to prevent them from escaping.

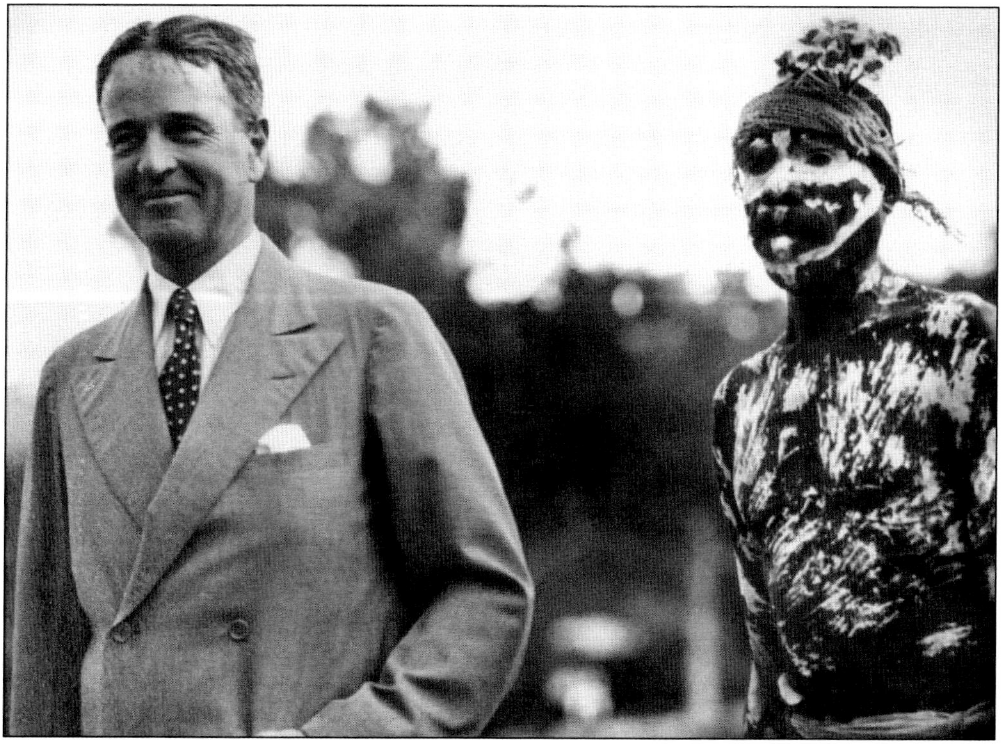

Willie K. is pictured here with an inhabitant of Great Palm Island whose skin is decorated with dried clay. These islands were populated by expatriate Australians of aboriginal descent who were banished by the government. They were hospitable to their guests and performed dances and demonstrations of spear and boomerang throwing that were described by Willie K. as impressive.

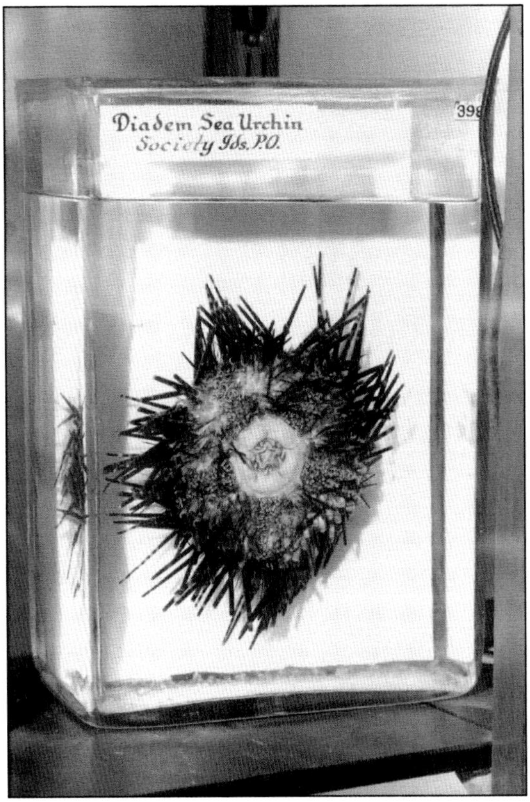

This sea urchin from the Society Islands is an example of the preparation of the specimens to be placed in Willie K.'s museum. After being sketched or painted by Belanske, they were scientifically classified, placed in a fixative called formalin, and labeled by Clifford Pope from the American Museum of Natural History. At a later date, the fluid would be drained and replaced with a mixture of alcohol and distilled water for long-term preservation.

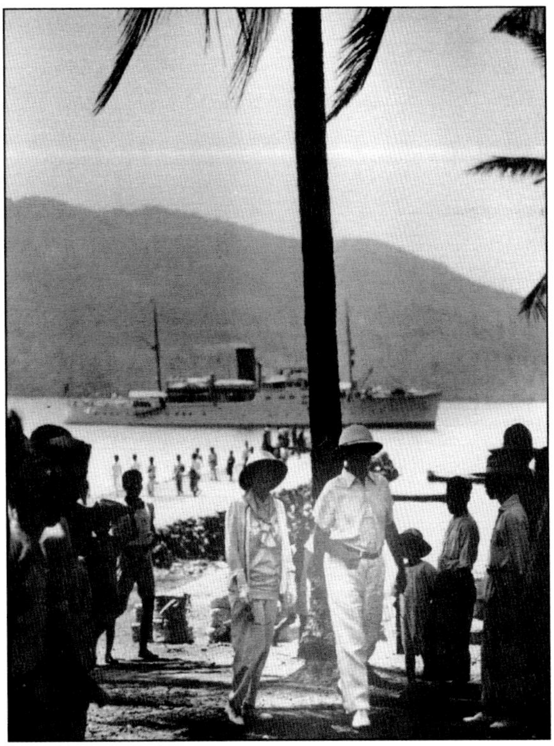

Alva lies out in deeper water, and Willie K. and Rose are shown landing at Larantuka on Flores Island. Willie K. described this location as a Dutch settlement that was "disappointingly Europeanized." During his visit, he was preoccupied with navigating the dangerously narrow strait here, which is less than a quarter of a mile in width. Of all the achievements during his life, he was most proud of his sailing prowess.

Five

Life Events Expressed in Architecture

Architect Ronald Hoyt Pearce was assigned to work on the Eagle's Nest estate by Warren and Wetmore, and he corresponded with Willie K. on every detail and decision. By 1932, his name appears on plans for the first time, and he addresses his correspondence to "Willie" rather than the formal Mr. Vanderbilt, as in earlier days. He was integral in the design and construction of the later phases of Eagle's Nest and traveled to Europe in pursuit of furnishings and architectural elements for the estate. Eagle's Nest is filled with brightly painted floor tiles, hand-carved wooden doors, and the contents of monasteries and estates resulting from Pearce's purchases.

Willie K. married Rosemund Lancaster Warburton (Rose, as Willie K. called her) in 1927 during one of his voyages. Her influence can be seen, particularly in the second-floor interior treatments of Eagle's Nest. Formerly married to Barclay Warburton II and considered to be one of the 20 best-dressed women in the world, Rose had discriminating tastes. While the earlier interiors of Eagle's Nest are heavy, dark, and masculine, the newer additions are decidedly feminine and French. The walls of the upstairs bedrooms are covered in light-colored panels, some with whimsically painted insets.

The early 1930s brought many tragic events to Willie K.'s life: the death of his mother, the death of Birdie, and the untimely death of his only son, William K. Vanderbilt III. The latter tragedy prompted Willie K. to erect an entire wing onto his home in memory of his son, which closed in the final side to the Eagle's Nest courtyard. The Memorial Wing contains a religious triptych set into the facade of the structure. Another religious architectural element mysteriously appears at this time in photographs of the wall near the entrance to the lower museum. Reported to be an authentic della Robbia Madonna, it lacks any explanation in the estate records.

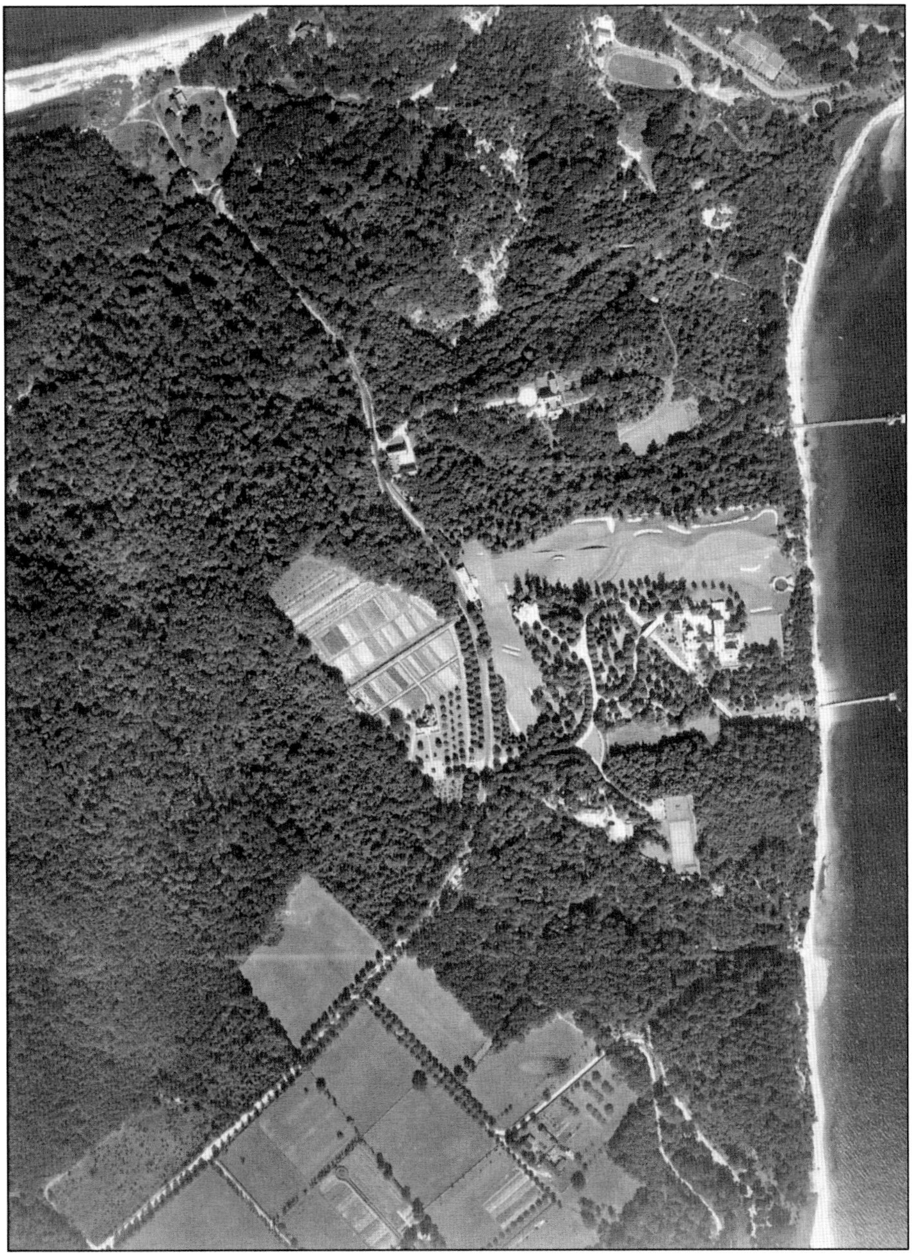

This aerial photograph shows the development of the Eagle's Nest estate property. On the west side of the road, the superintendent's cottage grounds look like a small farm, with manicured plots that provide vegetables and flowers for the estate. The remainder of the food and provisions were delivered by local suppliers like Cutter's Drug Store and the Huntington General Store. The Vanderbilts employed a full staff at Eagle's Nest, including a chef. All food was prepared in the basement kitchen and sent upstairs to the serving kitchen on the dumbwaiter to be plated and served in the formal dining room. Willie K., seated at the head of the dining room table, would step on a button located underneath the table to summon the staff. An annunciator board located in the kitchen would buzz and light up to display the number of the area in the house where the call originated.

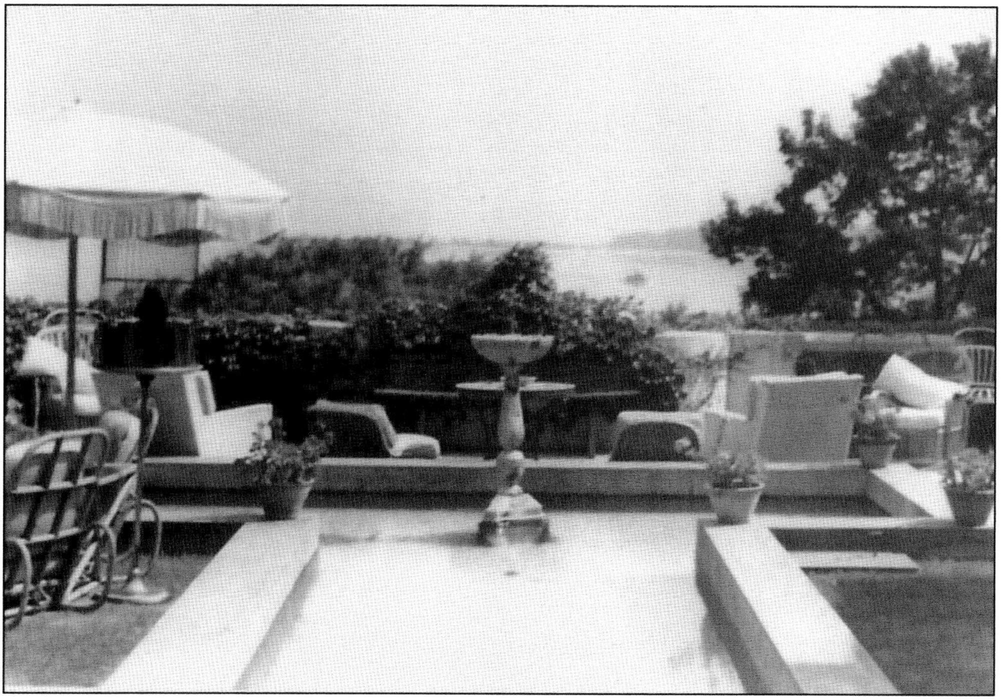

The circular fountain at the back of the house was changed to a *T*-shaped reflecting pool to complement the style of the house. Furnished for summer lounging, Willie K. and Rose had a spectacular view of the Northport Bay and the distant hills of Connecticut across the Long Island Sound. This garden area is adjacent to a porch with green Spanish-tile floors off of the back of the residence.

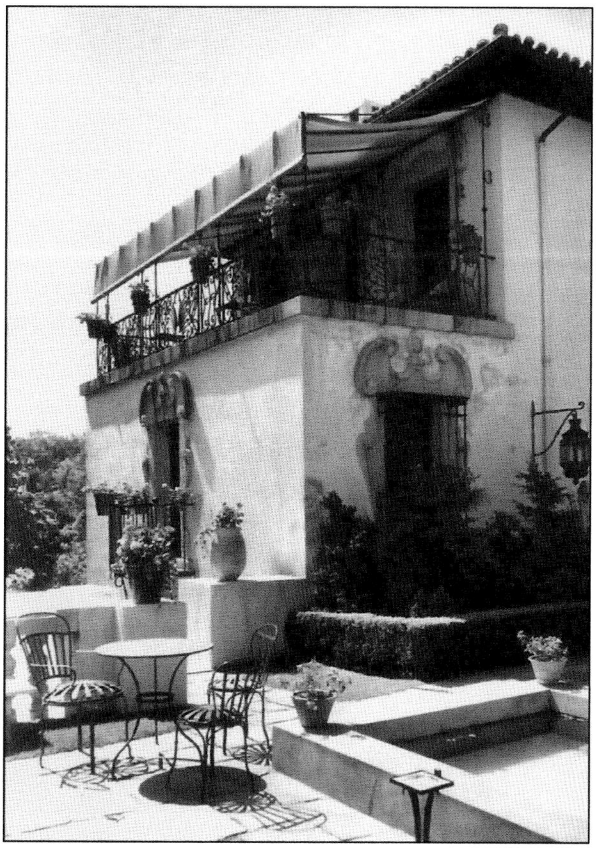

This view from the reflecting pool toward the house shows an awning-covered porch off of the main upstairs parlor known as the organ room. The squared-off edges of the boxwood gardens and new rectangular edges of the reflecting pool mirror the architectural forms. The potted plants with hanging vines sit in receptacles built into the balcony.

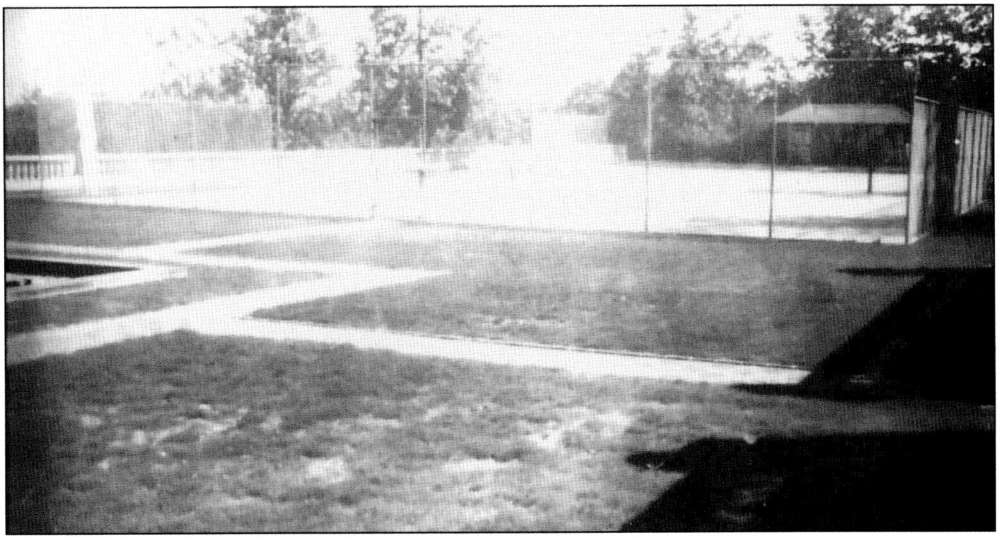

The tennis courts were located at the higher elevation of the property, to the right of the Corinthian columns and just past the structure known as the powerhouse. Right around the time that Willie K. married Rose, he had a building constructed to house equipment to generate his own power on the estate.

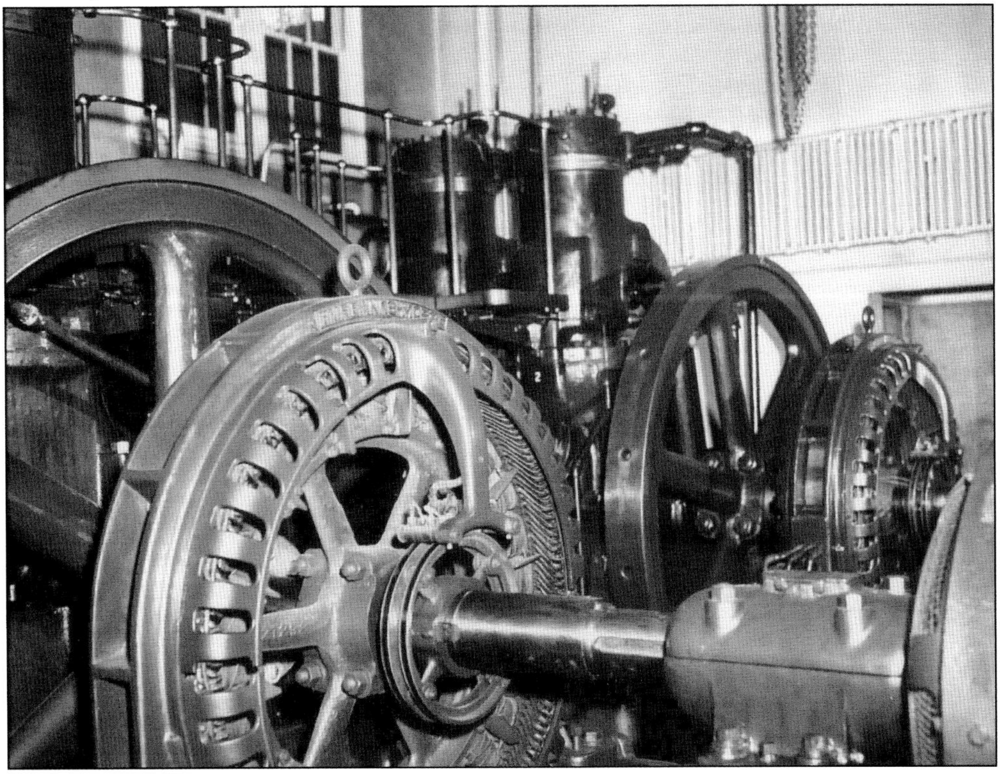

Two Fairbanks-Morse diesel engines were installed in a cavernous space in the lower level of the 1,800-square-foot powerhouse building. There were bedrooms, baths, and small sitting rooms upstairs. The wooden exterior was comparatively simple in design, indicative of the building's utilitarian purpose (see page 114 to view a photograph of the exterior of the powerhouse).

The top of the bell tower shows the weather vane made by ironworker Samuel Yellin. The custom design is a ship followed by sea serpents. Yellin's work at the estate reflected Willie K.'s personality through the use of sea creatures and natural forms. His work had an organic quality, enhanced by his purity of process, using only a hammer and anvil and no other equipment. The proliferation of black ironwork is integral to the Spanish style of the structure.

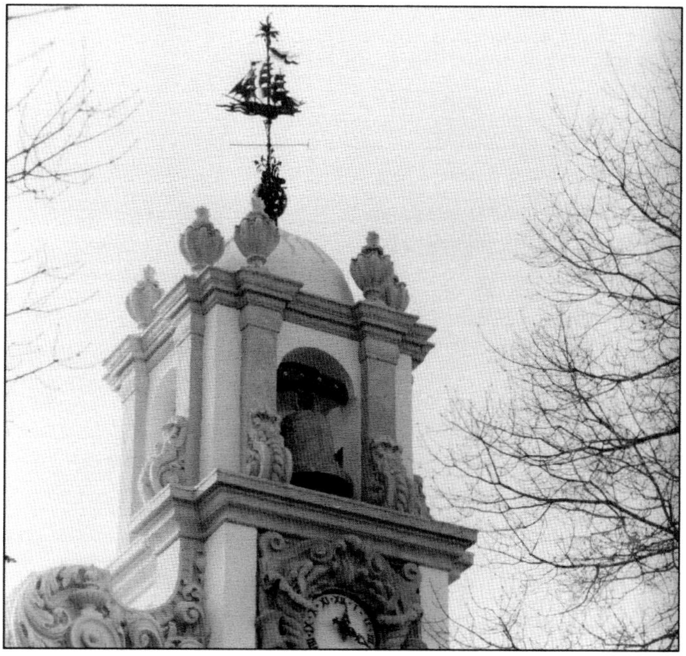

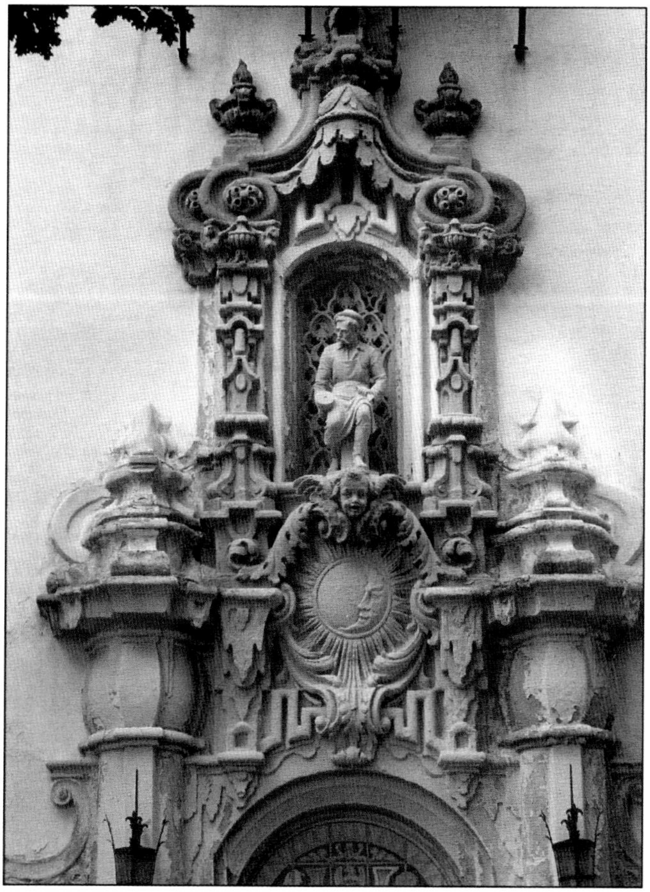

A statue of Richard Morris Hunt rests in a niche above the entrance to the laundry room underneath the mansion. This statue came from a Vanderbilt home in New York City that was being demolished. It was lifted off of the building by crane and placed into a box for shipping. Hunt was the architect of choice for Willie K.'s mother, Alva. Although the younger generation of Vanderbilts preferred the new American architects, placement of the statue pays homage to Hunt's work.

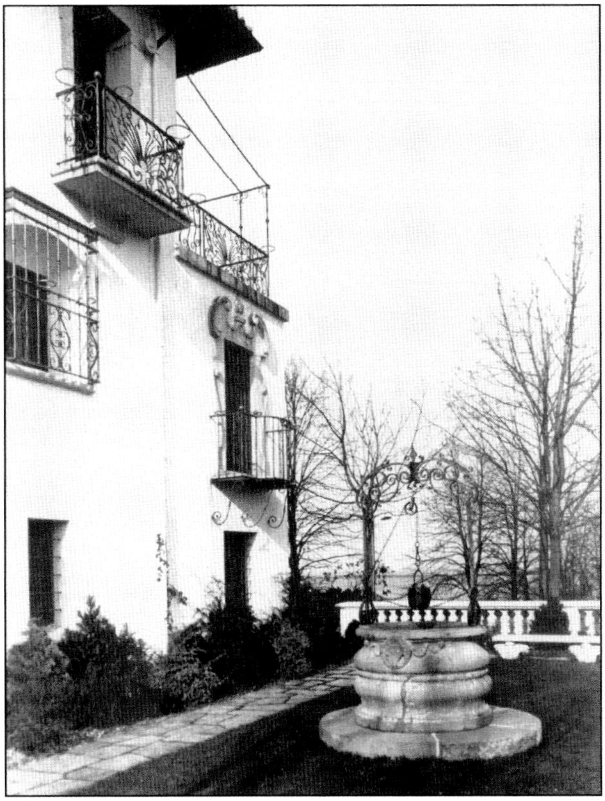

The wishing-well garden is a charming spot off of a lower level room used by the mansion staff to gather and eat their meals. Former staff members who worked at the estate in their younger years said that the staff was instructed to remain on the lower level of the house to carry out their duties unless specifically invited up to the main floor. The kitchen facilities, root cellar, and wine cellar were located on this level as well.

The area behind the staircase to the bell tower reveals the stepped walls down to the lower museum behind the nursery wing. The original landscape plantings on the property consisted chiefly of roses, evergreens, boxwood, and deciduous trees. Note that the plantings echo the height of the structures.

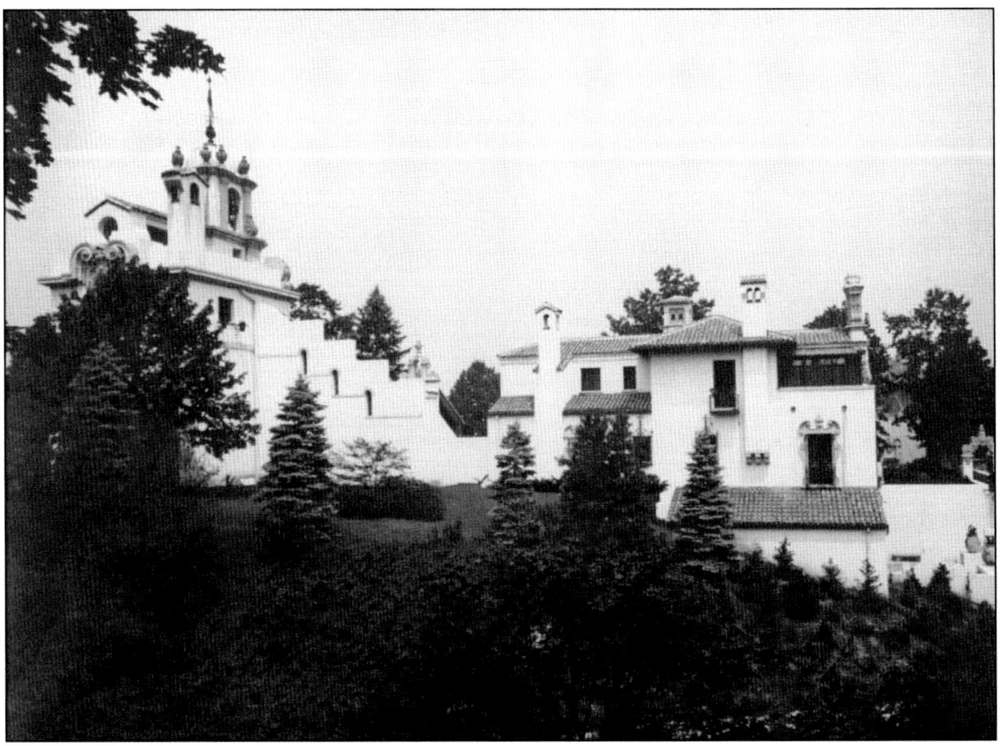

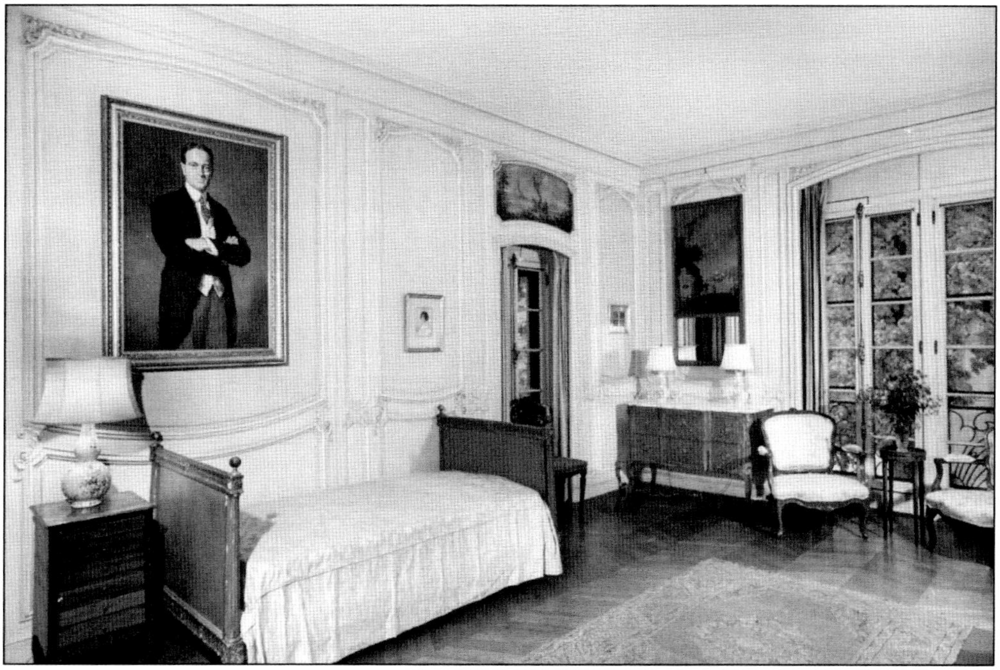

This is the lone guest room located upstairs with the family bedrooms, most likely occupied by a visiting adult relative, such as one of Willie K.'s siblings or daughters. A separate staircase located near the front entrance leads to the sleeping quarters. Another staircase off the porch leads only to the organ room. The portrait of Willie K. above the bed was painted by American artist Gari Melchers in 1925.

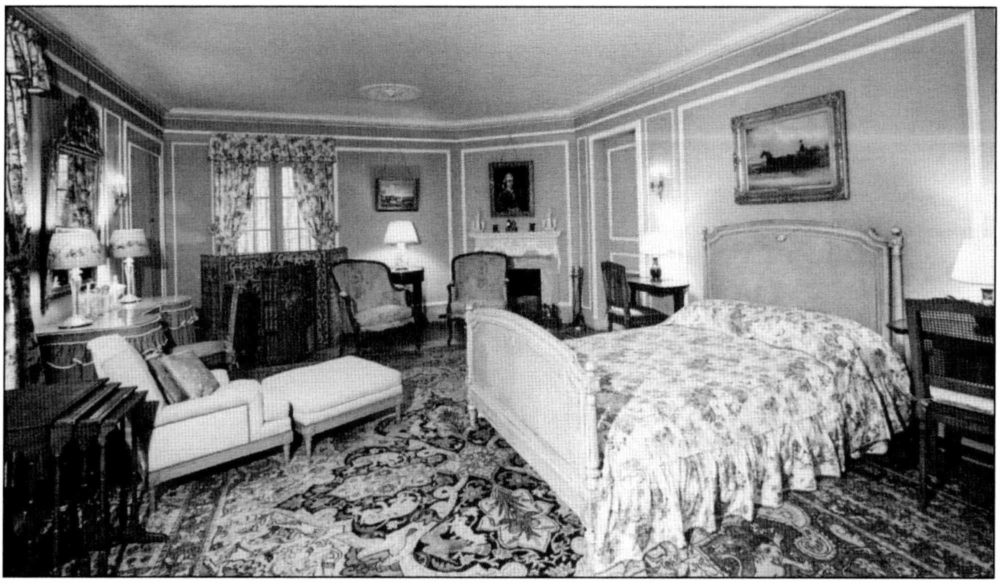

This is one of two quaint main-level guest rooms located in a small wing off of the covered porch at the back of the mansion. According to accounts passed down by former staff members, the Duke and Duchess of Windsor stayed here during their visits. It is the only room in the house that has a primitive form of air-conditioning. Decorative roundels in the ceiling allow cool air from the lower level to be pushed up through the use of fans.

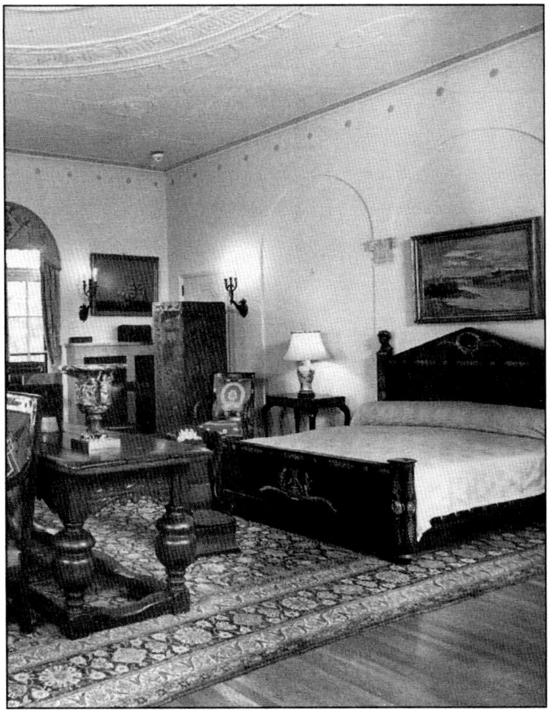

Willie K.'s bedroom (at left) is a large room located at the terminus of the second floor. This location provided him with a view of the courtyard on one side and the bay on the other. The furnishings are in the Napoleonic Empire style, characterized by a blend of neoclassical elements, imperial symbols, and Egyptian influences. A bust of Napoleon Bonaparte sits on Willie K.'s desk in the corner of the room, alluding to his admiration for the legendary emperor. The odd, small chair was a gift from the Duke and Duchess of Windsor. His bath, the door to which is behind the screen in the corner, has a marble floor with a custom-designed mosaic of a ship (below). This was a repeating theme on the estate, appearing in the weather vane and on the bell tower as well. Former staff reports that Willie K. requested that a bottle of champagne and a bottle of cola be left for him beside his bath each evening.

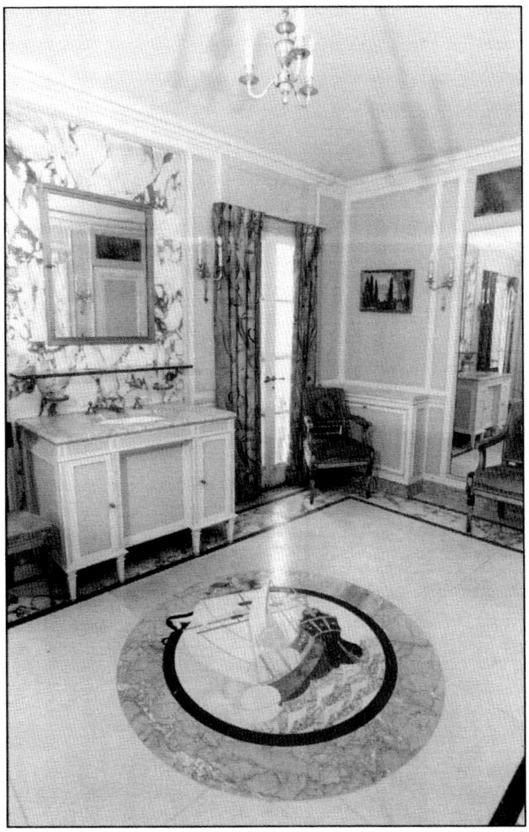

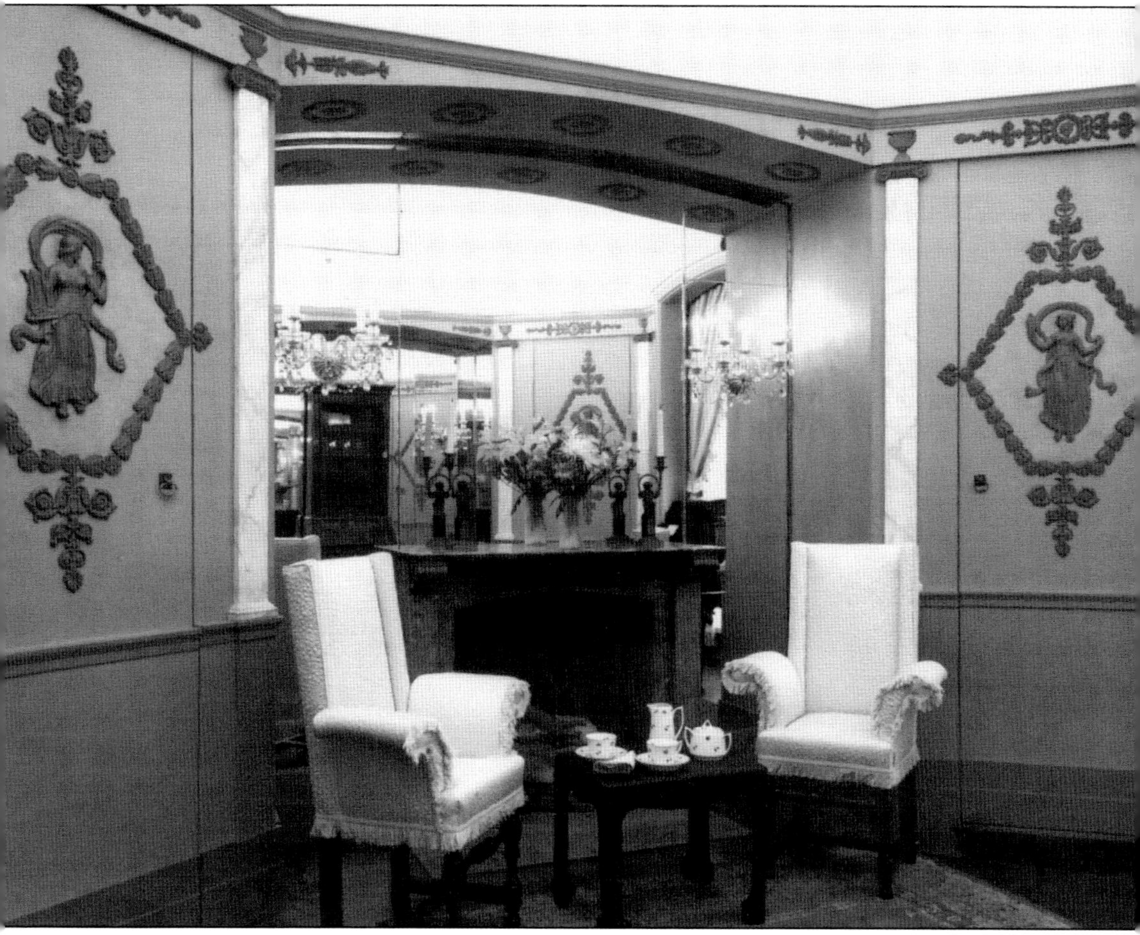

Rose Vanderbilt's dressing room and bath are located at the end of the living quarters on the second floor, immediately after her bedroom chamber. The dressing area is a symmetrical, octagonal space with three mirrored sides, one of which is a set of sliding doors concealing her bath area. Four sides of the octagon are closet doors with neoclassical appliqué designs, and the eighth side of the space has a window to view the courtyard. Painted in pale blue, mauve, and taupe, it is decorated in a romanticized Art Deco style, with theatricality worthy of Hollywood. Faux-painted wooden moldings that appear to be marble flank the mirrored fireplace inset. Rose was acquainted with the work of important interior designers, one of whom was Syrie Maugham, wife of author Somerset Maugham. Syrie was a guest of the Vanderbilts at their Fisher Island residence known as Alva Base.

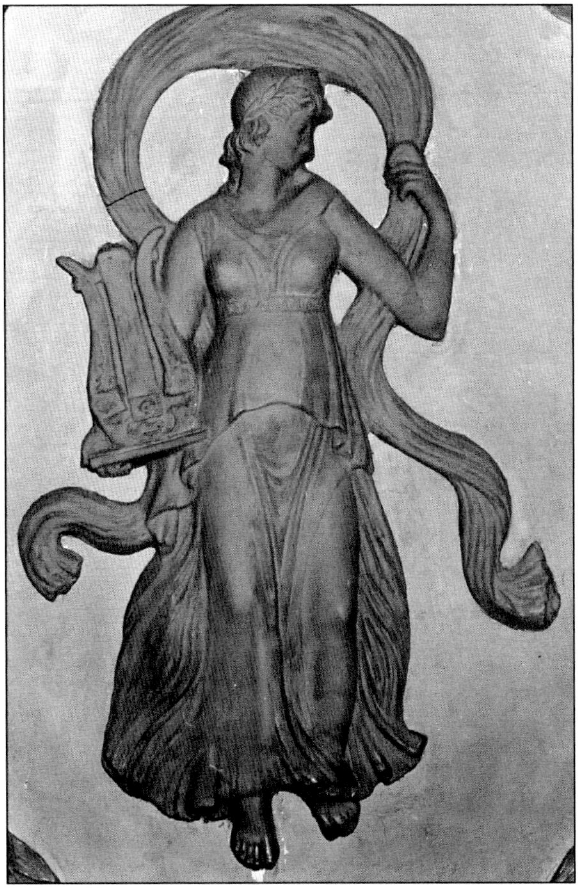

This is one of the figures from Rose's dressing room closet doors. Note in the previous and following photographs that each of the figures is unique. Their heads are turned to face different directions depending upon their placement, illustrating the level of detail required to carry out these design elements.

The opposite view of Rose's dressing room provides a peek into the wash area of the bathroom. On the other side of that room is a water closet with a scale built into the floor and the weight read-out at eye level, inset into the wall. There is also a built-in soaking tub carved from a single slab of rose marble.

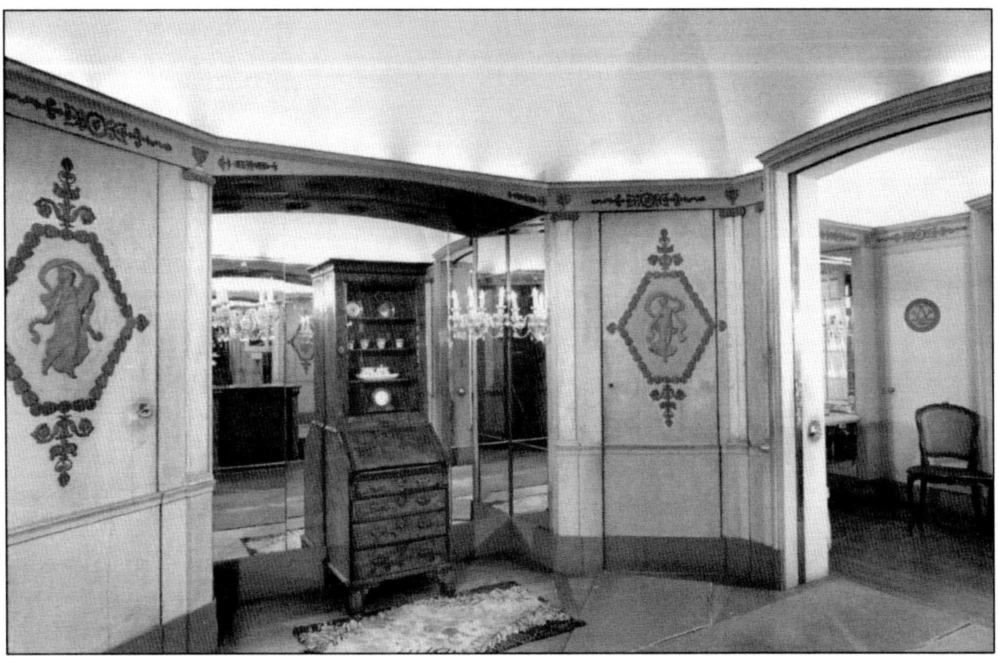

Rose's paneled bedroom is inspired by the Louis XV style, first popularized by his mistress Madame de Pompadour. Perhaps originally installed at another estate and reassembled for this room, it is difficult to attribute a specific date to the panels. The furnishings as photographed here postdate the ones original to the room, which were removed by Rose's children after her death.

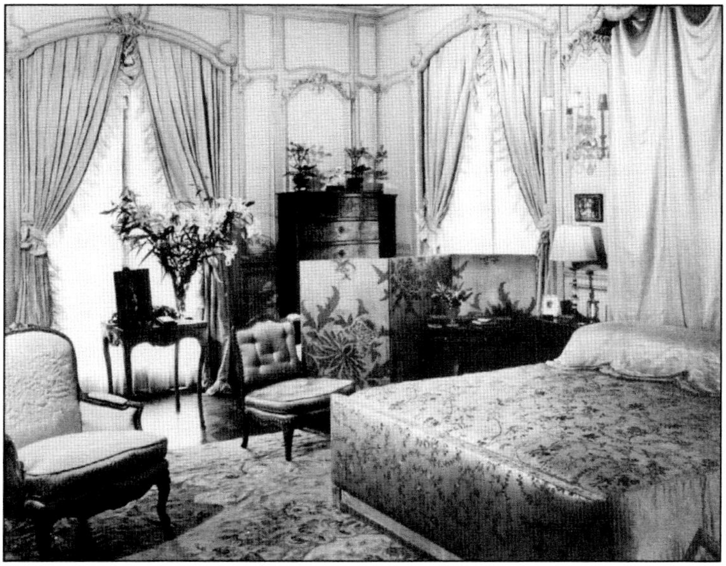

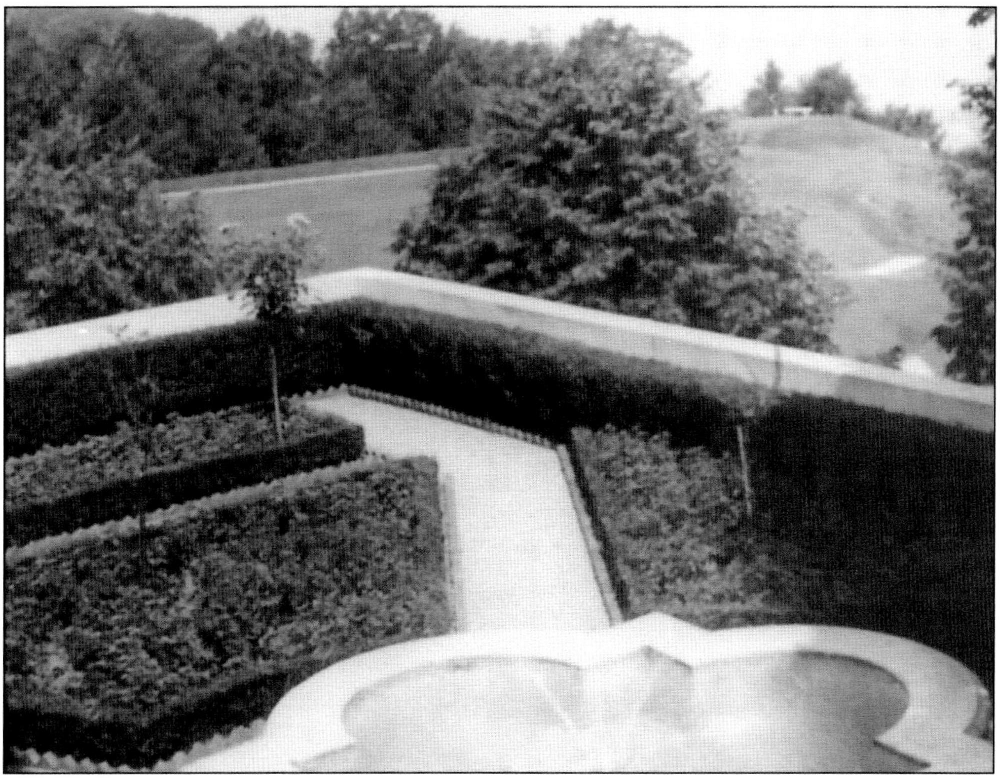

This is the view of the garden just below the window to Rose's bedroom. Water sprays from the fountain in the quatrefoil pool, and the gardens are planted with low boxwoods and roses. From this vantage point, there is a good view of the golf course, the saltwater pool, and the bay.

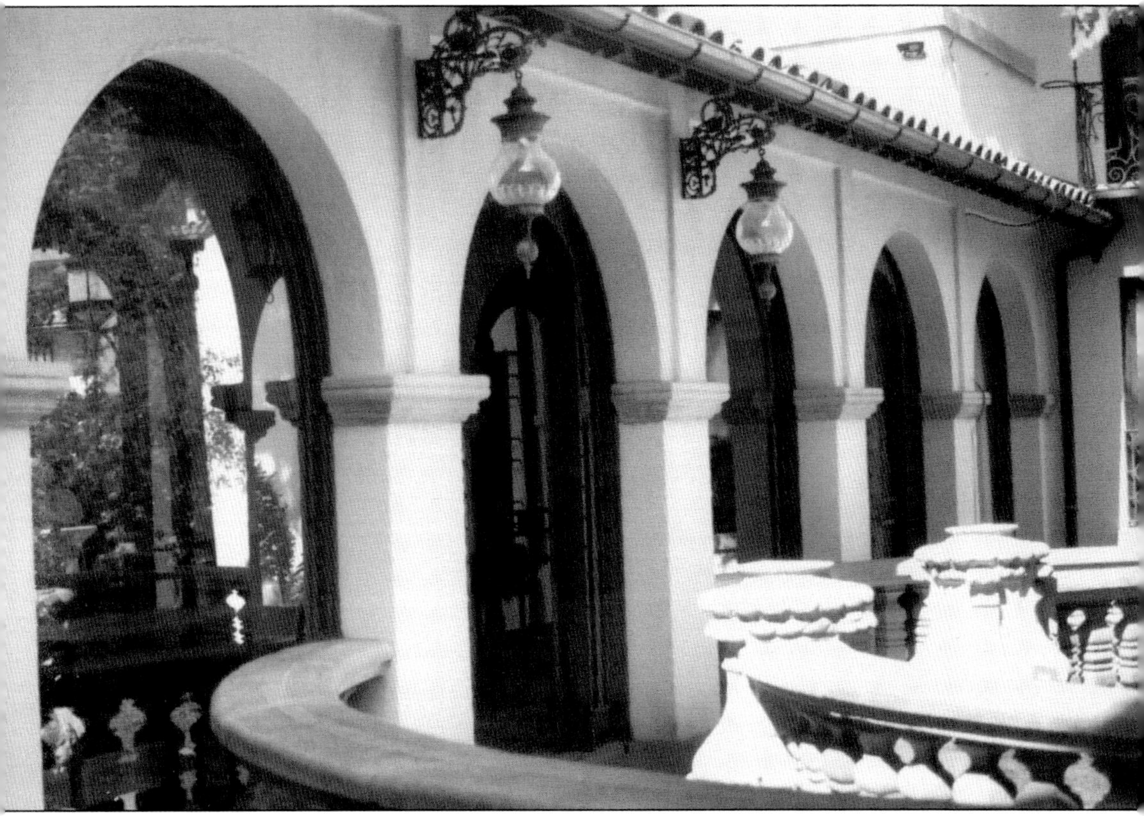

This is the arcade connecting the main residence with the nursery wing as viewed from the boxwood garden. The arches are now trimmed in painted black iron and glazed, the center ones fitted with opening sets of doors to pass through to the courtyard.

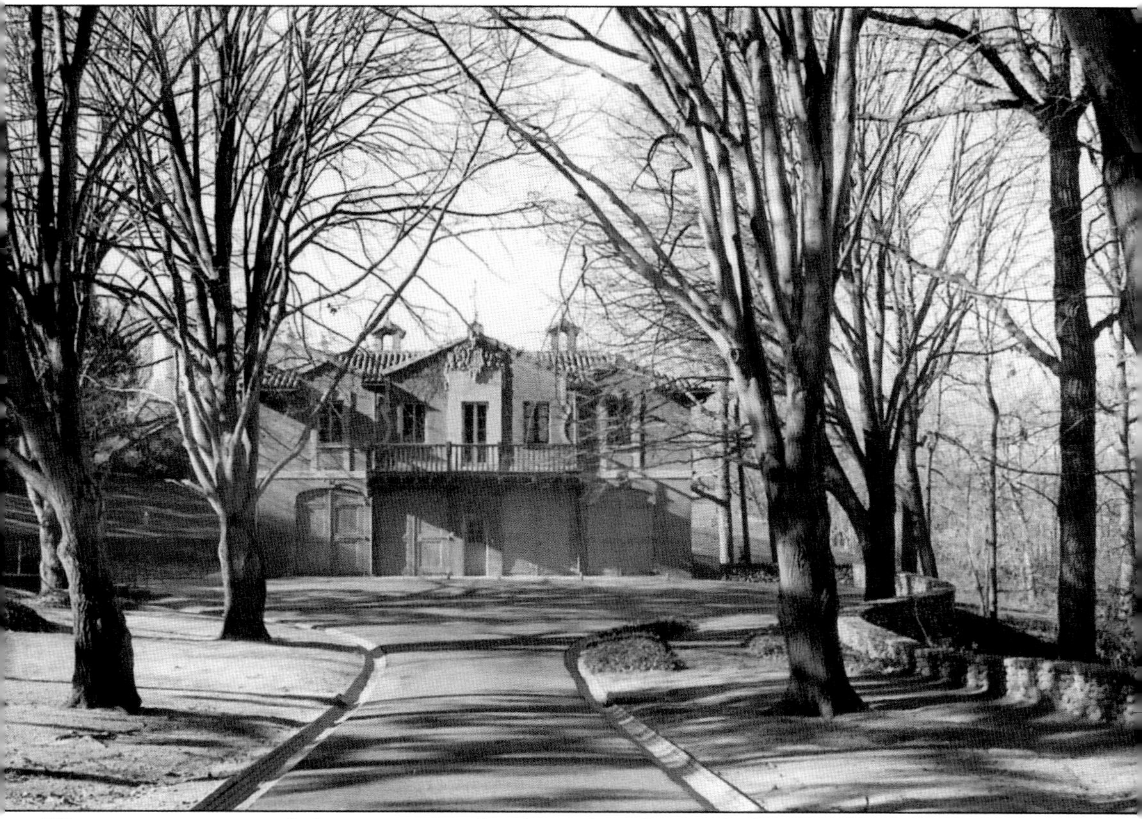

The garage was expanded to two stories by the early 1930s, with the upper story housing the chauffeurs of the visiting guests or male staff members at Eagle's Nest. This building has some interesting features not found elsewhere on the property. There are Elizabethan-style grotesqueries carved under the upper wooden balcony and an original Morris Lapidus design at the peak of the structure. Lapidus said that he arrived at the design by reinterpreting the radiator grille from a 1926 Packard automobile as Spanish plateresque. He showed the design to estate architect Ronald Pearce, who liked it enough to incorporate it into one of the structures.

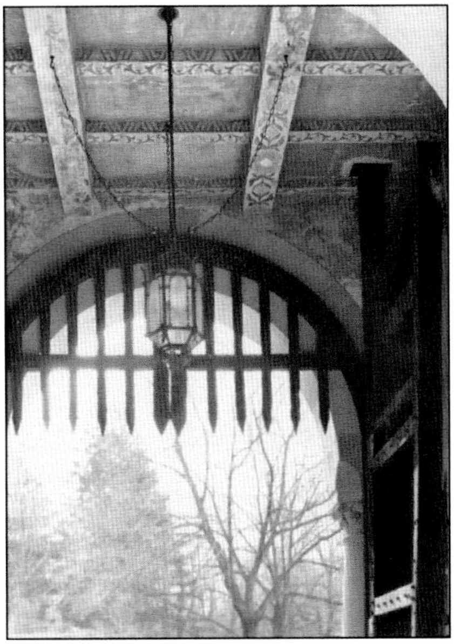

Underneath the bell tower arch, the ceiling was brightly stenciled in a vine and flower design. The hanging lantern lights the approach. Designs were incorporated into and hidden everywhere in unexpected places on the estate structures, leaving something new to discover with every visit.

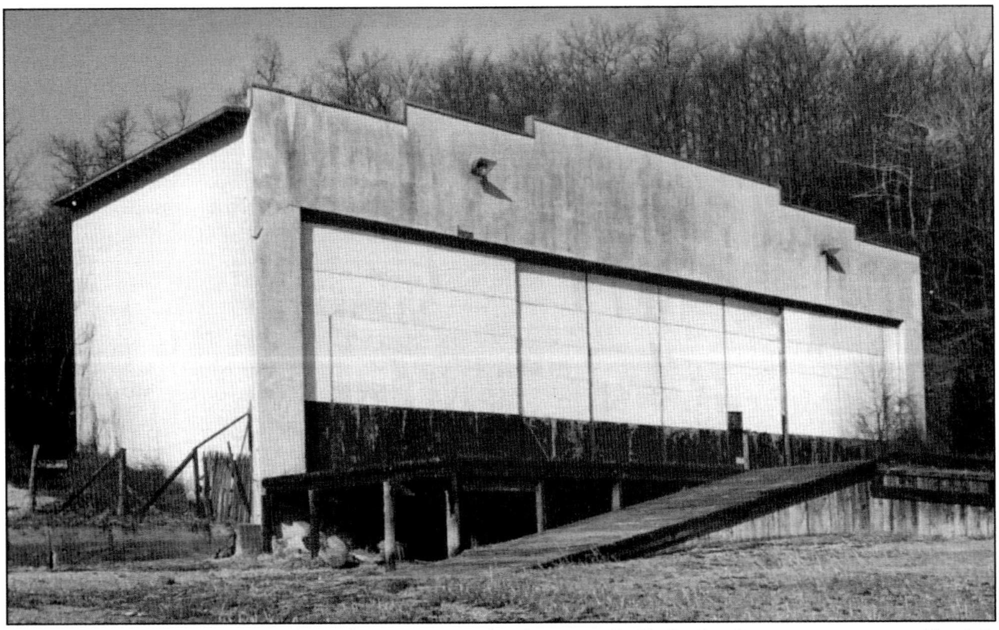

The 8,085-square-foot seaplane hangar was the least embellished of any structure at Eagle's Nest. It was built in the mid-1930s in an extremely simple, industrial Art Deco style, somewhat incongruous with the rest of the estate. The interior of the lower level housed Willie K.'s planes and the mechanical equipment to work on them. The interior of the top level contained a residence apartment consisting of two bedrooms, a living room, kitchen, and bath. Henry Gerstung, employed by Willie K. as a flight engineer and mechanic, occupied the space with his wife, Florence, in the late 1930s. According to an oral history account provided in 1998 by his niece Elizabeth Young, Gerstung referred to the apartment as "my blue heaven" for the color of the walls. He is credited with inventing and installing a de-icer for the airplanes. Unlike the boathouse, which is constructed of stone on the waterside, the materials used to construct the hangar did not weather well on the shore.

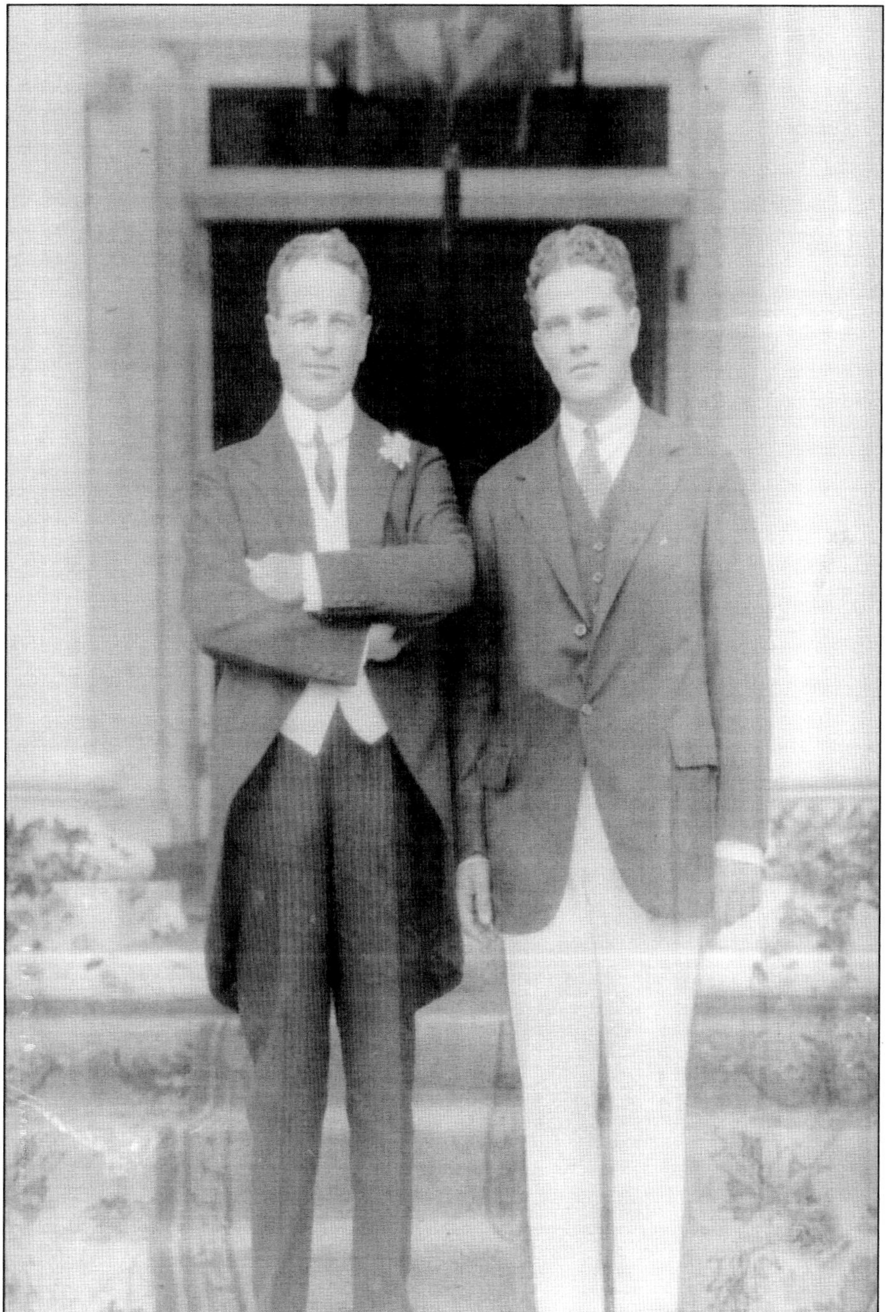

Willie K. is pictured in Newport, Rhode Island, with his son, William, at the wedding reception for his daughter Muriel, who married Frederick Church in the summer of 1925. Dressed in a formal suit, William appears older than his 17 years. His mother, Virginia, would not permit him to attend the church ceremony because it was not performed by a Catholic priest. The Vanderbilt family was of the Episcopal faith; however, Willie K.'s first wife was Catholic. Perhaps this is one of the reasons that although they were separated in 1910, Virginia and Willie K. did not divorce until 17 years later. (Courtesy of the Consuelo Vanderbilt Earl Estate.)

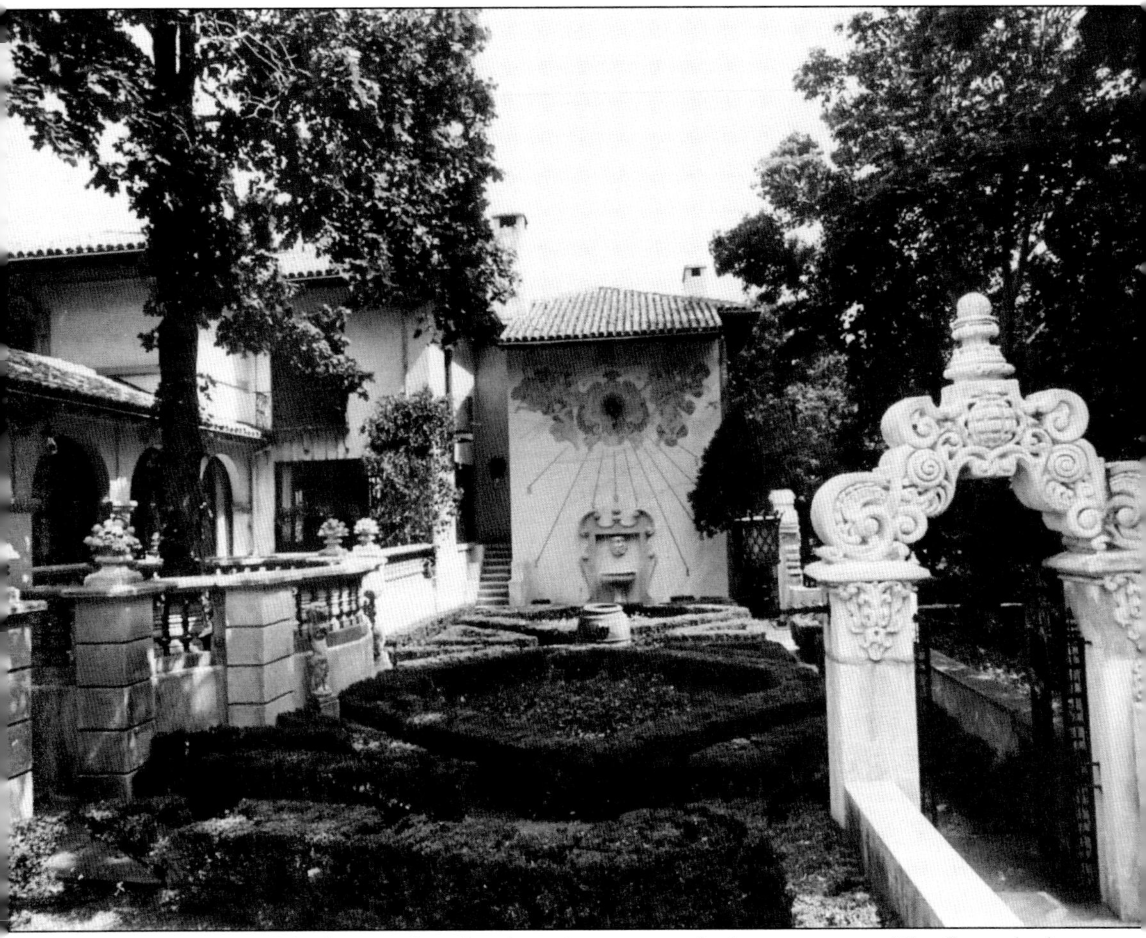

This is a view of the boxwood garden from the stairs to the lower museum. The flower beds are bordered by neatly trimmed, low boxwood hedgerows in simple geometric designs, giving the outdoor space a neatness and sense of order. Decorative elements are well spaced, and a stone balustrade parallels the window arcade. The sundial is visible from this vantage point. Located at a central point in the fresco scene, King Neptune's trident casts a shadow on the wall that reaches the clock-like markings, giving the correct time of day. The sundial was inspired by the designs at the Palace of Versailles in France.

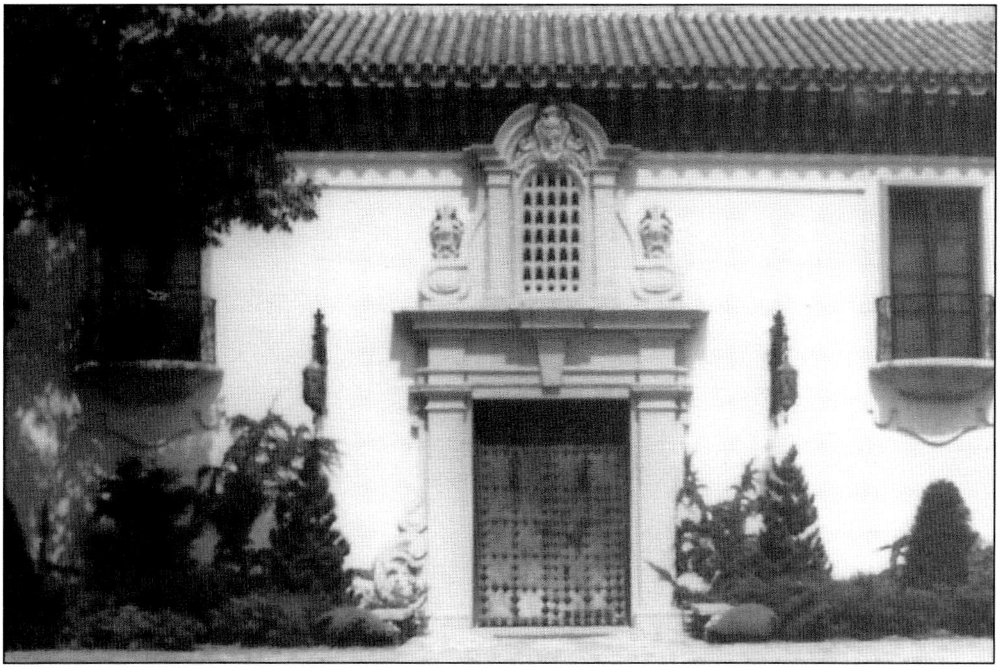

With the addition of this wing in 1935, the final side of the courtyard is closed. Built in memory of Willie K.'s son, William, who died in a car accident in 1933, it appropriately lacks whimsical elements and has a mausoleum-like facade. The decorative iron and stone embellishments on this wing are greatly toned down. Behind the grid-like fenestration above the entrance door is Rose's closet, and the window to the right of it is her dressing area. The window to the left is for the trophy room dedicated to Willie K.'s son.

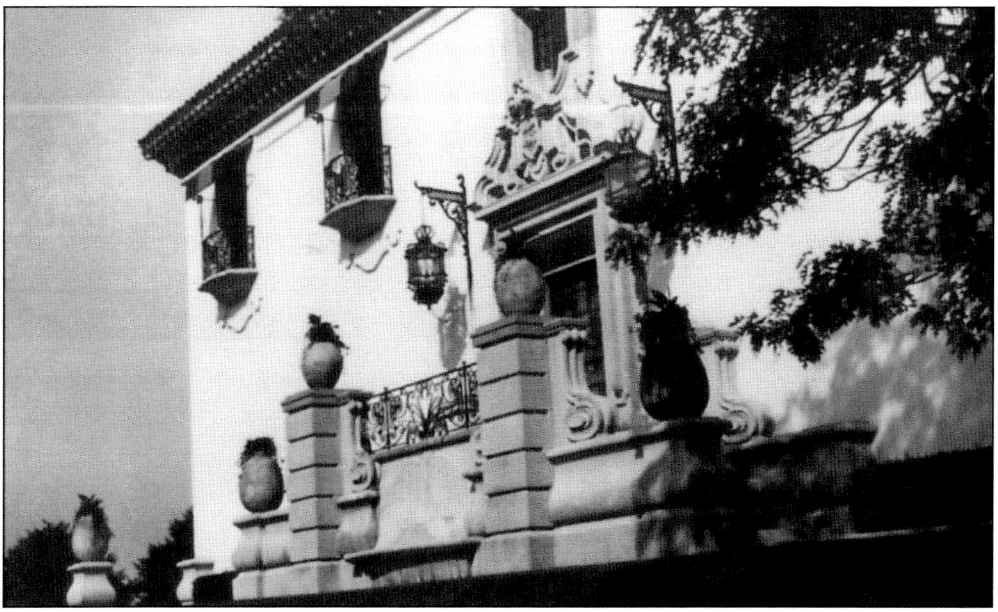

The back of this wing faces the estate's golf course. The style of this side of the structure is different than that of the front. It hints at Art Deco influences, with cleaner lines and less flourishes. The two windows to the left on the upper level are for Rose's bath and bedroom, respectively.

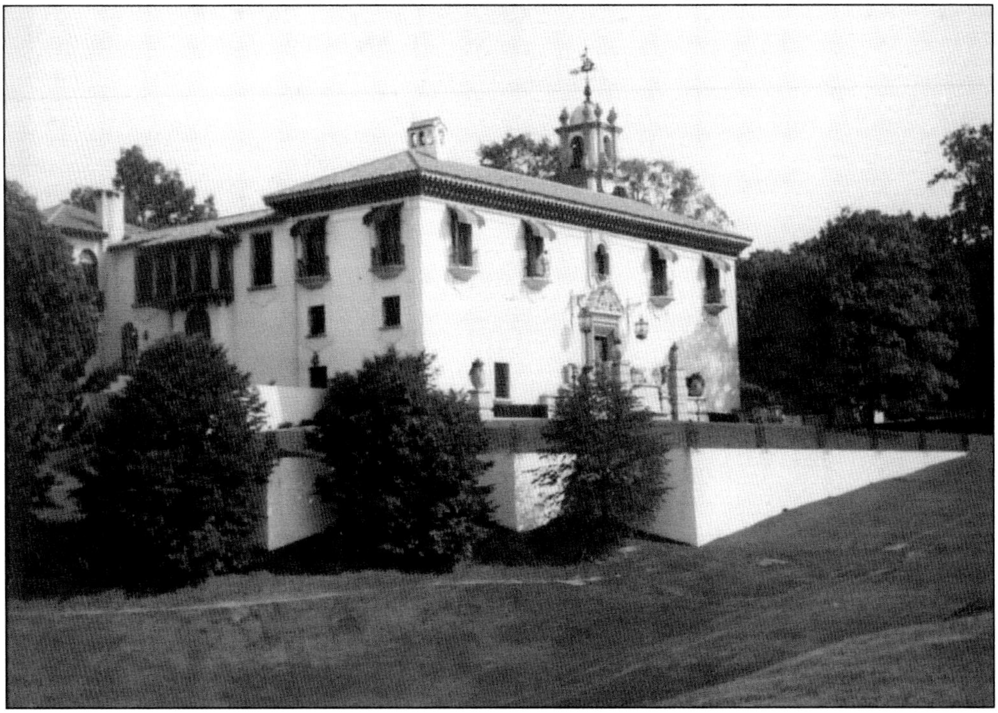

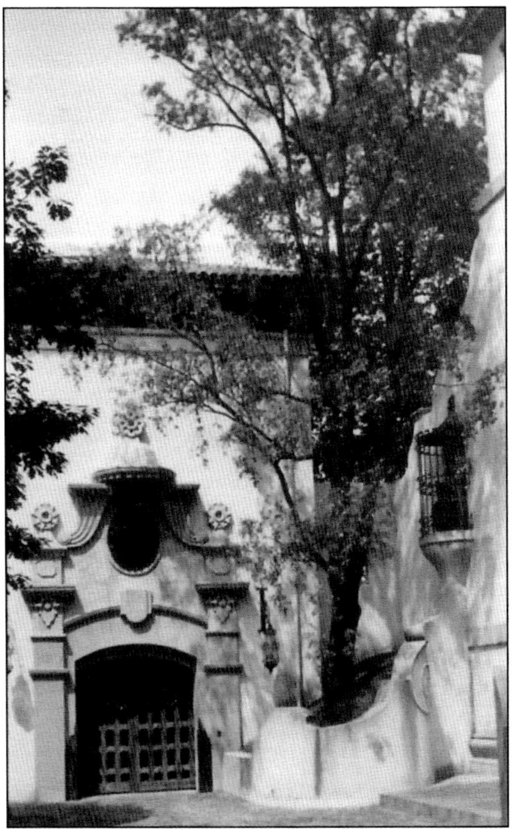

The view of the house from the northwestern side shows the back corner of the Memorial Wing and the retaining walls behind it where plantings were used to conceal and soften their sharp edges. Iron fencing runs the length of the wall. The porch extending from the left side of the second floor is the breakfast hallway.

This is a view of the lower side of the Memorial Wing, adjacent to the laundry room entrance. The wooden doors open to a garage with a large, round, metal turntable built into the floor. By pushing on the side of an automobile parked squarely upon it, it will turn around, and the car can drive back out.

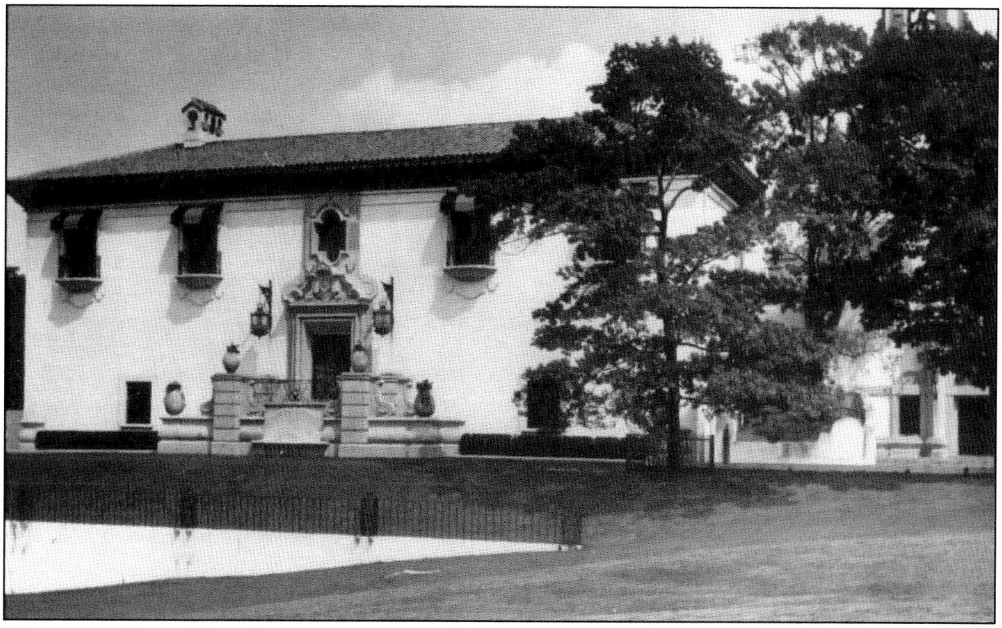

The turntable and laundry entrances as viewed from the golf course appear in the lower right of the photograph. The road on the estate leading down to this area came to be used for deliveries and maintenance vehicles and as an entrance for the estate staff.

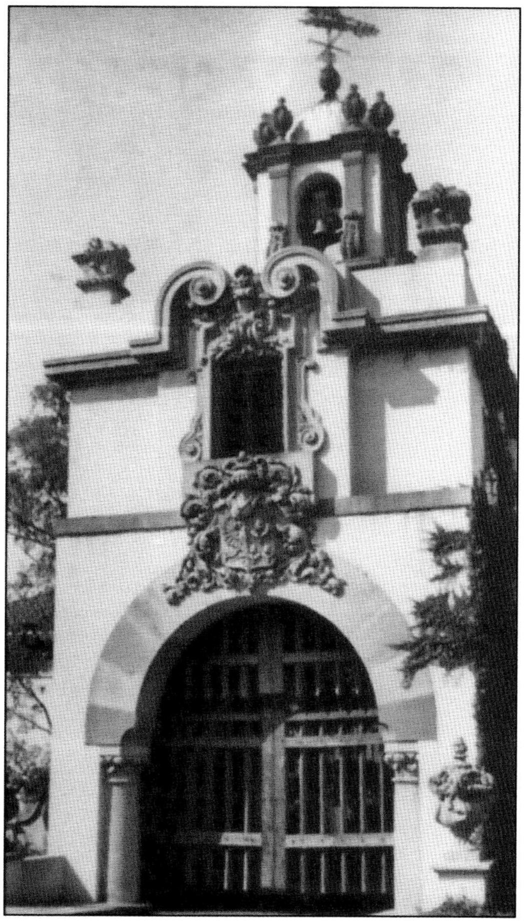

With the heavy wooden gates closed, the bell tower appears more imposing and solid. The portcullis is an applied effect, not an actual sliding wooden gate. The bell at the top of the tower, cast in Russia in 1725, rings on the hour and half hour through the use of electric motors. The Memorial Wing roof is visible in the upper-left corner of the photograph.

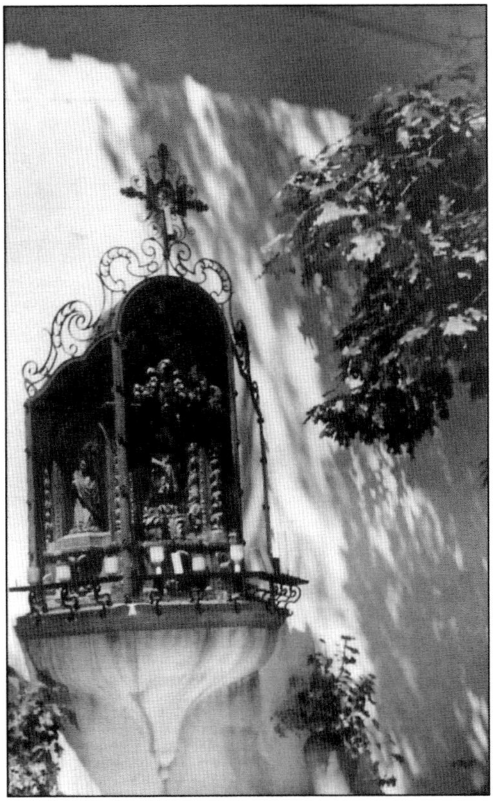

A religious triptych was installed in the facade of the Memorial Wing, on the bell tower entrance side, as if to announce the purpose of this wing of the house. It is an elaborate piece containing three-dimensional figures, surrounded by glass, and trimmed in ornamental ironwork.

In this view of the lower museum entrance from the access road to the boathouse, the retaining wall from the garden above is large and blank on this side. One of the few places on the estate that lacks any ornamentation or landscape treatment, it is somewhat of an anomaly in the architectural plan.

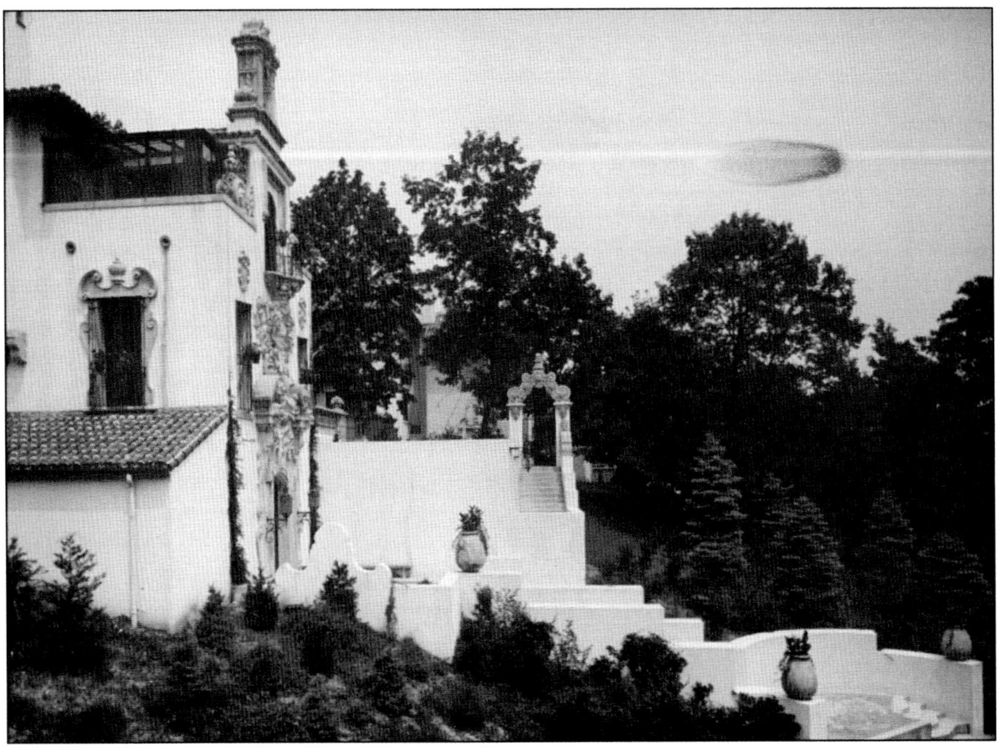

A Madonna and child sculpture is pictured on the grotto wall outside the lower museum. This wall is blank in the previous estate photograph, and there is no information or explanation for the sudden appearance of this piece, which is reported to be an authentic creation of the della Robbia atelier. The timing of its appearance may be related to the 1933 deaths of Vanderbilt's son, William, or mother, Alva. It is known that Alva had an affinity for della Robbia's work, having a Madonna and child piece in her Gothic room at Marble House.

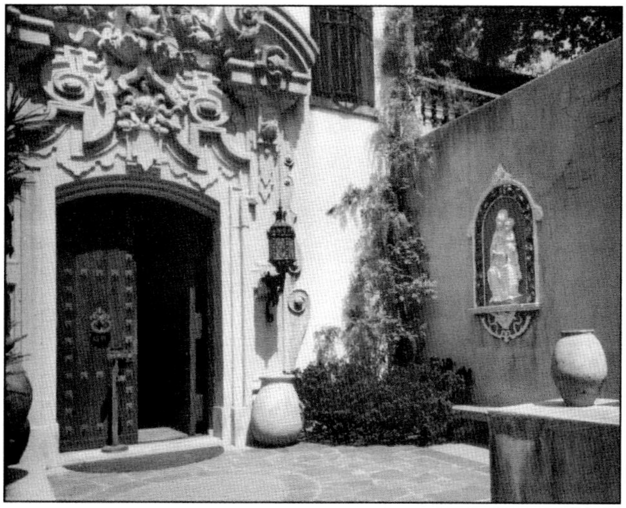

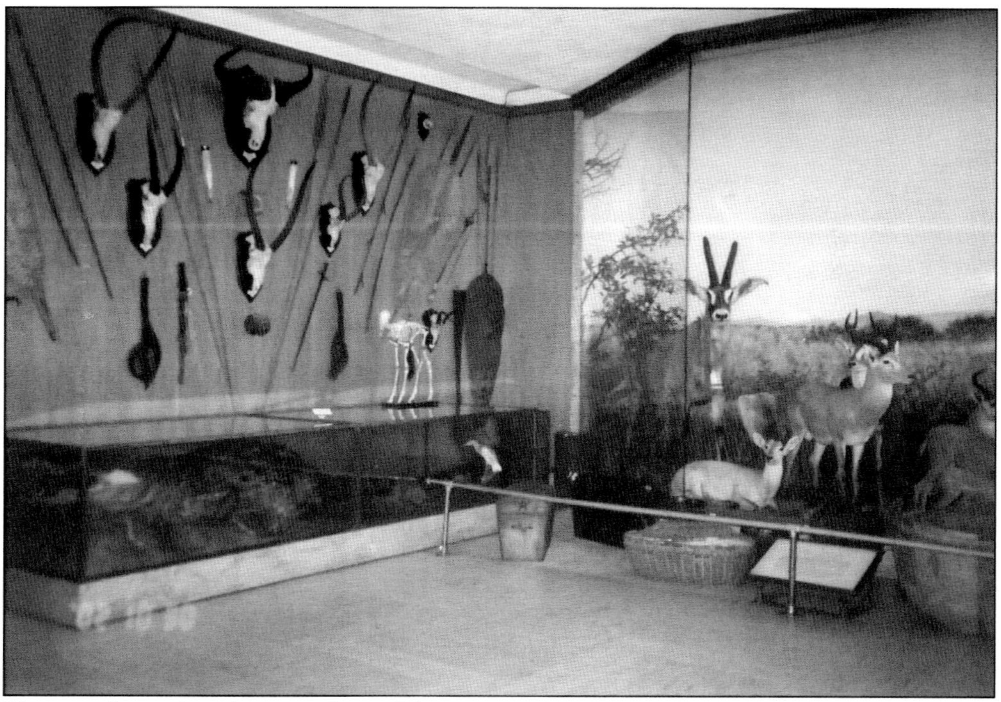

The room located on the upper floor of the Memorial Wing at Eagle's Nest contains trophies from William's 1931 safari to the Anglo-Egyptian Sudan. The animal trophies were shipped directly to London taxidermist Roland Ward for mounting from Africa and then sent back to New York for the museum.

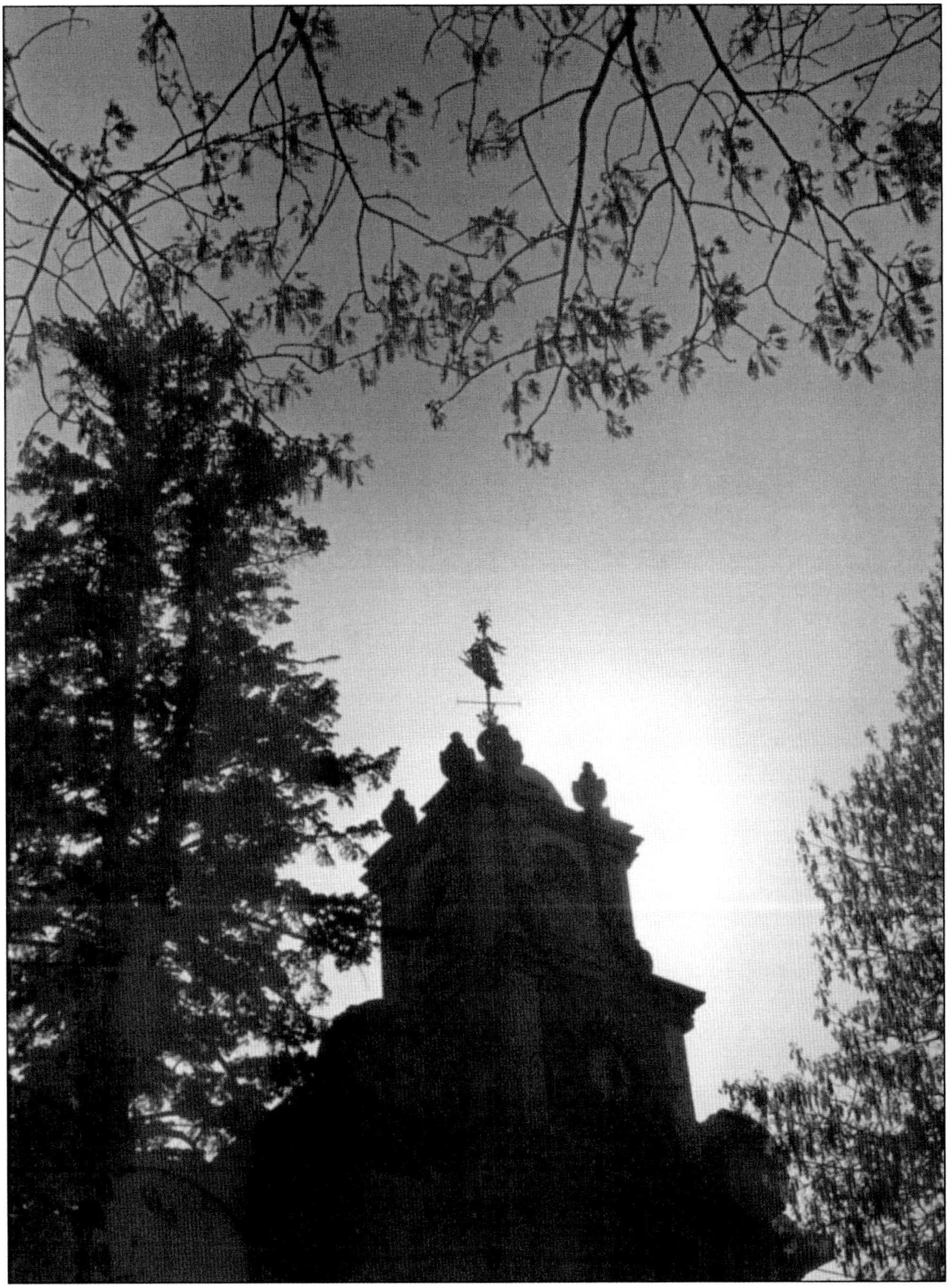

The bell tower silhouetted in the late afternoon sun signals the end of this chapter in the life of Willie K., awaiting the dawn of another. Between 1925 and 1935, he circumnavigated the globe twice, got remarried, commissioned a custom-made luxury yacht, built an estate with two museums, and lost three close family members.

Six

VANDERBILT'S FINAL SUMMERS AT EAGLE'S NEST

The last architectural changes to the estate residence were made between 1935 and 1940. The Memorial Wing exhibits were completed, a large library was added off of the nursery wing with an adjacent Moroccan-tiled room, and the central courtyard was paved with cobblestones. The lower museum, which became known as the Habitat, had a new addition as well. A whale shark of almost 32 feet was acquired by Willie K. after becoming tangled in the net of a commercial fisherman off the Fire Island coast of Long Island, New York. He had a taxidermist prepare it and suspend it from the ceiling of the room.

Willie K. produced *Over the Seven Seas*, a movie of his final circumnavigation of the globe in his yacht *Alva.* He shared his adventures with the community by arranging movie showings in local public venues. He purchased and donated the first rescue vehicle for the Centerport Fire Department. And, as other Vanderbilts before him, he turned his beloved custom-made yacht *Alva* over to the US Navy when World War II began. De-outfitted and renamed the *Plymouth*, it served as an escort ship before it was sunk in the Atlantic Ocean by a German submarine off the coast of the Carolinas.

With his beloved mother, son, and ship now gone, Willie K. turned to other activities to occupy himself. He purchased a Sikorsky aircraft and traveled with Rose and friends to his home on Fisher Island, Florida. When he felt more adventurous, he traveled to South America with a skilled pilot at the controls. He published his final book, *Flying Lanes*, in 1937, to chronicle that trip.

Willie K. was visibly frail in his last few years but could still be seen frequently in his tuxedo at the El Morocco nightclub in New York City. He had a table in a prime spot there, where he listened to Latin orchestras and drank champagne with Rose. Succumbing to a chronic heart ailment, Willie K. died in his New York City home in 1944 at the age of 66.

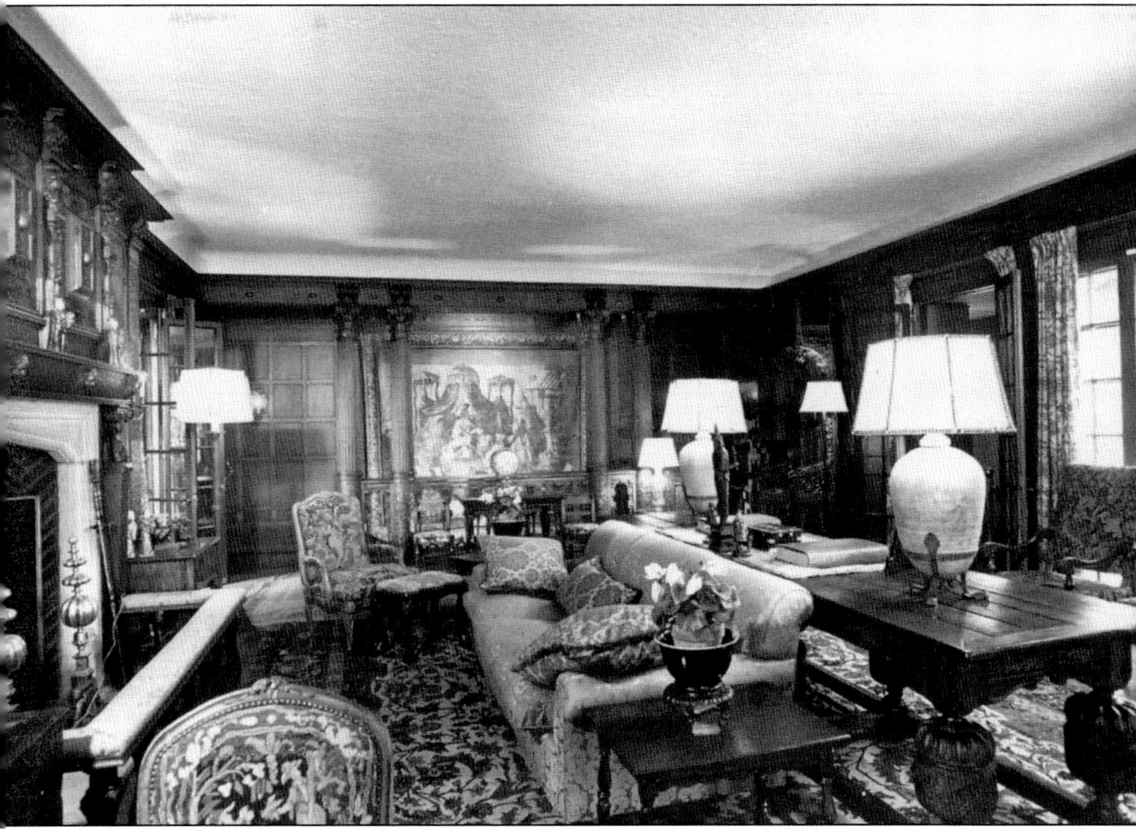

The upstairs parlor of Eagle's Nest was a gathering place where the family watched home movies on their Bell and Howell projector, played parlor games, or listened to organ music. The Aeolian pipe organ installed there in 1932 has 1,476 pipes that span three stories and are hidden in the wall behind a woolen Brussels tapestry. Many large estates had pipe organs, as they were popular during the 1930s. The dark, stained-oak walls of the room are paneled in Jacobean style and are said to be from an English manor house and reassembled for the room. A staircase flanked by intricately carved columns hides the view of the room, enhancing the dramatic effect once the top landing is reached. The furnishings are eclectic, with a large balloon-leg refectory table behind the sofa and a bishop's chair next to the pipe organ.

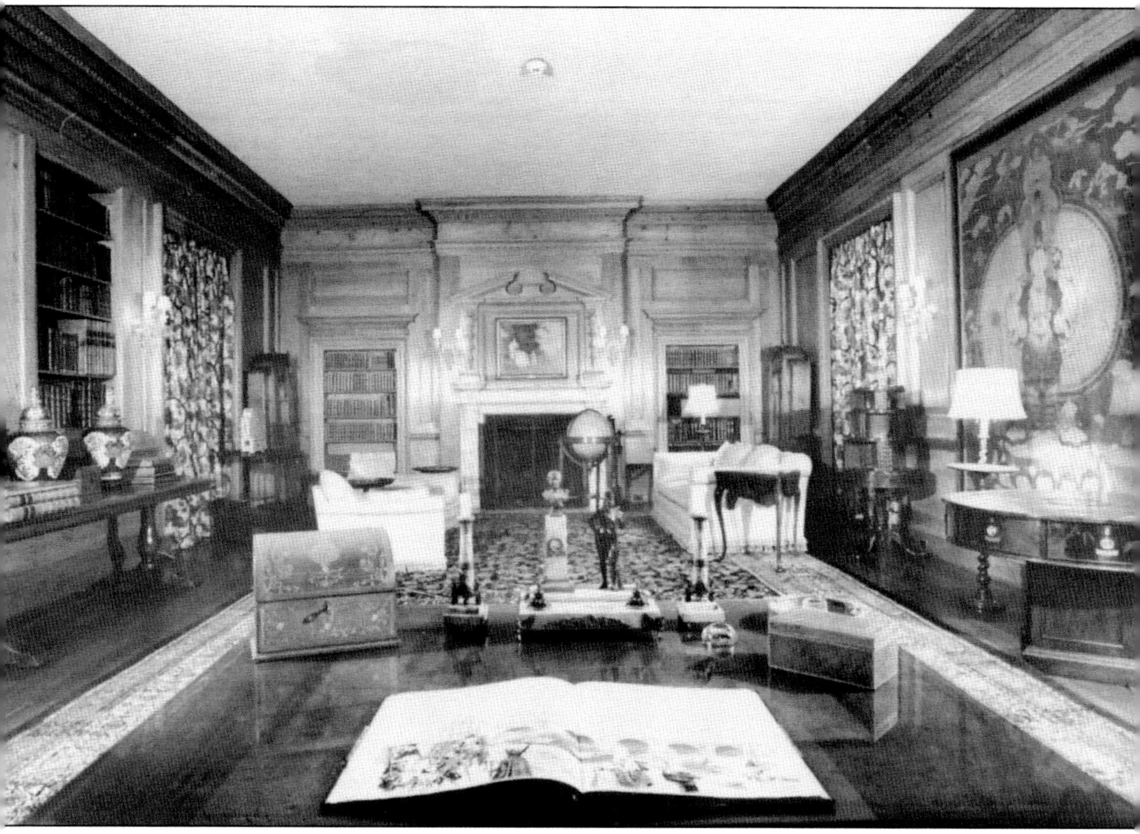

Vanderbilt's library was one of the last additions to Eagle's Nest, built off of the first floor of the nursery wing atop the lower museum area. A beautifully appointed room with light, paneled walls and a grand fireplace, Willie K. kept his large collection of books in the built-in shelving units. A Tibetan silk tapestry depicting a seated Buddha hangs on one of the long walls, and an antique Persian Bibikabad carpet in midnight blue with an ivory border covers the entire floor of the large room. Willie K. received sound decorating advice, for this particular type of carpet is known for its durability. Willie K. conducted railroad business and kept an eye on his stock portfolio in his library and was known to retreat to the adjacent open-air Moroccan courtyard to enjoy a cigar.

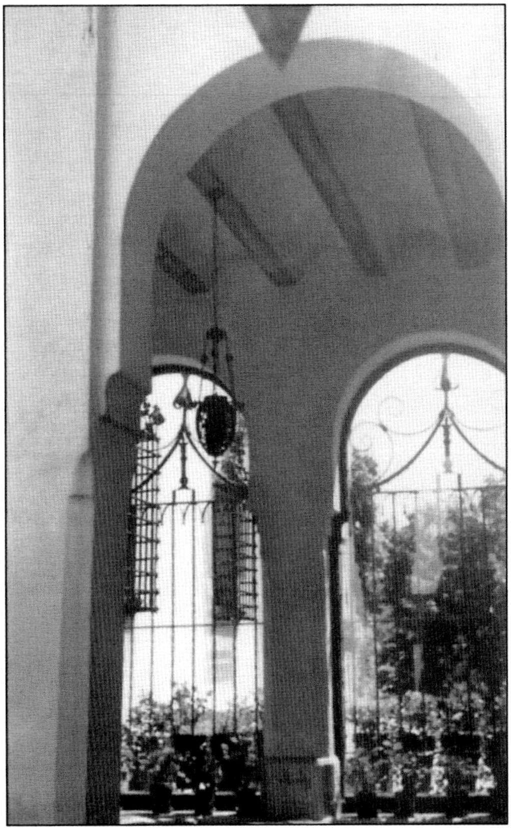

The space known as the Moroccan court connects the nursery wing to Willie K.'s library. The name derives from the style of the tiles, although they were purchased in Spain according to the archival records. The room was built as an outdoor courtyard, open to the elements with a running fountain. A covered roof was added, and the arched openings were glazed at a later date. A view of the opposite side of the court shows a massive square support column.

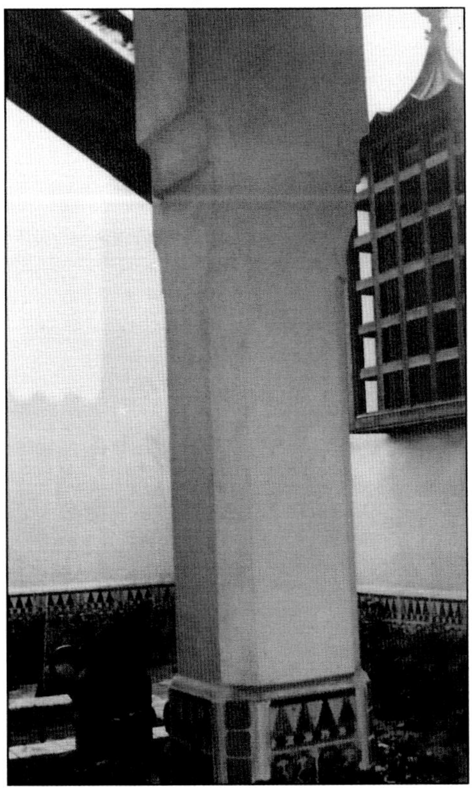

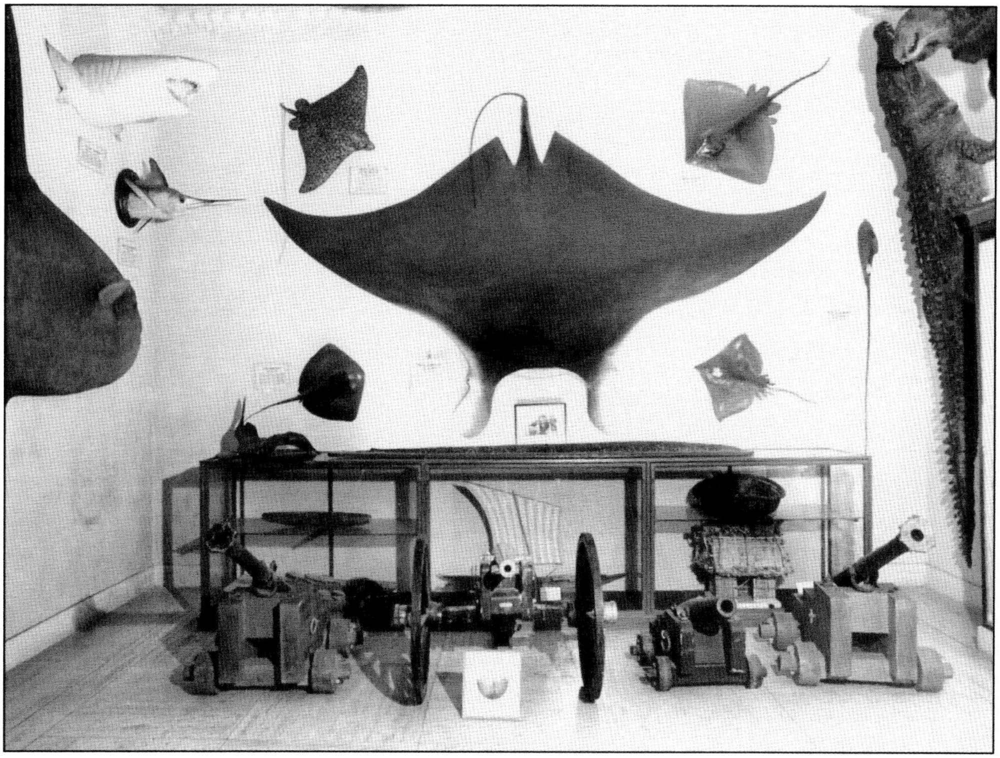

This photograph of the short wall on the left side of the first floor of the Hall of Fishes shows that it is now dominated by marine specimens. At its inception, a variety of objects and specimens were displayed side by side in this space. As Willie K.'s collections grew, and with the addition of the museum's second floor, exhibit spaces were organized by collection types.

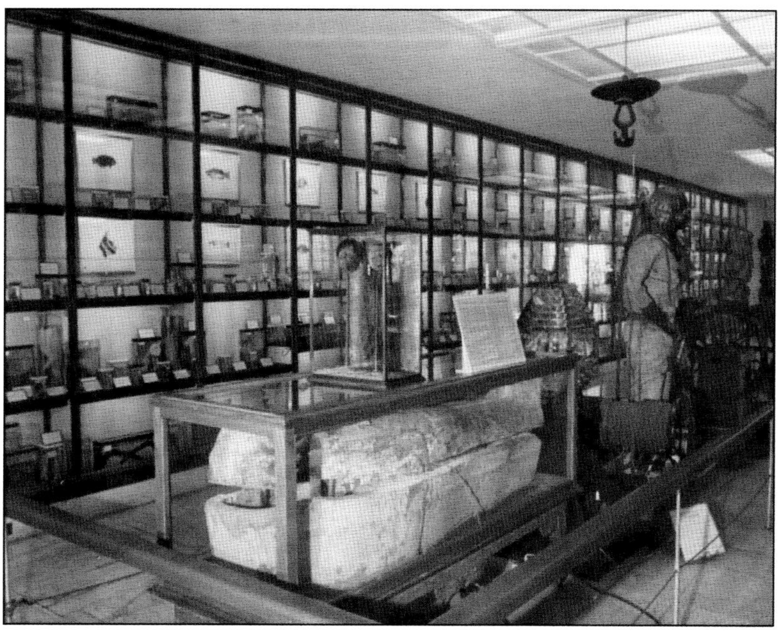

The upper floor of the museum was outfitted with wall-to-wall exhibit cases to display Belanske's artwork and the endless specimen jars holding thousands of fish. Willie K. added an Egyptian mummy, acquired on the *Alva* cruise in 1931, to his collection as well.

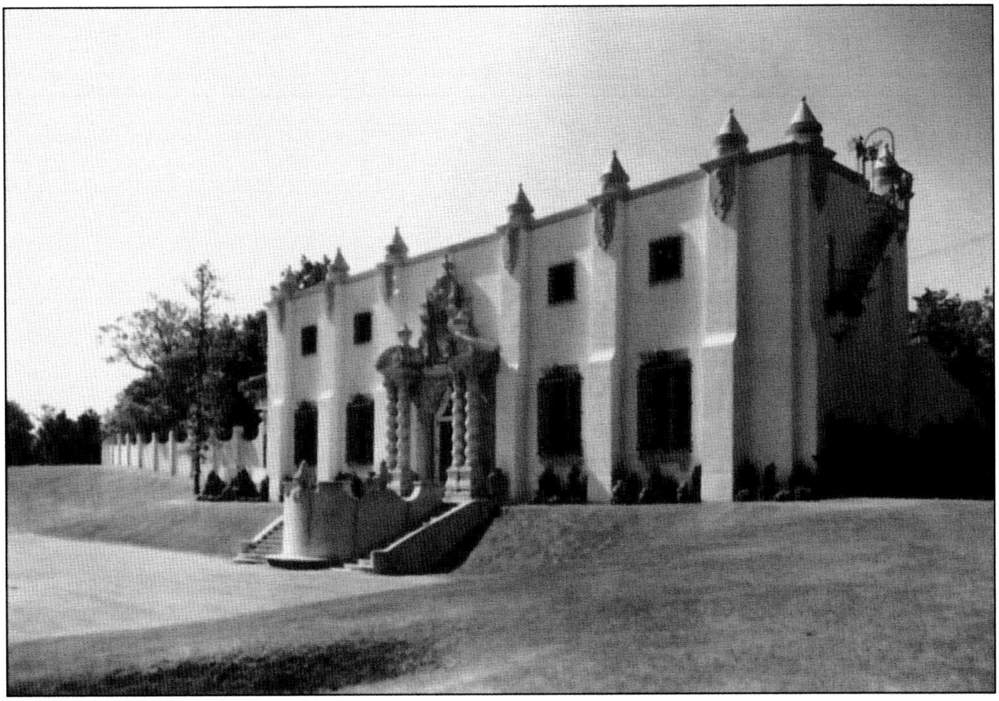

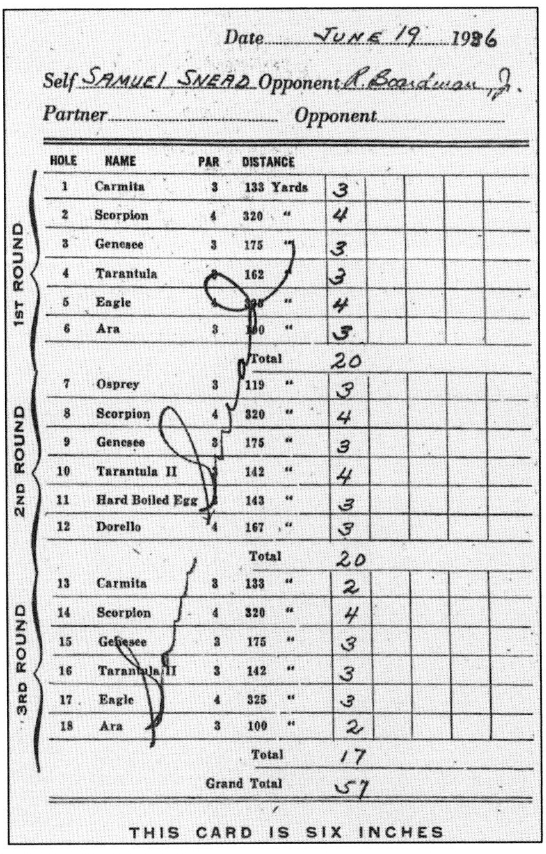

Date JUNE 19 1936

Self SAMUEL SNEAD Opponent R. Boardman, Jr.

Partner Opponent

	HOLE	NAME	PAR	DISTANCE	
1ST ROUND	1	Carmita	3	133 Yards	3
	2	Scorpion	4	320 "	4
	3	Genesee	3	175 "	3
	4	Tarantula	3	162	3
	5	Eagle	4	325 "	4
	6	Ara	3	100 "	3
				Total	20
2ND ROUND	7	Osprey	3	119 "	3
	8	Scorpion	4	320 "	4
	9	Genesee	3	175 "	3
	10	Tarantula II	3	142 "	4
	11	Hard Boiled Egg	[illegible]	143 "	3
	12	Dorello	4	167 "	3
				Total	20
3RD ROUND	13	Carmita	3	133 "	2
	14	Scorpion	4	320 "	4
	15	Genesee	3	175 "	3
	16	Tarantula II	3	142 "	3
	17	Eagle	4	325 "	3
	18	Ara	3	100 "	2
				Total	17
				Grand Total	57

THIS CARD IS SIX INCHES

The second floor of the Hall of Fishes had an unintended benefit: it provided Willie K. with a new tee for his golf course. Accessible by a precarious-looking metal staircase applied to the side of the structure, the roof also provided spectacular views of Northport Bay and the shores of Connecticut on clear days.

Professional golfer Sam Snead played the course at Eagle's Nest in 1936. His scorecard shows a score of 57 and lists each hole named for one of Willie K.'s ships. When interviewed via telephone by a local newspaper in 1995, he fondly recalled his visit and said the course was not an easy one to play. He also recounts his "old-fashioned picnic dinner" with Willie K. and remembered him as a "very, very nice man."

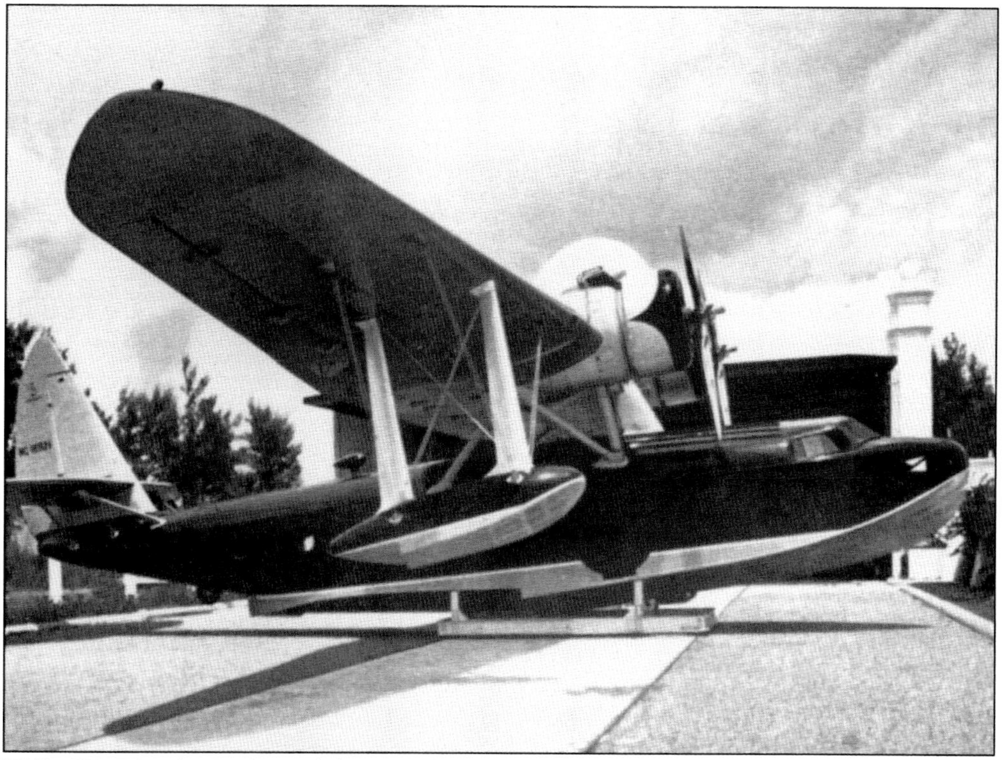

Willie K.'s Sikorsky S-43 Amphibian airplane is pictured at his winter home Alva Base in Fisher Island, Florida. It had twin Pratt and Whitney air-cooled radial engines and held three crew members and 15 passengers. He sold this airplane to the US government in 1941, at the onset of World War II, for $175,000. It crashed on a flight to Trinidad.

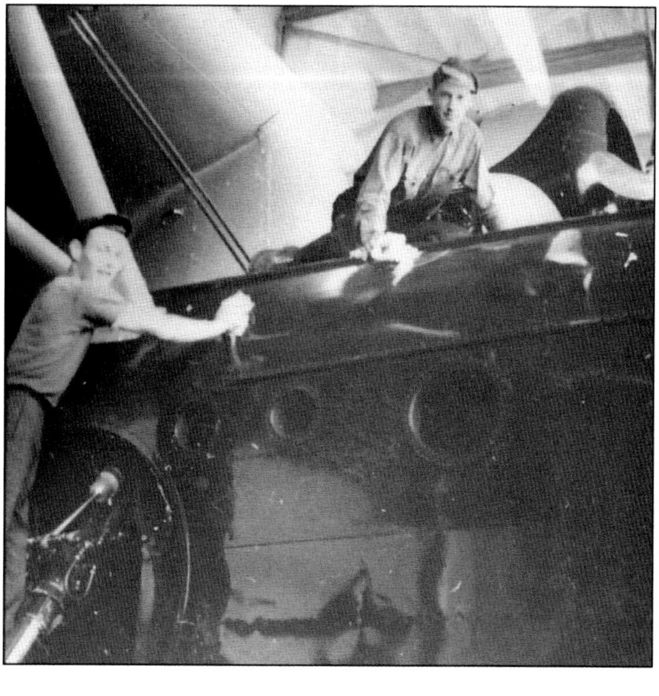

Two young mechanics service the Sikorsky at the seaplane hangar at Eagle's Nest. Air travel had become a new convenience, and a pilot was employed at the estate as well. A former employee recalls that Willie K. would remove his trousers for the flight to keep them from wrinkling and put them back on upon arriving at his destination.

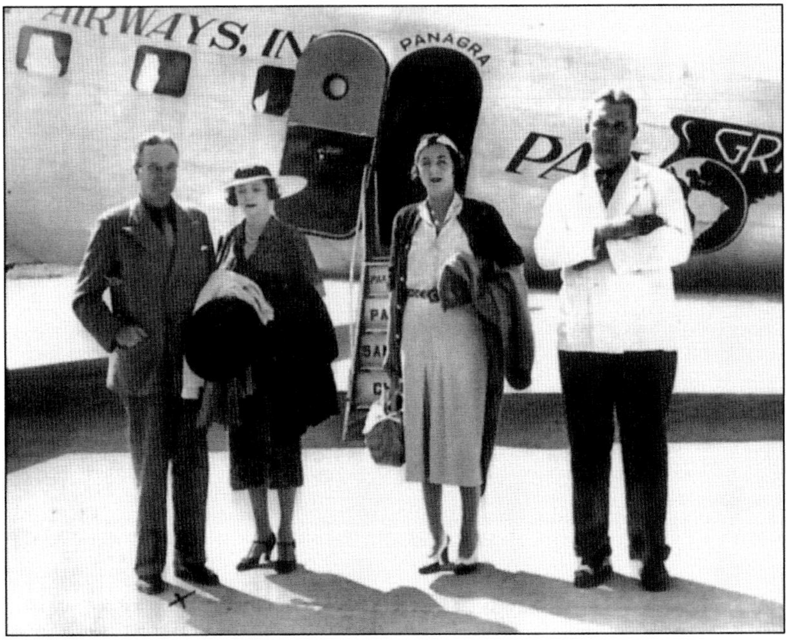

Pictured here are Willie K., Rose, and Robert and Edie Huntington in Santiago, Chile, in 1937 during their trip on the twin-engine Sikorsky. Along with pilot Earl F. White and mechanic Henry Gerstung, who also served as copilot, they flew round-trip from Miami, Florida, to Central America and Cuba.

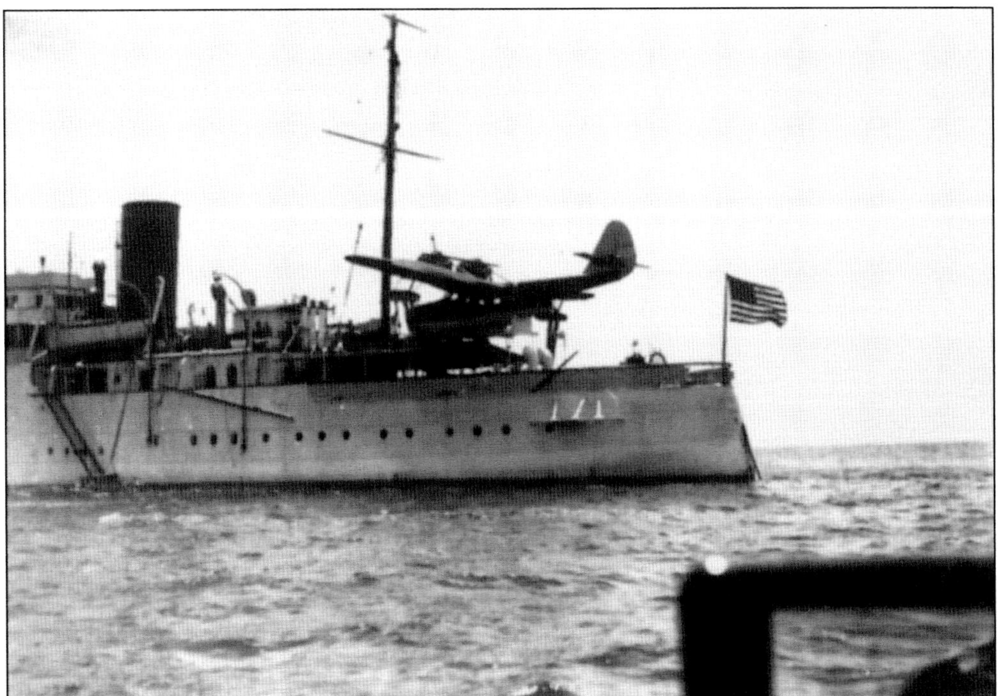

In 1934, Willie K. purchased a Douglas Dolphin Amphibian that held two crew members and eight passengers. It is pictured here perched atop the *Alva*, along with a smaller launch boat to the left. There were five boats kept on the ship in all, four of which were lifeboats.

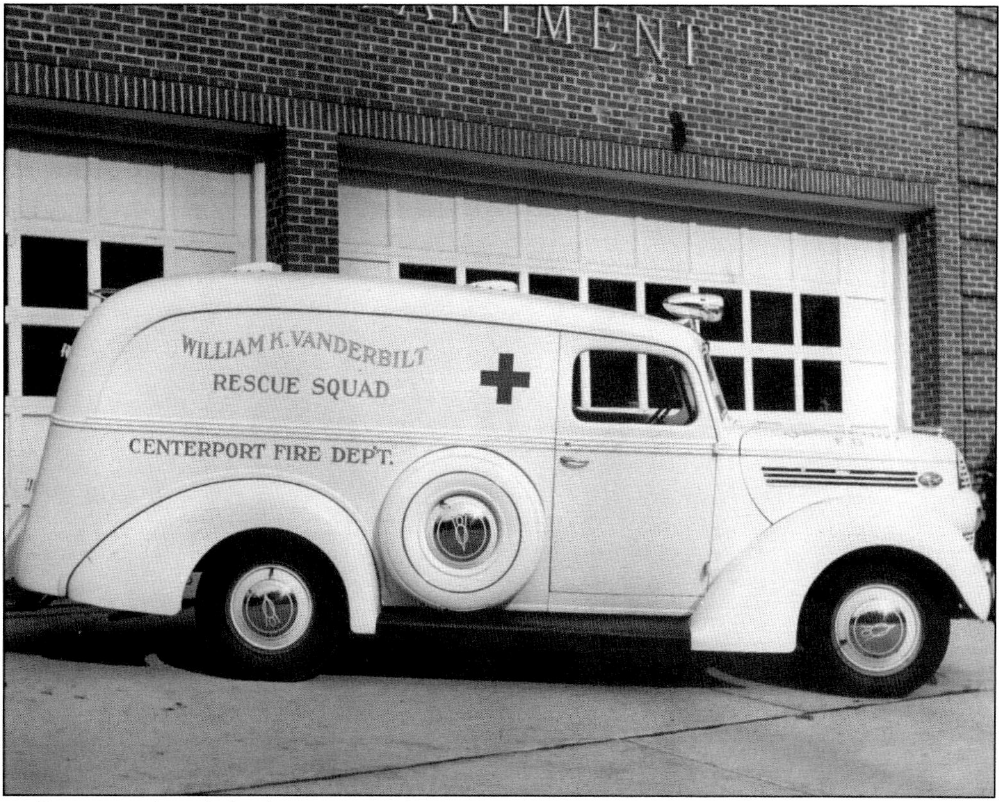

Willie K. purchased the first rescue vehicle for the Centerport Fire Department in 1938. They named the rescue squad for him and emblazoned his name on the side of the Ford vehicle. Many homes on Long Island were lost to fires in the early 20th century, prompting the development of extensive volunteer fire departments. Willie K. served as a volunteer for 43 years overall in the Great Neck and Centerport Fire Departments. (Courtesy of John Cristine and the Centerport Fire Department.)

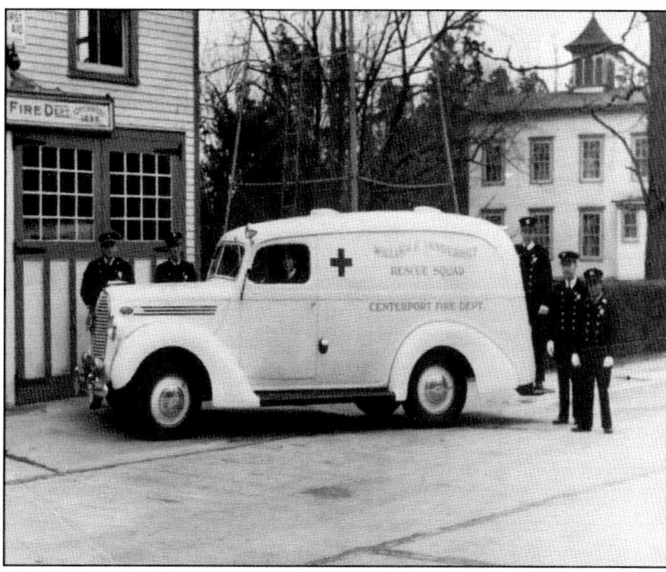

Six members of the original first-aid squad in Suffolk County are photographed with Willie K.'s donated vehicle in 1938. He hosted a mock fire drill to illustrate the importance of the volunteer fire departments to members of the community. In typical Willie K. humor, he had one fireman dressed in women's clothes to play the part of the proverbial damsel in distress. (Courtesy of John Cristine and the Centerport Fire Department.)

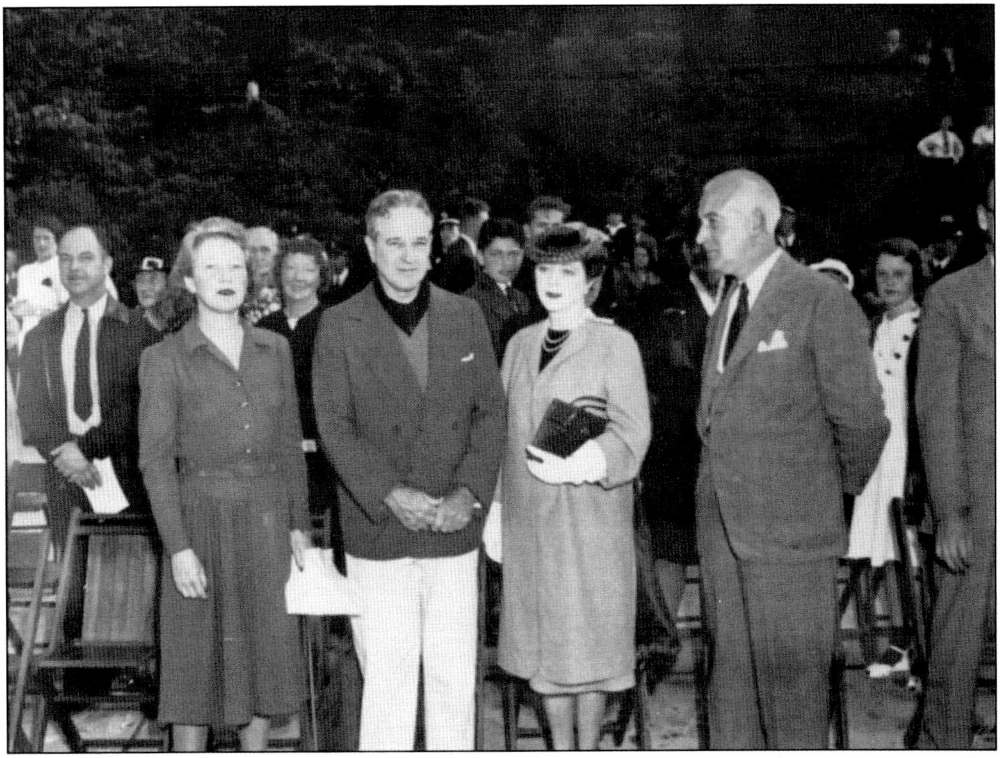

An aging Willie K. is pictured here, flanked by officials at a ceremony honoring him at the Centerport Fire Department station. Stylish Rose is by his side, and there appears to be hundreds of people in attendance. He was arguably the most prestigious member of their community. The Vanderbilts were generous donors to the fire department. (Courtesy of the Huntington Historical Society.)

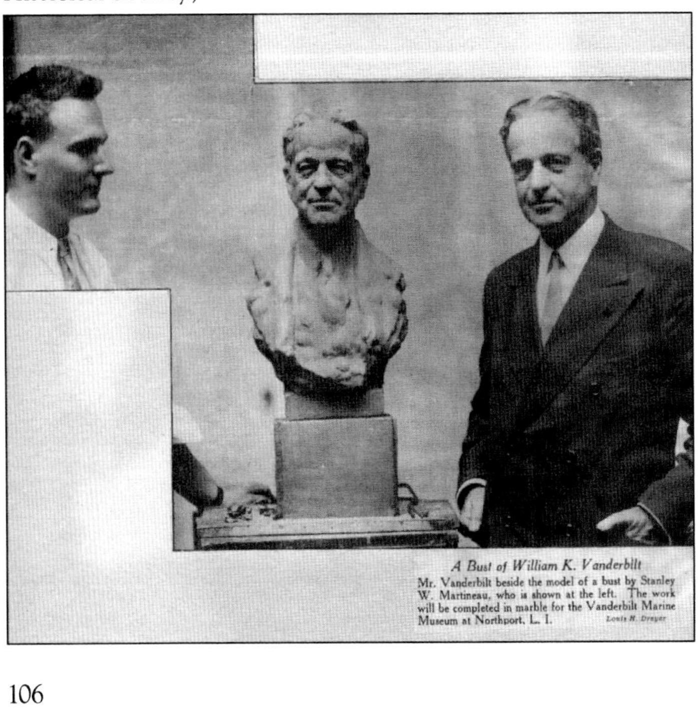

A Bust of William K. Vanderbilt

Mr. Vanderbilt beside the model of a bust by Stanley W. Martineau, who is shown at the left. The work will be completed in marble for the Vanderbilt Marine Museum at Northport, L. I. *Louis H. Dreyer*

This news clipping with the date and publication omitted was found among with Willie K.'s papers. It depicts him with a model of his newly commissioned bust and sculptor Stanley Martineau, who will create it in marble. The bust was positioned inside the entrance door with Willie K. looking out of the museum toward his golf course and the water view.

During summer stays at Eagle's Nest, Willie K. and Rose had a morning ritual: Willie K. would rise early for a round or two of golf, while Rose slept a bit or took her time to dress. She would retreat to the breakfast hallway between their bedrooms to catch up on correspondence while waiting for Willie K. to join her so they could dine together. The corridor is paneled in bleached pickled pine and has floral draperies.

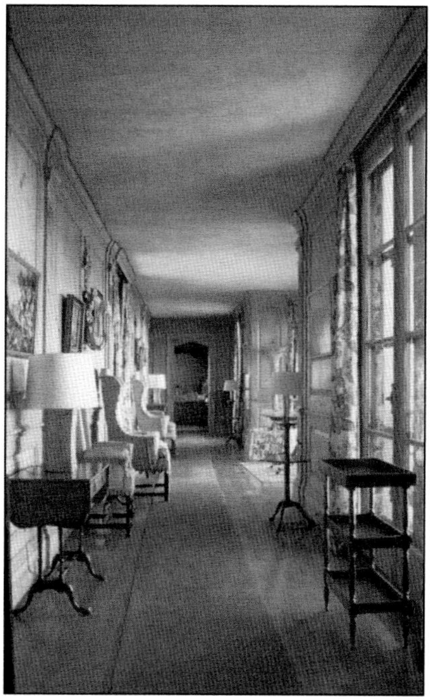

Willie K. and Rose continued to be photographed by the press wherever they went. They were known to frequent the supper club called El Morocco, along with many other celebrities. The interior was decorated in distinctive zebra-striped banquette seating in blue and white and white glass palm trees. They are pictured here enjoying their cigarettes and demitasse in a news clipping from Willie K.'s scrapbooks.

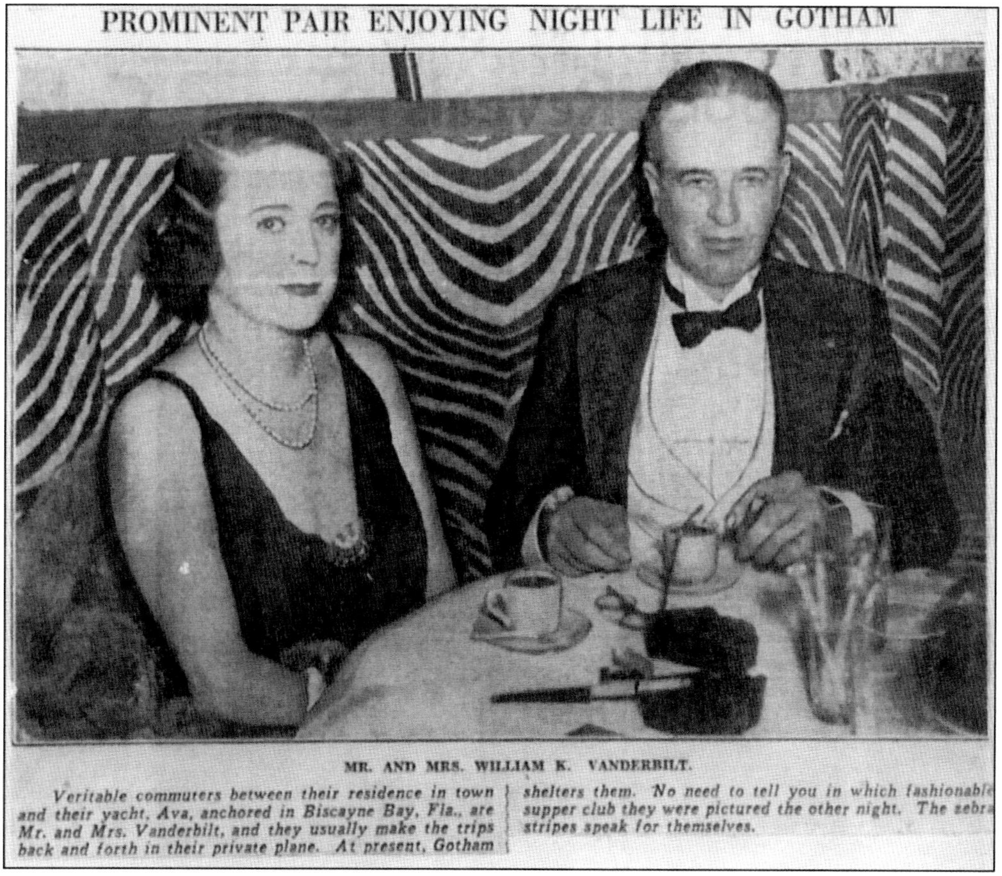

PROMINENT PAIR ENJOYING NIGHT LIFE IN GOTHAM

MR. AND MRS. WILLIAM K. VANDERBILT.

Veritable commuters between their residence in town and their yacht, Ava, anchored in Biscayne Bay, Fla., are Mr. and Mrs. Vanderbilt, and they usually make the trips back and forth in their private plane. At present, Gotham shelters them. No need to tell you in which fashionabl supper club they were pictured the other night. The zebr stripes speak for themselves.

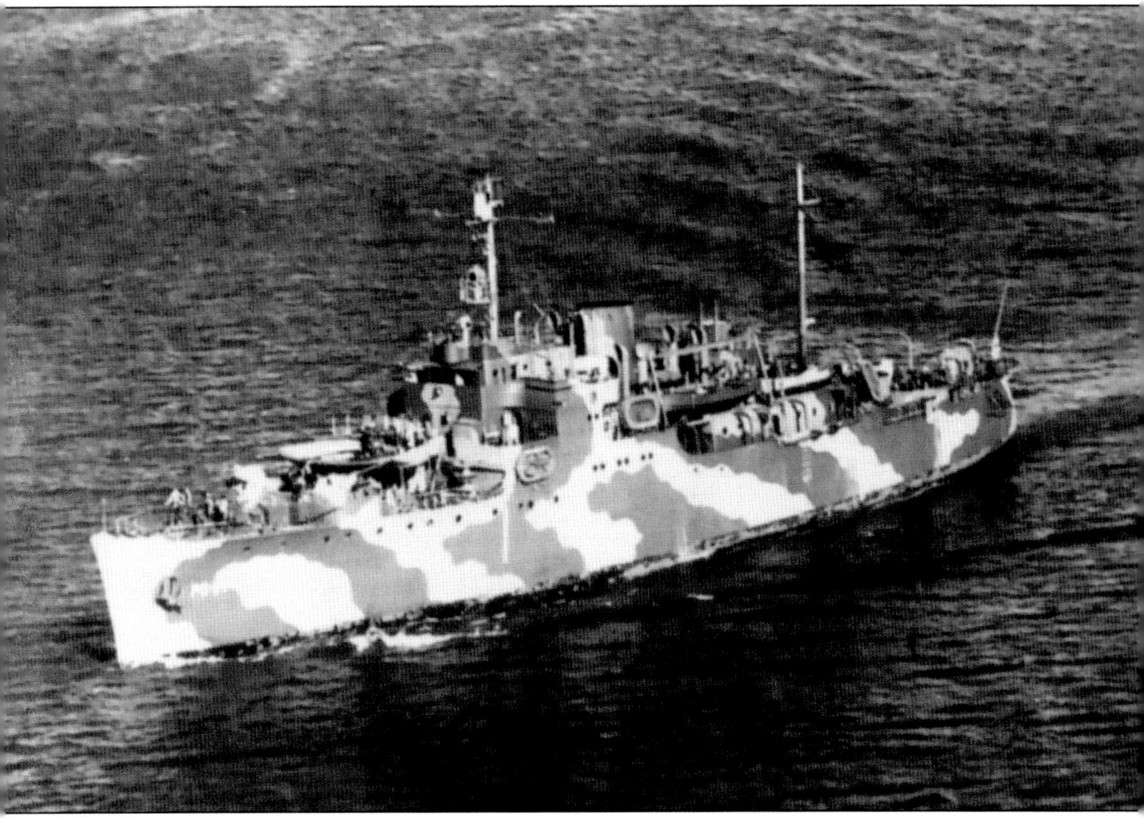

Renamed the *Plymouth* by the US Navy, the former identity of Willie K.'s steam yacht *Alva* is barely recognizable. De-outfitted and painted in camouflage, it served as an escort ship until torpedoed by a German submarine off the coast of the Carolinas. A fiercely patriotic family, each generation of Vanderbilts donated ships to aid in the wars during their respective lifetimes. (Courtesy of the National Archives.)

Seven

From Private Estate to Public Park

In his last will and testament, Willie K. set forth his wishes for the Eagle's Nest estate. Rose would live at Eagle's Nest for as long as she would like, or the rest of her natural life, and then it would be given over to the public. He stipulated the various amounts to be left to his daughters, employees, and friends. Willie K. also provided an endowment for the operation of the estate in the amount of $2 million. His daughter Muriel would add several million dollars to that amount a few decades later.

Rose continued to live at Eagle's Nest until her death in 1947. The estate was initially offered to New York State, and when they declined, Eagle's Nest became part of the Suffolk County Parks System. The mission for the new museum was set forth by Willie K. himself: "Eagle's Nest was to be a recreational park and museum dedicated in perpetuity to the education and enjoyment of the public."

The transition from an exclusive enclave for one of the wealthiest families to a public park required much perseverance and the efforts of many. By the time Eagle's Nest was officially turned over to Suffolk County in 1950, it had fallen into disrepair. The original architectural firm of Warren and Wetmore were called upon to assess the condition of the facility in the early 1950s and made appropriate recommendations. For a short time, Rose's son from her first marriage, Barclay Warburton III, helped with administrative matters. Architect Ronald Pearce also provided a written outline with future suggestions for the museum.

The board of supervisors of Suffolk County assumed governance of Eagle's Nest and appointed a board of trustees to oversee its interests. A gatehouse was constructed at the front gate and staffed around the clock by uniformed guards.

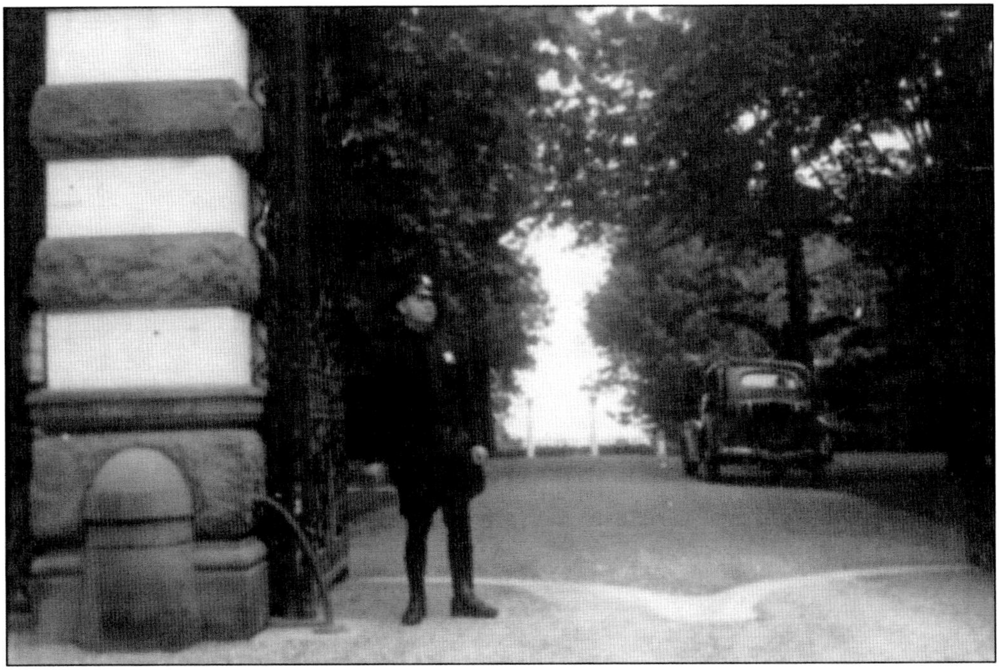

Above, a uniformed guard stands watch at the front gate of Eagle's Nest. This undated photograph shows the entrance to the estate, now decades old, with mature plantings that partially obscure the vista and the entrance colonnade. Below, an unidentified Eagle's Nest employee poses next to the fountain outside of the lower museum. Many staff members who were employed during Willie K.'s last decade there remained at the estate during its next transitional phase. The estate was cared for and prepared to receive crowds of public visitors. (Both, courtesy of Norman Bowden.)

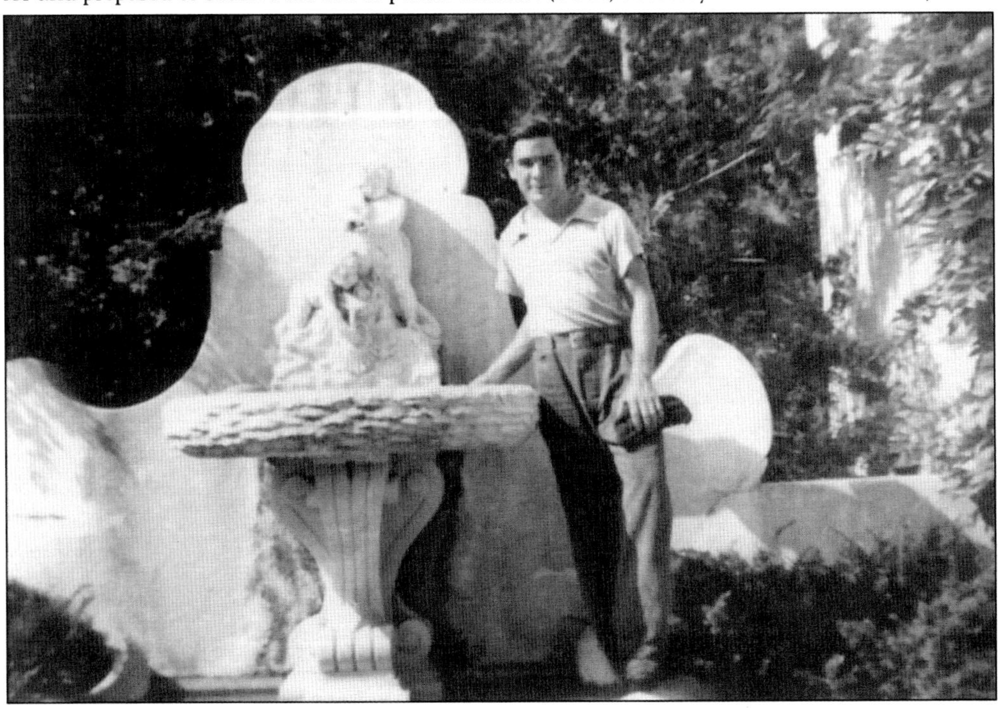

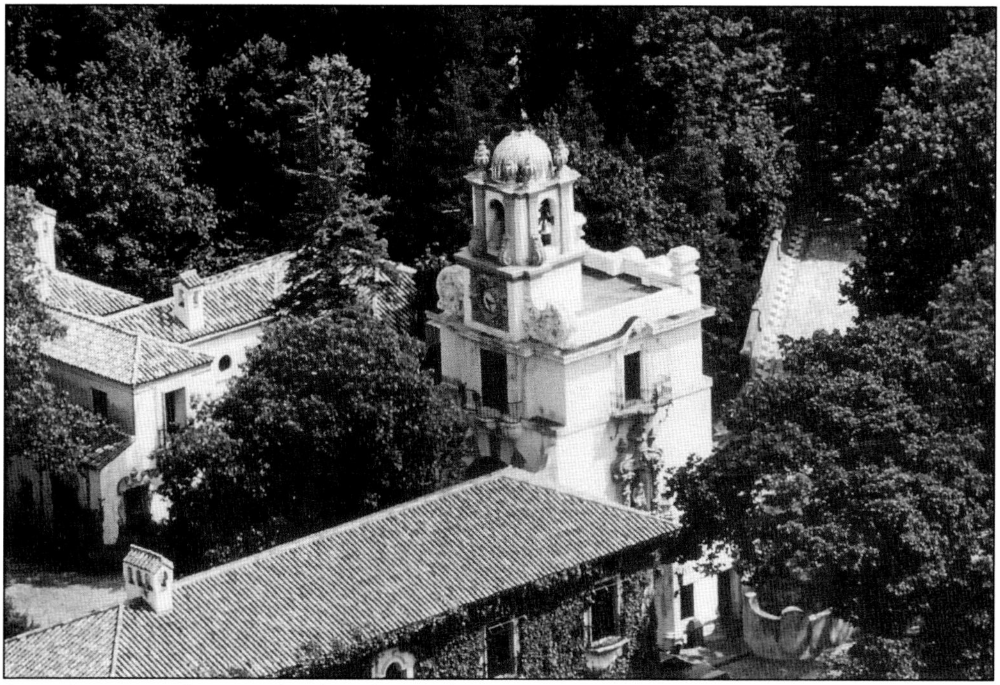

A rooftop-view photograph taken from behind the Memorial Wing shows the aging structure overgrown with ivy and the plantings dominating the landscape. The once-pristine stucco facades are stained by years of rainwater running down from the roofs. More a normal part of aging than neglect, the maintenance of an old estate can be overwhelming. The estate is well constructed and even endured the New England hurricane of 1938 unscathed.

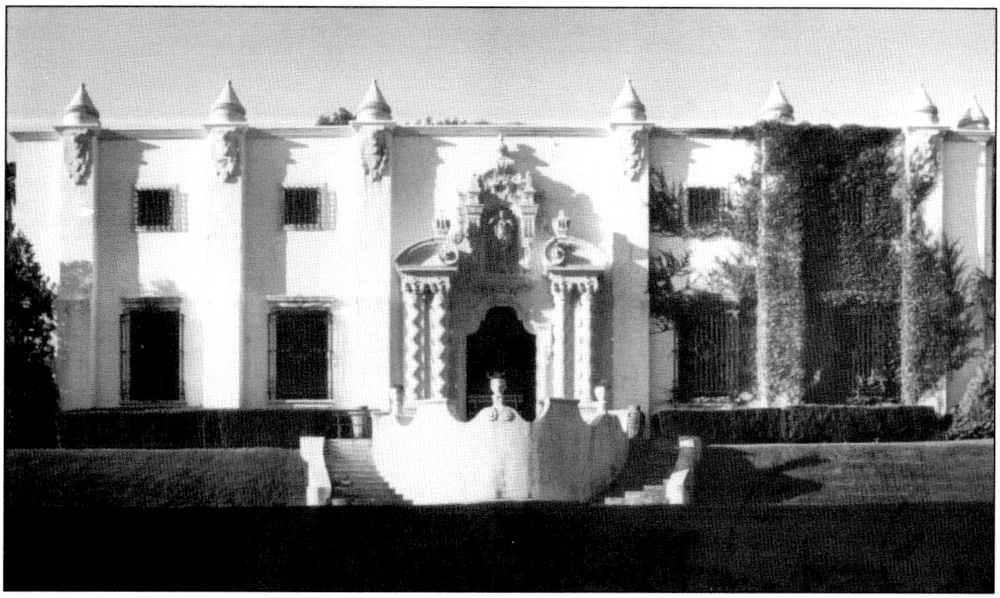

Like the house, the Hall of Fishes had also fallen victim to creeping vines and large, overgrown trees. The staircases were discolored and beginning to crumble from the freezing and swelling due to normal changes in weather conditions. For this reason, Spanish-style structures such as the ones at Eagle's Nest are customarily found in warmer southern climates.

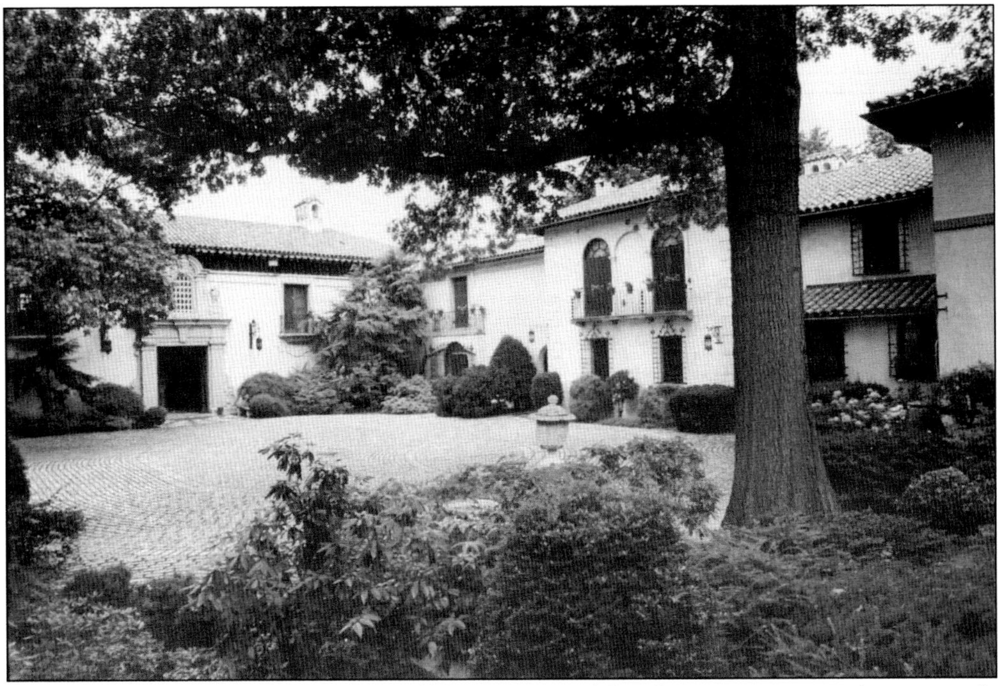

The courtyard of the estate shows the cobblestone pavers (above), an improvement that was made in Willie K.'s time. The overgrown plantings are evidence of the passing years, but the aging buildings are still quite beautiful. Scaffolding was installed in the courtyard of Eagle's Nest for the resurfacing of the stucco exteriors that took place in the early 1980s (below). Sandblasting of the building facade was part of an exterior restoration project. During the summer months, work was performed on the less-visible sides of the mansion, and the courtyard work was performed in the colder months when the museum was not as busy. While museum revenue is used for regular maintenance, major capital improvement projects are made possible through funds appropriated by Suffolk County.

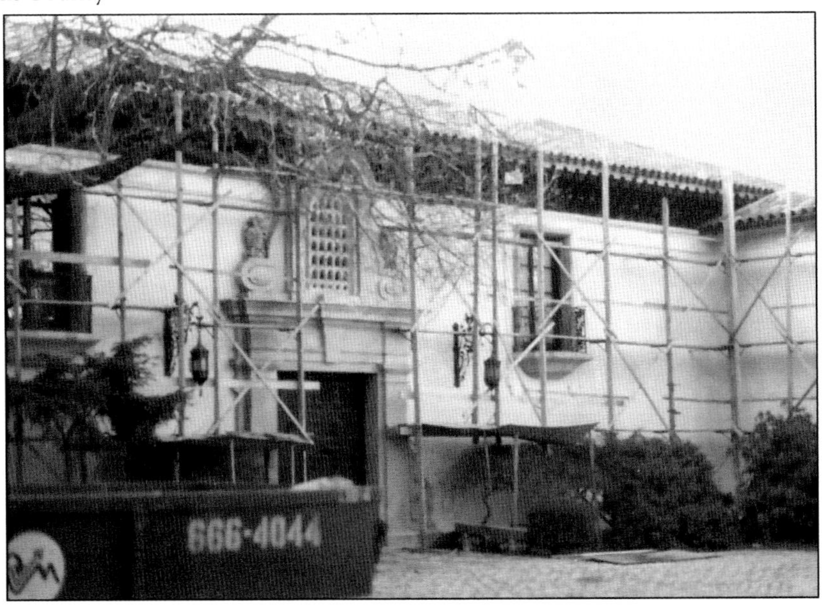

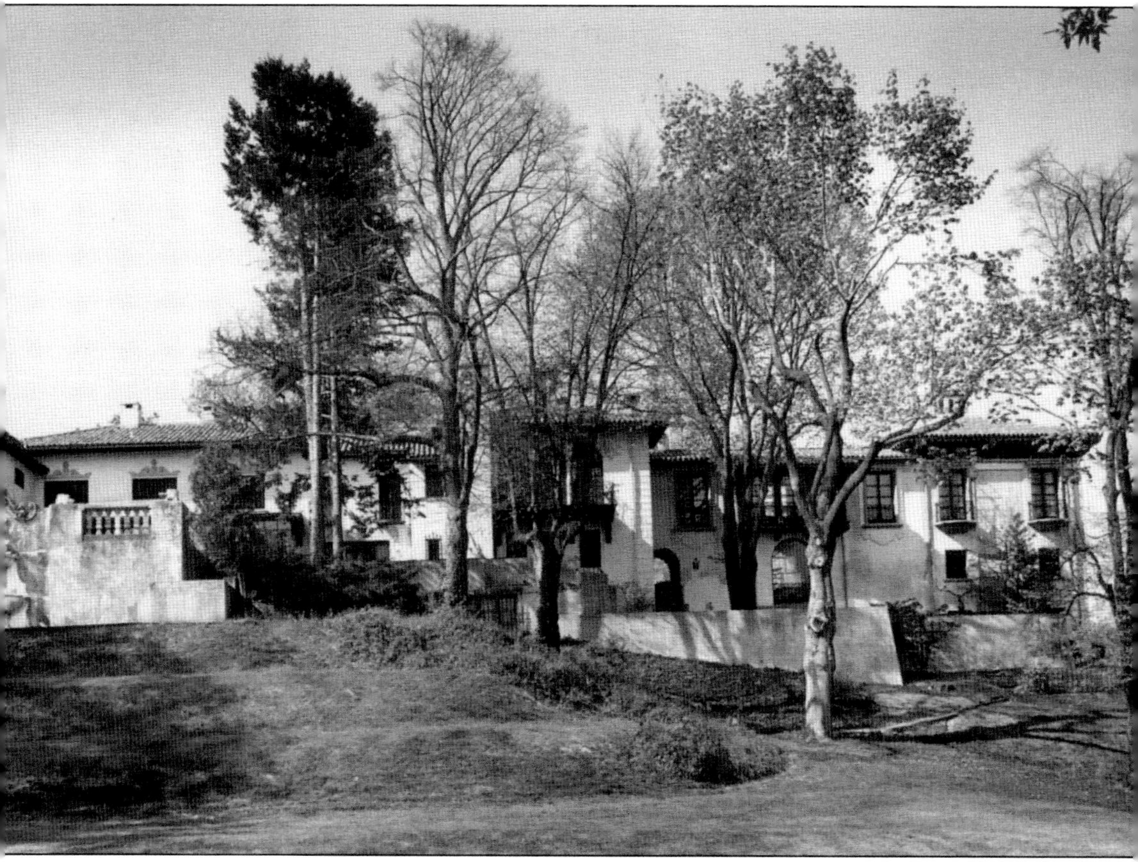

A view from the back of the now 37,600-square-foot Eagle's Nest residence reveals that while it is also in good condition, it suffers from the same issues such as overgrowth of the plantings, crumbling architectural elements, and discolored facades. At the center of the photograph, the view of the balcony of Willie K.'s bedroom is obscured by a large tree, and stucco walls appear dingy. The grilled window on the lower level at the center of the photograph is the kitchen where the meals were prepared. A fallen tree in front of the mansion porch completely hides it from view, save for a peek of the upper corner of its glass enclosure.

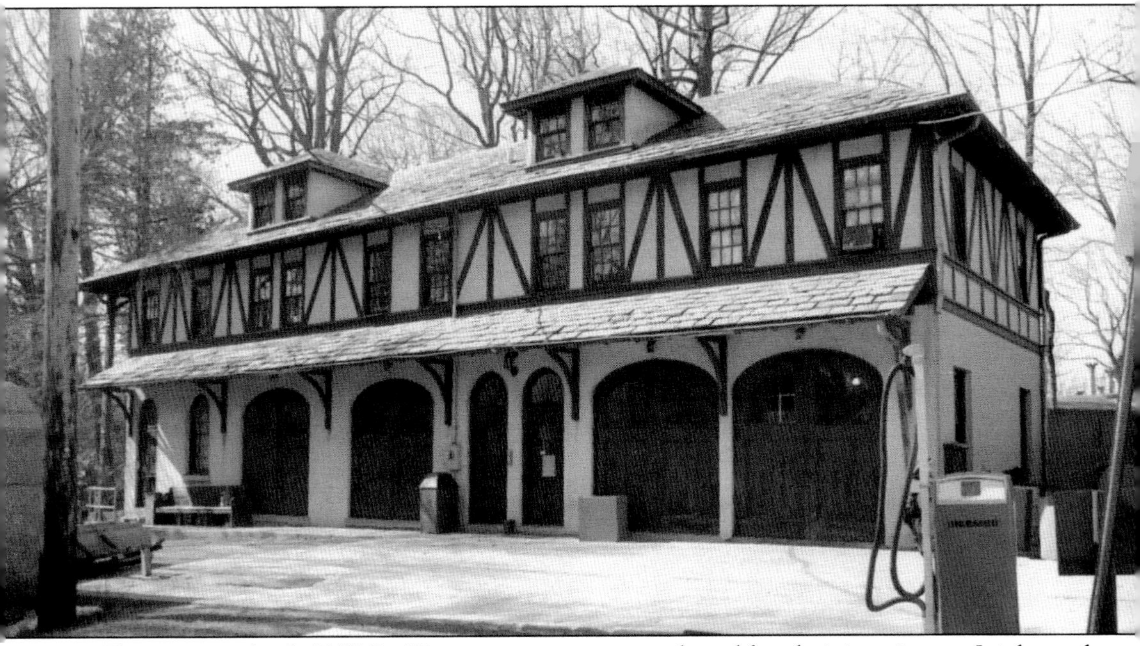

The structure that held Willie K.'s power generators was adapted for administrative use. It is located away from the more decorative structures and has smaller rooms suitable for offices. The power equipment may still be usable, but according to museum records the fuel lines leading to it were damaged in the 1960s by grading of the property during the construction of a lower parking lot. Adjacent to this structure on the west side there was a peacock pool, and there are stories about a rare black swan that lived on the property as well.

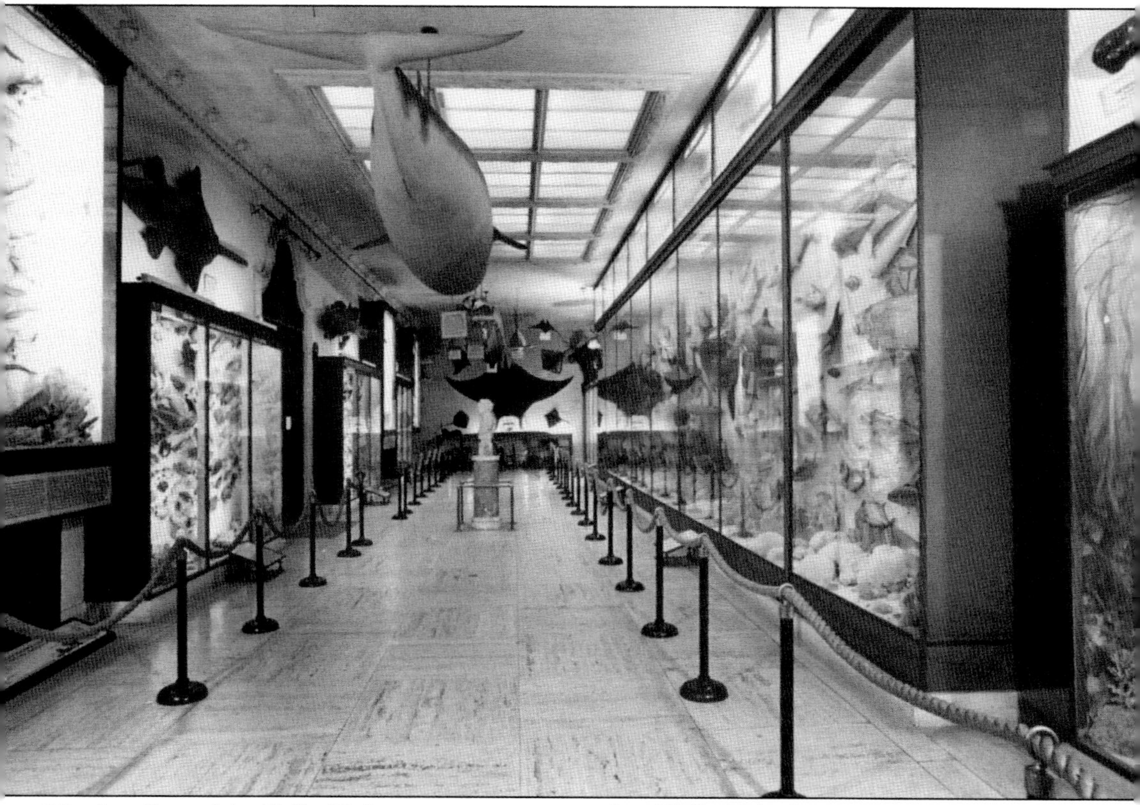

The first floor of the Hall of Fishes is as impressive as when Willie K. built it in 1922. Most of the exhibits have fared well, and those that did not have either been removed from display, replaced, or repaired. The first floor was completely refurbished approximately 20 years ago. Most of the fish specimens originally prepared by Belanske remain as he left them. He used a fascinating process whereby he repainted the actual fish skins based on his color sketches and paintings and mounted them on forms for display. The specimens were then arranged according to the waters in which they were caught. The larger specimens were prepared similarly and placed around the room. Other cases were artfully prepared by Belanske to showcase the ethnographic artifacts from Willie K.'s travels.

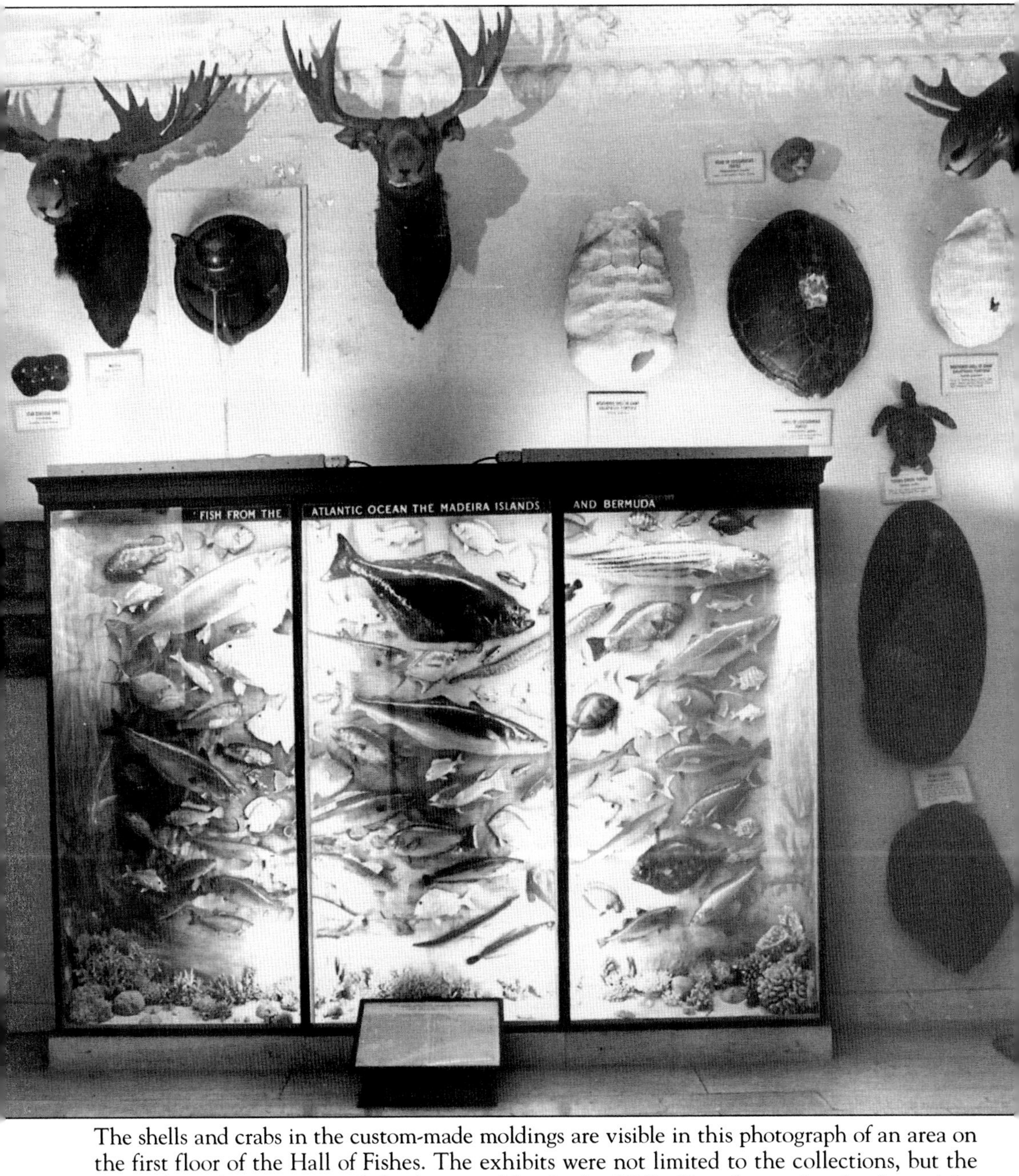

The shells and crabs in the custom-made moldings are visible in this photograph of an area on the first floor of the Hall of Fishes. The exhibits were not limited to the collections, but the rooms themselves were intended to be part of the display. Willie K. understood and embraced the blending of art and science, as well as the capacity of his museum to educate and entertain.

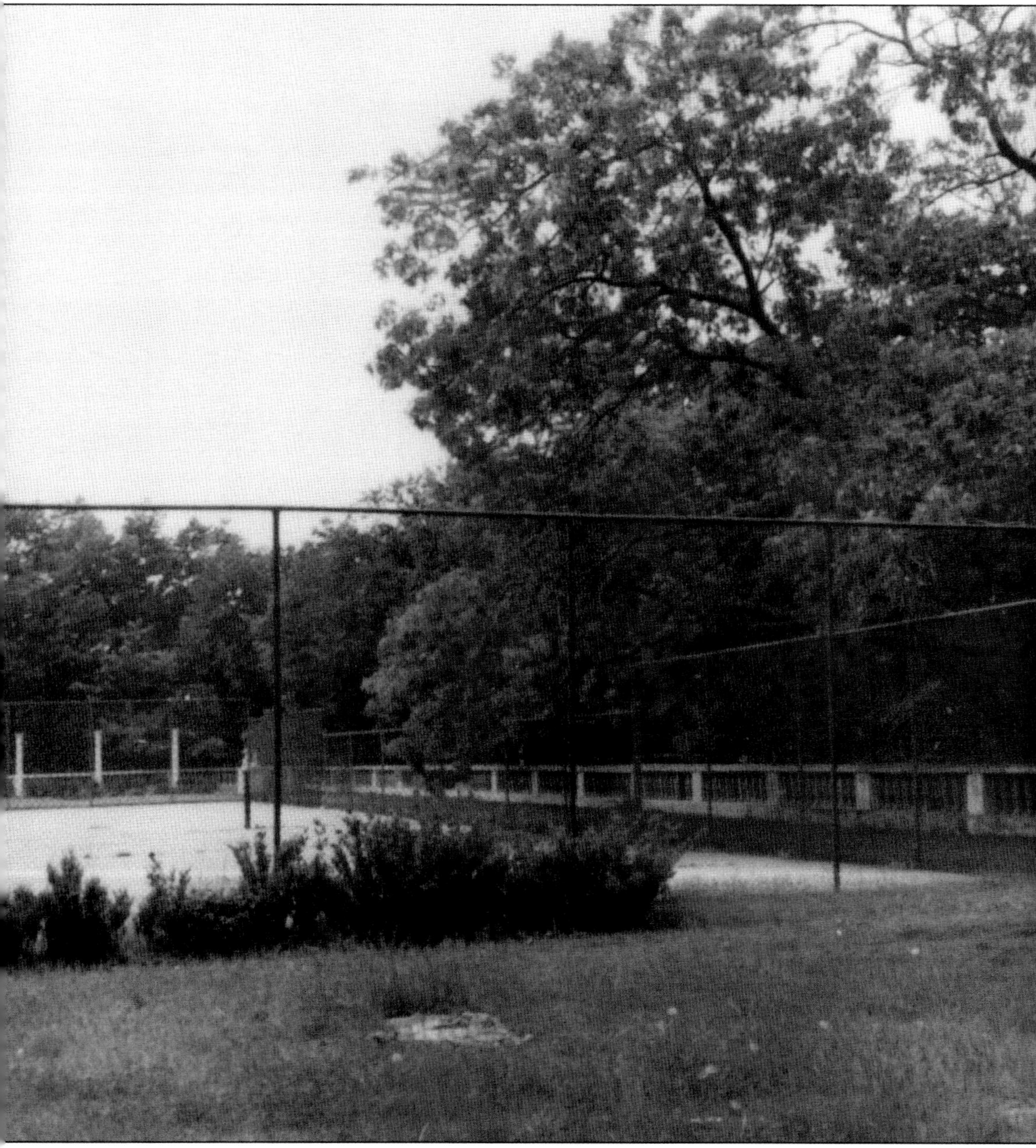

This is a view of Willie K.'s original tennis court just before it was razed to make way for the new planetarium. The columns at the far end remained in place and are still part of the rose garden's landscape. The addition of the planetarium made it possible to offer more types of educational and public programs.

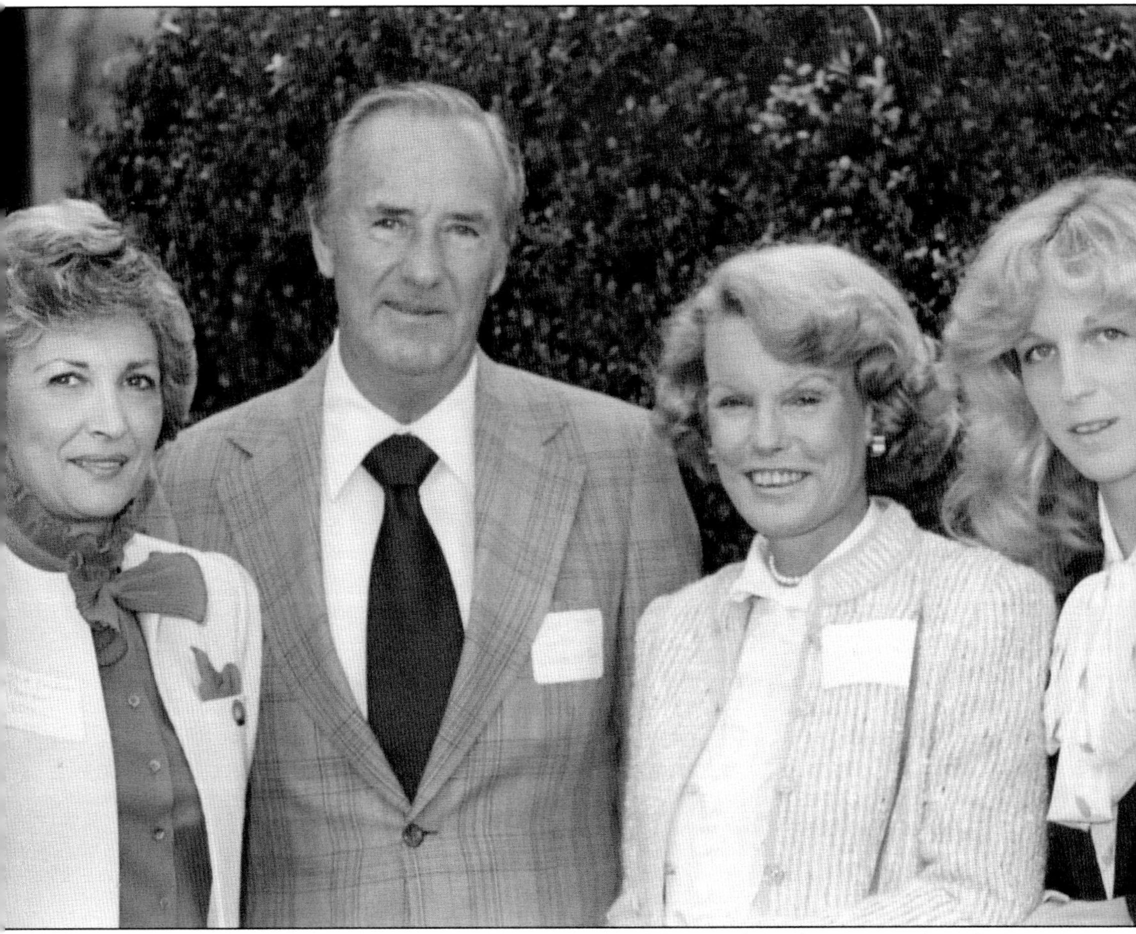

Willie K.'s granddaughter Iris Christ (second from right) served on the museum board of trustees during the 1980s. She shared her recollections of her grandfather with the employees, saying that he was a nice man and that she fondly remembered swimming in the saltwater pool with him during her summers here as a child.

Eight

The Suffolk County Vanderbilt Museum

Although most of Willie K.'s original exhibits remain much as he designed them, there were a few changes made to the Eagle's Nest estate. Two of those changes occurred nearly concurrently in 1970 and 1971 and were significant: the addition of a full-dome planetarium and a diorama hall known as the Stoll Wing. The trustees of the museum and Suffolk County officials began discussing the addition of a planetarium shortly after the museum became public. Since Willie K. was always on the cutting edge of the latest mode of transport, space travel seemed like a natural progression of his original mission. The Vanderbilts made their fortune through a transportation empire, and space travel would have been the next frontier to conquer. Those who have learned about Willie K. believe that he would have tried to fly to space if he had the opportunity.

The Stoll Wing was built by a fellow world explorer and museum trustee by the name of Charles H. Stoll. Stoll embarked on Arctic expeditions sanctioned by the American Museum of Natural History and traveled to collect specimens much as Vanderbilt did. He financed the only addition to the mansion and stocked it with trophies from his expeditions. This new wing has eight dioramas representing every habitat on earth. Like Vanderbilt, Stoll retained artists from major museums to carry out the design of these dioramas and their background scenes. Stoll was the president of the museum board of trustees in 1971 and officiated at the dedication ceremony for the planetarium.

Much to the credit of Willie K., Eagle's Nest continues to fulfill his intended mission. Visitors from all over the world come to see one of the few remaining Long Island Gold Coast estates with its original furnishings. His collections remain on display and continue to fascinate and entertain. Collections-based education programs have been developed to complement New York State school curriculum. Concerts and car shows take place on the scenic grounds during the warmer months, and his history lives on through an enthusiastic staff.

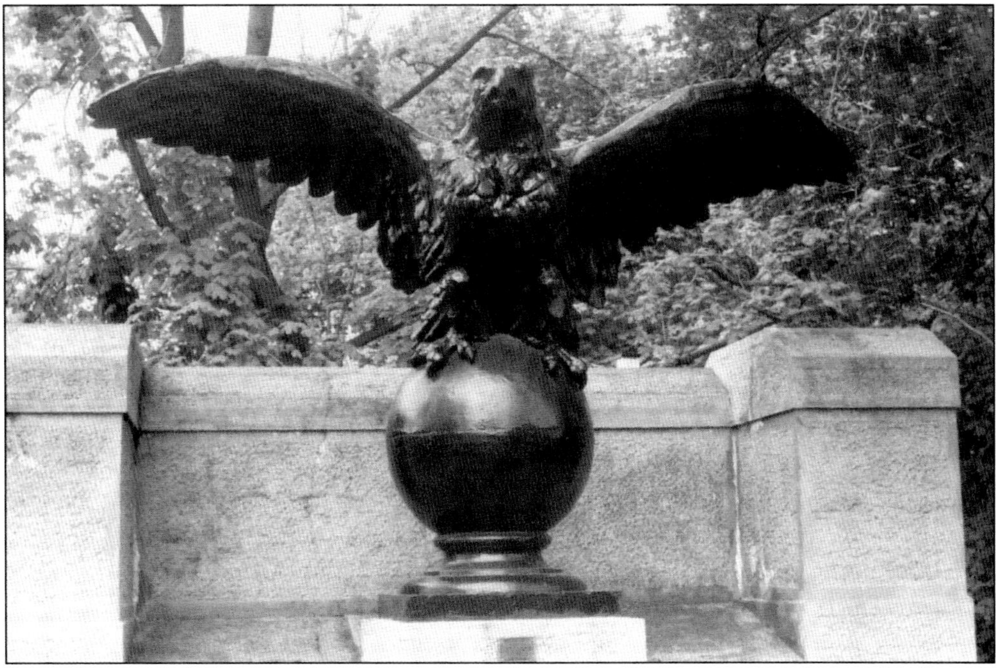

The same pair of eagles from Grand Central Terminal has been welcoming visitors to Eagle's Nest since 1910. While the site is still known by that name, it is more commonly referred to as the Suffolk County Vanderbilt Museum (SCVM). Now a not-for-profit organization, it has earned both a New York State charter and an accreditation from the American Alliance of Museums. Its collections include an Egyptian mummy and full-dome planetarium.

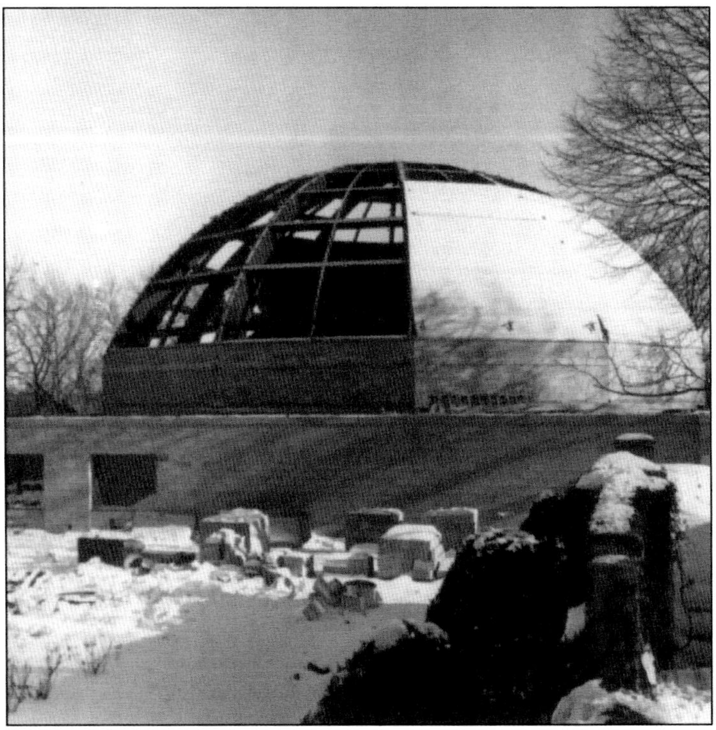

Construction of the planetarium began in 1970 and was completed in 1971. The grand opening was in June of that year. A state-of-the-art GOTO projector was installed to re-create the night sky in any season of the year underneath the planetarium's 60-foot-diameter dome.

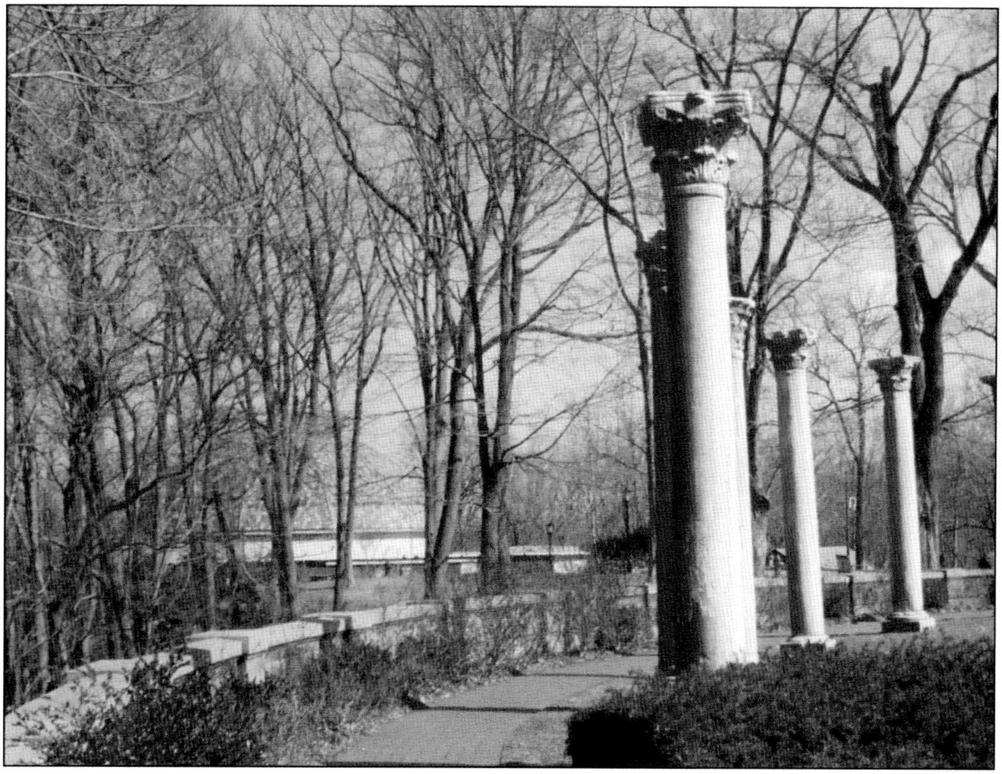

When the planetarium opened, the SCVM was able to expand the programming offered to the public and astronomy education programs to the schools. There are live educational lectures for school groups, entertaining public shows, and stargazing sessions through the high-powered telescope in the roof's observatory.

In 2013, the 42-year-old GOTO equipment was removed and replaced with a Konica-Minolta GeminiStar III star projector with upgraded video and sound systems. The new equipment provides superior visual effects compared with the older technology. The planetarium was reconfigured and outfitted with new seats and carpeting.

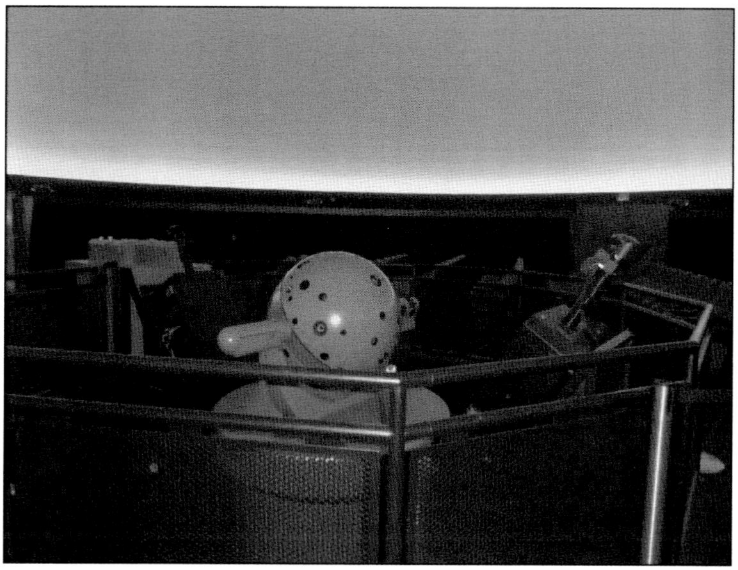

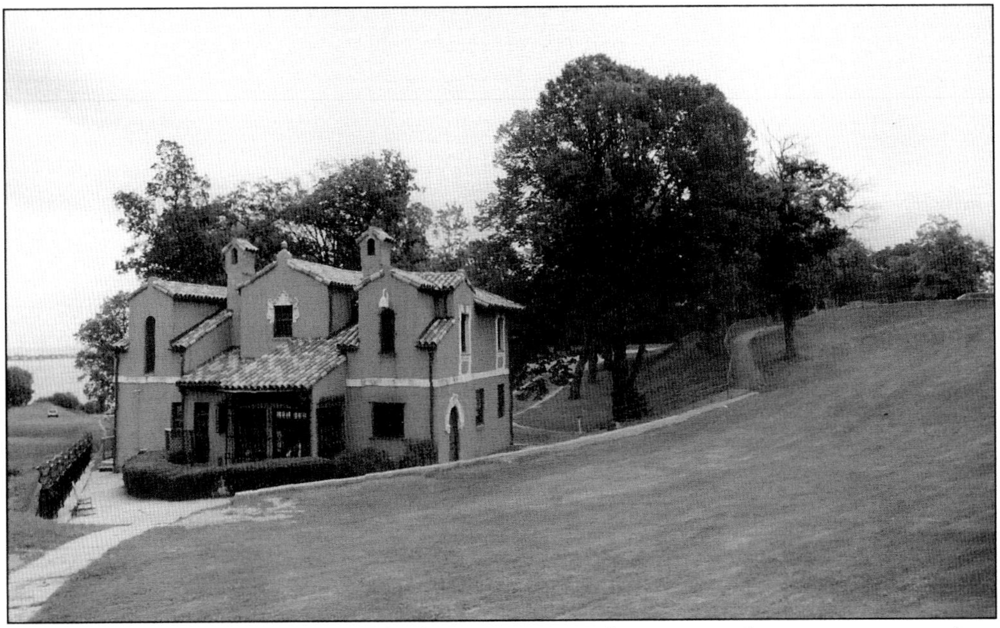

The garage building that was one of the first structures on the property plays an important role at the SCVM. The building is used for the museum education programs, which are based on Willie K.'s original collections. These programs were designed to enhance classroom learning and align with New York State curriculum; they form the basis for the museum's New York State charter. On the weekends, an acting troupe uses the space for live performances.

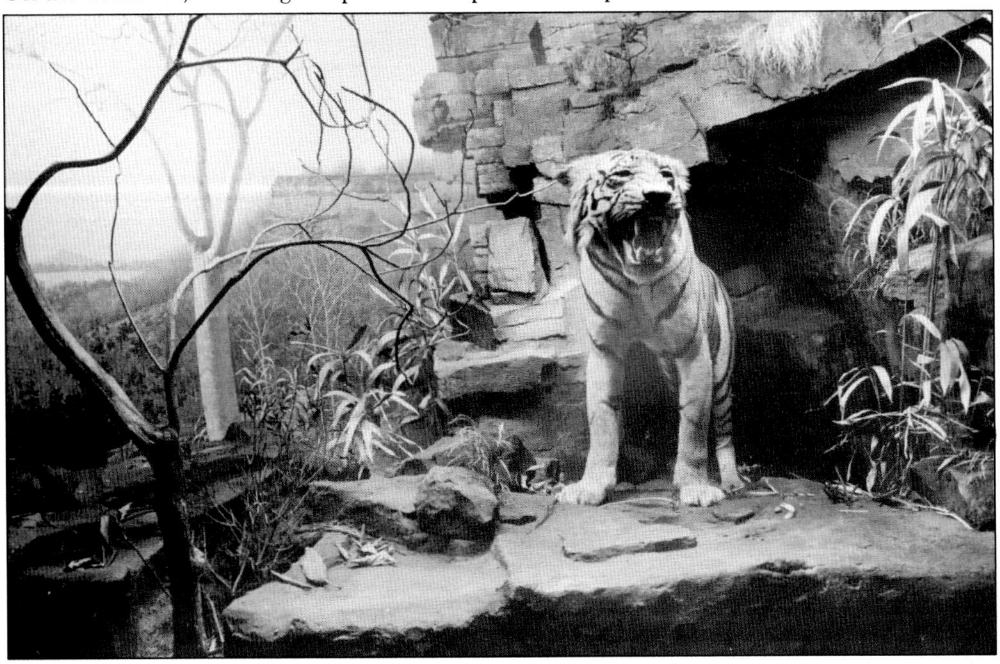

The natural history dioramas are integral to many of the education programs and are popular with visitors as well. In addition to Willie K.'s Hall of Fishes, there are two natural history exhibit halls containing a total of 17 diorama scenes. The backgrounds were all painted by talented artists from the American Museum of Natural History in New York.

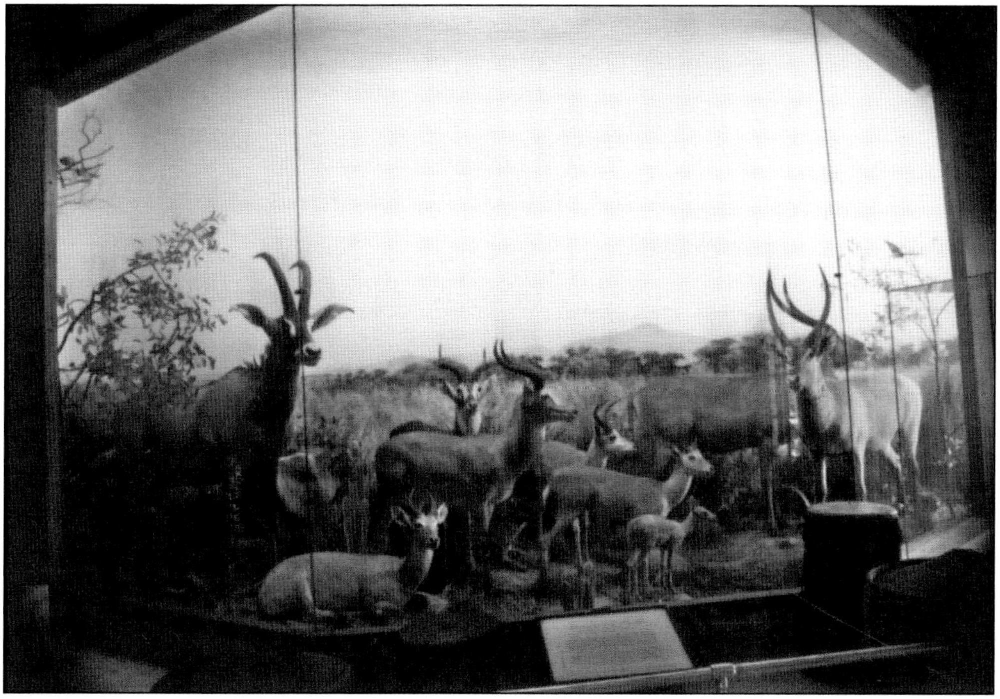

In addition to the Hall of Fishes and two diorama halls, there are three exhibit galleries in the Memorial Wing of the SCVM. One of them features natural history specimens from Africa collected by Willie K.'s son. This antelope diorama is located in that room and was completed in 1936 by artists from the American Museum of Natural History.

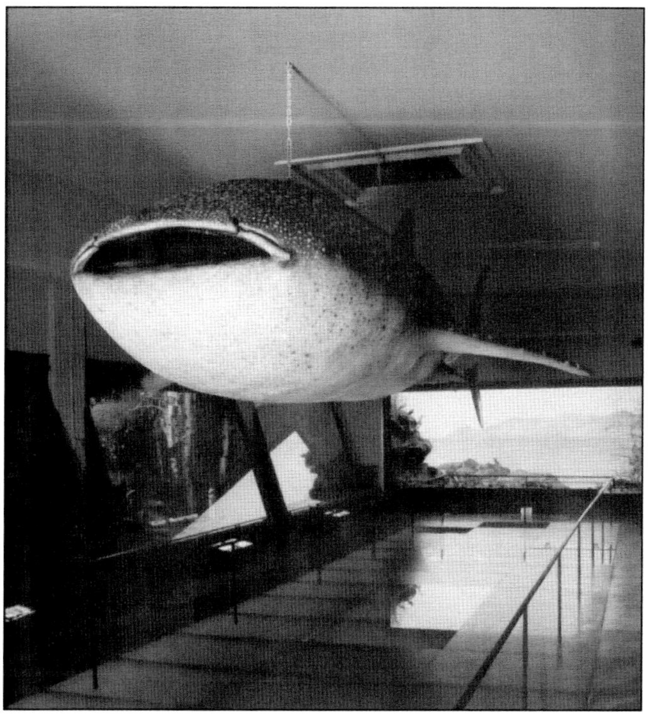

The lower museum, now called the Habitat, was Willie K.'s private exhibit during the years he lived at Eagle's Nest. It has a glass floor, illuminated in blue, and nine diorama scenes representing his travels. The whale shark suspended above the room is almost 32 feet long and was added in 1935. This exhibit hall underwent a total restoration and was reopened in 2009 after being closed to the public since 1996 due to deterioration.

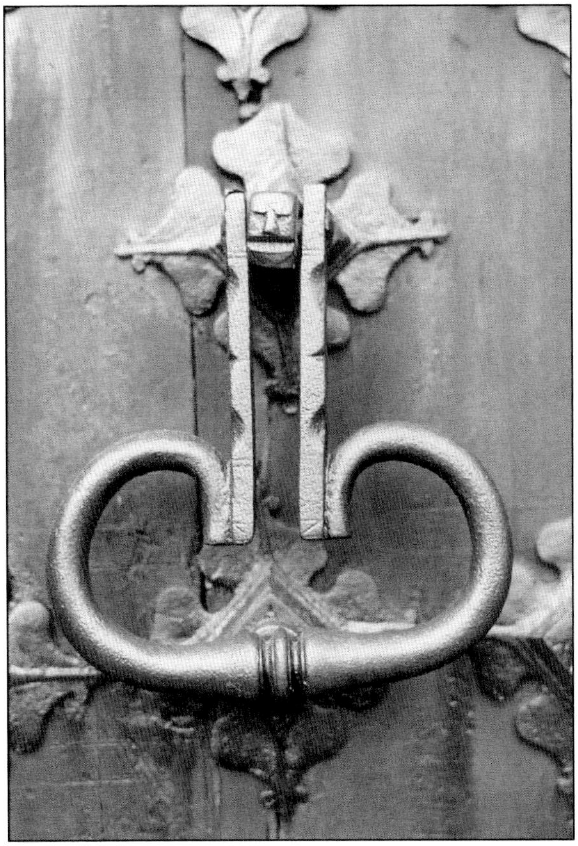

Visitors enjoy learning about the historical features at the museum. The detail on this door knocker on the Memorial Wing entrance is a visitor favorite. This door has two door knockers: a higher one with a horse's face in the center and the one pictured here with a human face. The museum staff explains that the doors are very old, from a time when there where no automobiles; therefore, the upper door knocker is for visitors arriving on horseback.

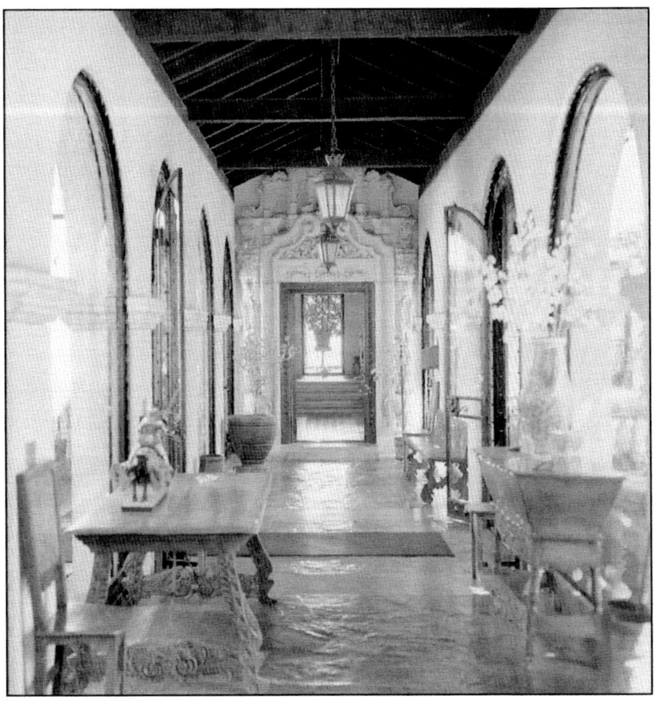

The arcade interior, a serene space during Willie K.'s life here, is now a busy corridor to the historical house at one end and the nursery wing at the other. Visitors pass through the center doors from the courtyard and down through the boxwood garden to visit the Habitat and Stoll Wing exhibit halls.

This is the view from the second-floor landing of the Hall of Fishes building. No longer used as a golf course, the vast lawn is the site of many community events and private parties during the warm months of the year. The SCVM hosts several car shows each year, along with concerts, weddings, and parties.

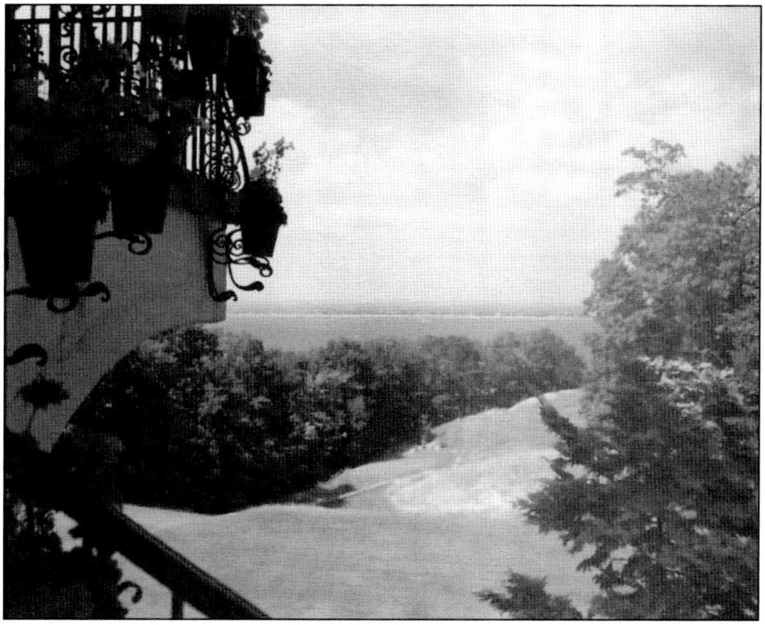

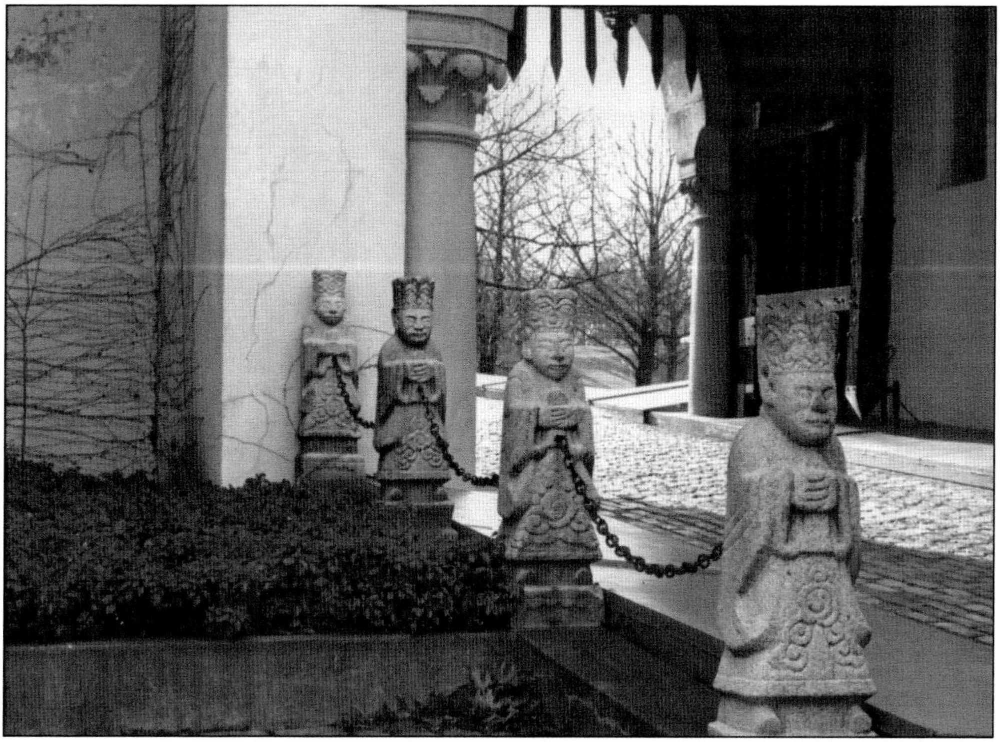

Four Asian stone statues usher visitors into the courtyard. They were added in the late 1930s at about the same time as the cobblestones. Like many of the indoor furnishings and outdoor sculptures purchased by the architects during European excursions, any documentation of their origin does not remain.

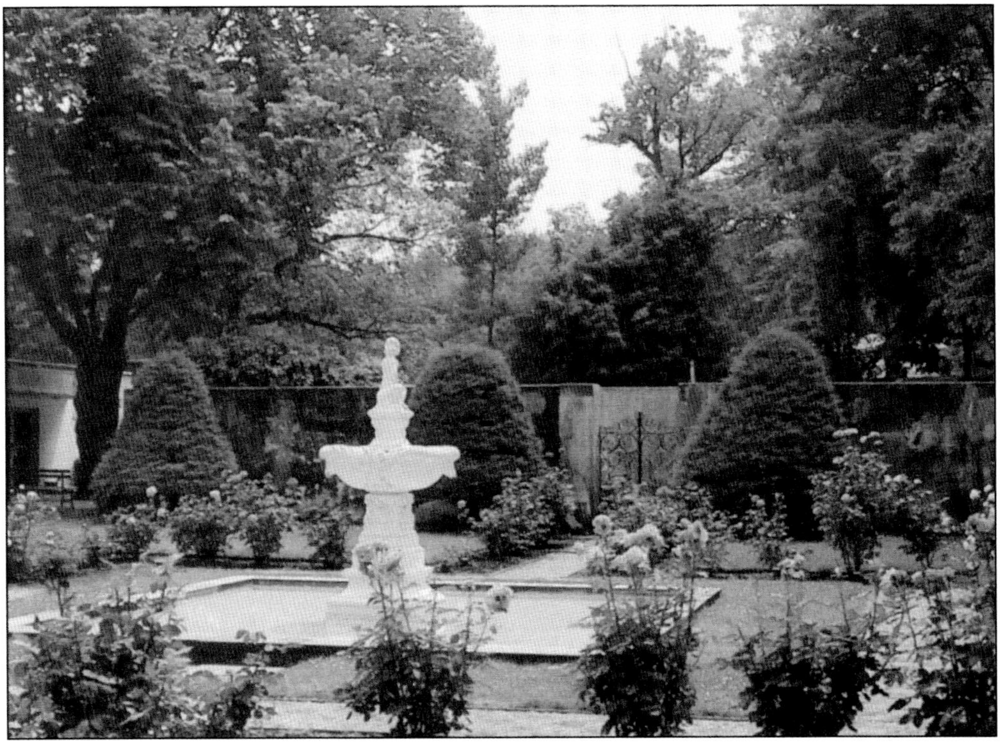

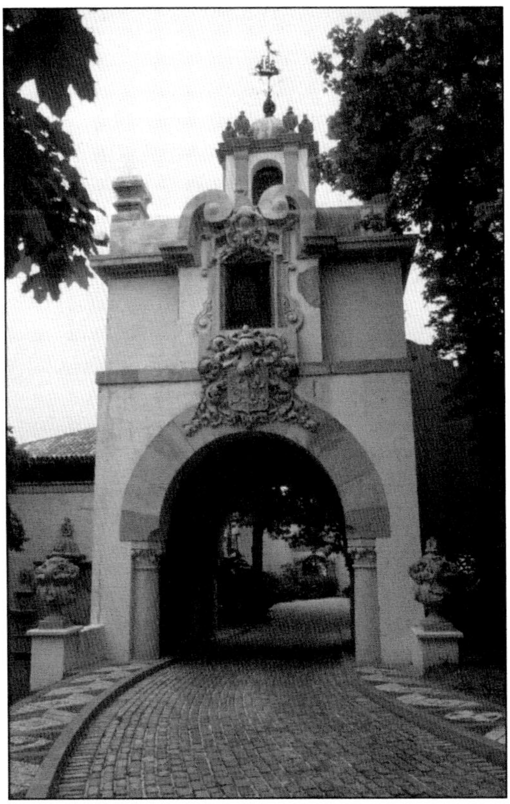

The rose garden located outside of the planetarium is faithfully maintained by volunteers from the local community. A variety of roses grow here, identified by species and given name. Overlooking Northport Harbor on one side, with a reflecting pool fountain, historical columns, and decorative iron gates, this site is used by visitors, private parties, and education groups.

Instantly recognizable for it unique style, the bell tower at Eagle's Nest is possibly one of the most iconic structures on all of Long Island. Passing through it and entering the courtyard of the estate transports visitors to a different place in time, allowing them to experience what it was like to live like a Vanderbilt, if only for an afternoon.

BIBLIOGRAPHY

Balsan, Consuelo Vanderbilt. *The Glitter and the Gold*. New York: Harper Brothers, 1952.

Boone, Lee. *Bulletin of the Vanderbilt Marine Museum*, Vols. I–VII, 1933–1938.

Croffut, W.A. *The Vanderbilts and the Story of Their Fortune*. Chicago and New York: Belford, Clarke & Company, 1886.

Lapidus, Morris. *Too Much Is Never Enough*. New York: Rizzoli, 1996.

Pennoyer/Walker. *The Architecture of Warren & Wetmore*. New York and London: W.W. Norton & Company, 2006.

Society for the Preservation of Long Island Antiquities, Eagle's Nest. *The William K. Vanderbilt Jr. Estate: An Historic Structure Report*. New York: September, 1982.

Vanderbilt, William K. II. Unless otherwise noted, self-published:

———. *Log of My Motor 1899–1908*, 1908.

———. *Log of My Motor 1908–1911*, 1912.

———. *Through Italy, Sicily, Tunisia and Algeria by Motor*, 1918.

———. *Across the Atlantic with Ara Summer 1924*. New York: Brentano's Publishers, 1925.

———. *To Galapagos on the Ara*, 1926.

———. *15,000 Miles Cruise with Ara 1927*, 1928.

———. *Taking One's Own Ship around the World*, 1929.

———. *West Made East with the Loss of a Day*, 1931.

———. *Flying Lanes*, 1937.

As with any historical site, there exists a collective institutional memory consisting of archival materials, secondary sources, and oral histories provided by original estate employees or their families.

Discover Thousands of Local History Books Featuring Millions of Vintage Images

Consistent with our mission to preserve history on a local level, this book was printed in South Carolina on American-made paper and manufactured entirely in the United States. Products carrying the accredited Forest Stewardship Council (FSC) label are printed on 100 percent FSC-certified paper.

MADE IN THE USA